8/79

JAMES MILL ON
PHILOSOPHY AND EDUCATION

JAMES MILL
ON PHILOSOPHY
AND EDUCATION

by

W. H. BURSTON

UNIVERSITY OF LONDON
THE ATHLONE PRESS
1973

Published by
THE ATHLONE PRESS
UNIVERSITY OF LONDON
at 4 Gower Street London WC1

Distributed by Tiptree Book Services Ltd
Tiptree, Essex

U.S.A. and Canada
Humanities Press Inc
New York

Set in Monotype Baskerville by
GLOUCESTER TYPESETTING CO LTD
Printed in Great Britain by
EBENEZER BAYLIS & SON LTD
The Trinity Press, Worcester, and London

PREFACE

This book is a study of James Mill as an educationist. As such, it concentrates on his philosophy of education as expounded in his long article on 'Education' for the 6th edition of the *Encyclopedia Britannica*. But it also includes his practical work for education and especially his work to spread popular education on the one hand, and his unique and single-handed education of his son, John Stuart Mill, and through him, of the rest of his family of nine, on the other.

In studying Mill's philosophy of education it is essential to refer also to his general philosophy for Mill was, on the whole, a consistent thinker, and much in his philosophical works throws light on the meaning of his educational theory. And there are times when the process works in reverse, for education held such a central place in Mill's thinking that his educational theories can clarify his moral and political philosophy. Chapters in this book are therefore devoted to his aims in education in relation to his Ethics, his psychological basis of education in relation to his Theory of Knowledge and Psychology, and to his theories of Social and Political Education in connexion with his general political theory.

All this, however, has to be seen in the historical context in which he lived and about which he wrote. This is, in my view, essential in the interpretation of any thinker of the past: it is particularly necessary when dealing with the Utilitarians who were very much pre-occupied with the problems of their time. The opening chapters therefore give some account of the historical background, and also of James Mill's life and career. I have argued that, in interpreting Mill, a major principle to observe, is to consider how his theories applied to his own time, and how they might stand when considered as a general ideal, and, in my view, unless we recognize this dualism in Mill's thought, at almost every stage, we shall not correctly understand what he was saying.

All students of Utilitarianism stand heavily in debt to Professor Halévy. If I have not been able to agree with him on some major matters, this does not imply that I have not learnt much, as has everyone, from his masterly survey. But the individual Utilitarian thinkers do deserve to be studied in their own right and a full understanding of the Utilitarian movement can only be gained by individual studies of the thinkers who produced it.

Many colleagues and friends have, over the years, helped me to clarify my mind on the various matters dealt with in this book. I would like particularly to thank my former colleagues Professor J. A. Noonan, Professor L. A. Reid, and Mr H. E. O. James who read the chapters on linguistic theory, philosophy and psychology respectively. Their expert help was invaluable. I would also like to record my indebtedness to my former tutor, the late Professor G. C. Field, and to Professor Michael Oakeshott: both have been most helpful, stimulating and encouraging.

December 1971   W.H.B.

CONTENTS

I

England at the time of
James Mill

James Mill was born in Scotland on 6 April 1773. In 1802 he came to London, and from then until his death he lived in or near London, except for the four years when Bentham was the tenant of Ford Abbey in Somerset, and Mill spent at least half of each year with him. What was the England in which Mill lived and worked and formed his theories for the improvement of mankind?

It was an age of great political events. The years while Mill was at the University of Edinburgh, saw the French Revolution, the Reign of Terror and the European war. His arrival in London in 1802 was followed by the renewal of the war, and the long struggle to overthrow Napoleon—by sea, by economic warfare, and by military action in the Peninsula, and in France. This war, though a mighty struggle, was not 'total' in the sense that we understand a European war to be. It was vital to England because all Europe was involved, rather than because all or a majority of Englishmen were directly affected. 'During half the years of the struggle with France', writes Trevelyan, 'England sent no expeditionary force to Europe, and even the seven campaigns of the Peninsular War cost less than 40,000 British dead.'[1] By contrast, England's command of the sea gave her an ever-increasing share of the export markets left uncontested by European rivals. The ebb and flow of economic war—of Orders in Council in England, of Berlin decrees in Europe and of non-Intercourse acts in the U.S.A.—all these produced painful fluctuations, especially in the north. But they were temporary and often local in their effects. For most of the

[1] G. M. Trevelyan, *English Social History*, Longmans, 1944, pp. 466-7.

1*

war, for most English people, 'the war was in the newspapers'.[2] Its very length reduced its impact as a conscious factor in their lives.

The end of the war in 1815 brought social distress, social disorder and attempts by Lord Liverpool's government to repress the malcontents by prosecution, punishment and emergency legislation such as the famous six 'gag' acts. To the student of affairs like Mill, these issues of social amelioration, liberty of speech and freedom of association, and the like, seemed much more vital than the war. The government's actions were dictated by fear of a revolution in England similar to that which had produced such violence in France. To the reformers, these actions looked differently: they demonstrated with unmistakeable clarity a government of a small and privileged group acting in its own interests and against the community as a whole. To Mill, and to many thoughtful people of his day, politics was 'the keystone of the arch': until political evils had been ended, until the system of government was reformed, no economic or social progress could be hoped for. Thus, though the years after 1821 witnessed modest but important reforms by Peel in the criminal law, by Huskisson in the direction of freer trade, the dominating theme to the politically conscious Englishman was the need for the reform of Parliament, and the Reform Act of 1832 the most important event.

This was also the period of economic and social change known as the 'Industrial Revolution'. This term 'Industrial Revolution' unfortunately calls to mind a number of different things—inventions, transition from water to steam power, improved roads, canals, railways, capitalist organization of industry, class rivalries, factories and factory towns with all their attendant social evils. With so much represented by a single phrase, ambiguity and inaccuracy in describing a particular point in the process is only too probable. To say that England between 1802 and 1830 was in the midst of the Industrial Revolution is thus to say very little. What actually happened in this period to the various different processes and events denoted by the blanket term 'Industrial Revolution'?

The inventions of the Industrial Revolution dated from the

[2] Ibid., p. 466.

early part of the eighteenth century. By 1800, some, in some industries, and in some localities had been widely adopted. 'It was in the manufacture of textiles', writes Professor Ashton, 'that the transformation was most rapid.'[3] Hargreaves' Spinning Jenny was invented in 1764: by 1788 it was estimated that about 20,000 of them were in use in England. But this device could be used with the domestic system of industry: Arkwright's frame, invented in 1768 was from the beginning used in mills or factories. Crompton's mule and Watt's steam engine came in 1790, and the rate at which these inventions were adopted can be seen by Manchester's development: in 1782, there were only two cotton mills in or about Manchester—in 1802 there were fifty-two. This was certainly rapid change, but it was confined to one locality and limited to one industry. It transformed Lancashire, and cotton, but not England. Other inventions in other industries were more slowly adopted and produced their results in the growth of factories and towns later in the century. England in Mill's day was not an industrial land: as late as 1831, 28 per cent of all English families were employed in agriculture, and at least 50 per cent lived in rural areas. There were more tailors and shoemakers in London alone than the whole mining population of Northumberland and Durham. There were, even in 1831, far more female domestic servants in England and Wales than all the people, adult and child, employed in the cotton industry.[4]

The age was an age of transition, prolific in invention, and confident of the future. Development in places was rapid, but new forms of transport accentuated the local character of industrial change. The real picture is portrayed by Clapham, when he writes of 1831: 'The representative Englishman, then, was not yet a townsman, though soon he would be. Nor was the representative townsman either a man tied to the wheels of iron of the new industrialism, or even a wage-earner in a business of considerable size. The townsmen were no doubt often connected with industries which had been undergoing transformation and becoming, as we say, more capitalistic; but

[3] T. S. Ashton, *The Industrial Revolution*, O.U.P., 1948, p. 70.
[4] J. H. Clapham, *Economic History of Modern Britain*, C.U.P., 1926, i, pp. 66–7 and 71–4.

generally such transformation had been neither rapid nor recent.'[5] The England of Mill's day may have been England in the midst of the Industrial Revolution in one sense but in many of the senses in which we understand the term 'Industrial Revolution' the process was only just beginning, and the majority of Englishmen knew little of large factories or large industrial towns with all their familiar social evils. Nowhere in Mill's private correspondence or published writings do we find any reference to these matters. The nearest is a passage in the *Essay on Education* advocating a minimum age of employment and minimum hours: both reforms were as urgently needed under the domestic system as under the later factory system.

In part this is to be explained by the fact that Mill lived in London. Then as now, perhaps, the Londoner regarded his problems as the nation's and the problems of the provinces as relatively unimportant. There was far more reason for this view in Mill's day, for London dwarfed all other towns by a considerable margin. Of the 25 per cent of the population living in towns larger than 20,000 inhabitants in 1831, 11 per cent or nearly half, lived in London. And London at this time, as the Hammonds remark, 'was scarcely touched by the Industrial Revolution'.[6] Mrs George agrees: 'London . . . is in a sense exceptional . . . the direct results of what is called the Industrial Revolution were not conspicuous there.'[7] But London was the scene before Mill's eyes, and if we are to see the historical context in which he wrote it is to London that we must turn.

In the first quarter of the nineteenth century London as a continuous built-up area was bounded in the north by Shoreditch, Finsbury Fields, Islington, Somers Town (developing during this period), and the 'new road' to Paddington roughly corresponding to the present Euston and Marylebone roads. To the west, the boundary was Park Lane and Hyde Park, continuing after the gap of Green Park and St James' Park to Westminster and Pimlico. Chelsea was small and relatively

[5] Clapham, op. cit., i, p. 67.

[6] J. L. and B. Hammond, *Town Labourer*, Preface to 1925 edn, Longmans, p. vii.

[7] M. Dorothy George, *London Life & Labour in 18th Century*, L.S.E., 1951, p. 1.

isolated, being separated by Neat House Gardens and Tothill Fields. So also were Kensington and Brompton. South of Chelsea the river formed the boundary with no building on the south side until one reached Kennington, and proceeded eastwards to Newington Butts, Walworth, Bermondsey, and Rotherhithe—the area of building becoming narrower and more confined to the river bank the farther east one went. There were docks and some houses at Deptford, and then came Greenwich. Camberwell, Peckham, and Brixton were small and separated communities. On the north side of the river the eastern boundary was roughly Stepney Fields and Bethnall Green, both open spaces. Kingsland, Dalston, and Bow were all separated communities, as were Shacklewell, Newington Green, Kentish Town, and Camden Town. It was a small London: a London where Chalk Farm was still a farm, containing a 'tavern and tea garden', quite isolated from any other building, and where, nearby, contemporary maps marked 'a pleasant path to Hampstead'.[8]

It was a small London, but very overcrowded. By contemporary maps its size varied little for the first quarter of the nineteenth century. But population was increasing at an unprecedented rate. 'The outstanding feature of the social history of the period [of the Industrial Revolution]', writes Professor Ashton, 'the thing that above all others distinguishes the age from its predecessors—is the rapid growth of population.'[9] It was a problem of which contemporaries were well aware. 'Only in the nineteen years 1798–1817 between the issue of the first edition of Malthus' *Essay* and of the fifth had it been finally decided, by the methods of the census, that the population was not merely growing, but growing fast.[10] From a 'possible 9,250,000 in 1781, the people of Great Britain had increased to a measured 10,943,000 in 1801, to 12,597,000 in 1811, and to 14,392,000 in 1821. In 1831, the return was to be 16,539,000'.[11] The main cause is generally thought to have been the increase in the net birth rate—i.e. not the numbers born, but the numbers

8 From Laurie & Whittle's New Map of London, 1813.
9 Ashton, op. cit., p. 3.
10 Clapham, op. cit., pp. 53–4.
11 Ibid., p. 55.

born who also survived. The death rate fell rapidly between 1790 and 1820,[12] and in so far as this affected infant mortality, it meant not only a rise in population, but a rise in the child and youth population. It is not possible to be certain of this, nor to distribute the increased population among age-groups. But Ashton remarks: 'By that time (1792–3) it is probable that the profuse waste of infant life was a little less . . . and if so, there would be a higher percentage of children and young people in the population. It is a matter to be borne in mind when considering the constitution of the labour force of the early factories.'[13] It is also relevant when considering the problem of education confronting those who lived in England at this time.

For various reasons, this rapid increase in population produced probably greater and certainly more noticeable social evils in London than elsewhere. Mrs George has written of attempts since the days of Elizabeth to restrict the growth of London by restricting building. She adds: 'It seems probable that the peculiar squalor and infamy of some of the courts and alleys built in the 17th century is partly due to the building policy begun by Elizabeth and carried on by the Stuarts and Cromwell. Buildings of a sort were put up in yards behind thoroughfares and in the courts of existing houses and by encroachments on waste land. The object must have been to escape notice and build in such a way that demolition would be no great loss. Overcrowding and poverty continued the process long after the restrictions had been given up.'[14] The result of restricting or prohibiting new building—a well-meant but entirely ineffectual measure to restrict London's population —was to produce worse buildings than would otherwise have been the case. Worse, because built in back yards and courts away from the public gaze and knowledge of the authorities: worse, too, because, in view of the evasion of the law involved, such buildings were constructed as cheaply as possible. And in addition, the general effect was less building than would have occurred in a free market, and more overcrowding, especially when the increase in population became rapid.

[12] Clapham, op. cit., p. 55.
[13] Ashton, op. cit., p. 5.
[14] George, op. cit., p. 72.

Mrs George concludes that 'although for want of statistics, generalisations on housing conditions are rash, yet certain conclusions may be drawn from the mass of miscellaneous and incidental information which is available. In the first place, overcrowding was general. Among its causes (besides the perennial one of poverty) was the necessity for workers to live near their place of work, owing to the absence of any means of cheap transport, and the unpleasantness and danger of walking through the streets, much more the outskirts, of London after nightfall ... Secondly, the standard dwelling of the artisan, even in a "genteel trade", seems to have been a single room and in very many cases a furnished room—while in many trades this was a workshop as well as living and sleeping place. Differences of social grade among the workers were marked by the part of the house occupied, by the respectability or otherwise of the street or court ... rather than by the number of rooms occupied.'[15]

A more detailed picture of life in central London at the end of the war is given by Francis Place, in a report shewing the need for education, and referring to the very crowded conditions in the small courts off the main streets. One such was Dumetta Court, near Drury Lane which 'had been condemned'. Rooms were let out to 'labourers and their families at 6/6 a week ... and again sublet to others ... Short's Garden's, nearly the whole of which we found occupied by poor roomkeepers—generally with families living in apparent wretchedness—it frequently happens that more than one house, sometimes as many as four, had been hired of their owner by one individual who let the house out in rooms—in some cases with furniture ... the room-keeper's change of abode is frequent ... The men were generally absent being labourers, and many of the women, particularly widows occupied in making soldiers' clothing, for which they stated being paid 5d for a pair of trousers, they

---

[15] M. D. George, op. cit., pp. 95–6. Mrs George's general conclusion is that there was a gradual improvement in housing from about the middle of the eighteenth century. But she takes 1840 as the date of comparison, and quotes 'in the reports of 1816–17 we read of forty in a cellar, and of cellars and rooms being shared with pigs and asses' (p. 107). In our period, it is these conditions which are relevant: whether they were worse in the eighteenth century is hardly apposite to our purpose. And the main improvement appears to have been later than 1816.

finding the thread . . .'[16] In this street, 412 families, including
829 children lived in 224 houses. This was one of the poorer
districts of London, although central, but it was by no means
the worst. According to one report it was common for a whole
family to live in a single room, and such rooms might be cellars
or garrets, according to the poverty of the family[17]—and 'from
three to eight individuals often sleep in the same bed'.

This was how the poor lived. But London was a city of con-
trasts. Mrs George quotes Archenholtz about 1780: 'The east
end, especially along the shores of the Thames, consists of old
houses, the streets there are narrow, dark and ill-paved;
inhabited by sailors and other workmen who are employed in
the construction of ships and by a great part of the Jews. The
contrast between this and the West End is astonishing: the
houses here are mostly new and elegant; the squares are
superb, the streets straight and open . . . If all London were
as well built there would be nothing in the world to compare
with it.'[18] But in Mill's day, it was not only the contrast
between East and West End which was striking, but the existence cheek by jowl in various districts of poverty and squalor
with wealth and magnificence. When Mill lived in Newington,
he took a weekly walk to Bentham's house in Queen's Square
Place, Westminster, calling on the way at Francis Place's shop
in Charing Cross Road. He would pass the relatively pleasant
districts of Islington and Pentonville and then what was one
of the worst districts, the area between St Sepulchre's, Clerken-
well, and Holborn, and the courts off Holborn and the Gray's
Inn Lane. He would touch the West End—Pall Mall was then
residential—and in Westminster itself find the contrast between
the large and spacious houses in Queen's Square Place, and, a
few steps further on, 'the older parts . . . notably Petty France
. . . which had long been ill-inhabited'.[19] London was almost
literally Plato's two cities—a city of the rich and a city of the

[16] B.M. Place Collection, vol. 60. This part of the report is by Edward Wakefield, based on personal visitation. Place says it was 'by far the best', and it is
extensively used in Brougham's Royal Commission on Education.

[17] Clapham quotes, 1,132 cellar tenements in Marylebone alone as late as 1854.

[18] George, op. cit., p. 66.

[19] George, op. cit., p. 83. The nearby Tothill Fields was 'almost if not quite
the last place in London where bull-baiting was regularly carried on' (p. 97).

poor. And although the East End can be regarded as wholly poor, London west of Temple Bar—the London Mill and Place knew and the London they surveyed in an attempt to discover its educational needs—this London exemplified the contrast in many districts and in places in adjacent streets.

It is almost impossible to generalize about the work and occupation of Londoners. There were 'four hundred or so different occupations in London'.[20] The chief ones were building, shoemaking, tailoring, cabinet-making, printing, clockmaking, jewellery, and baking.[21] There are two points to notice about the London worker in those days. First, the ratio of wage-earner to employer was low—'something less than ten to one' according to Clapham: a very large number of people worked directly for the consumer—it was an age of independence, of individual initiative. As a corollary of this, of course, businesses and factories were small concerns employing relatively small numbers of people. There were eleven great brewers of London, but there were seventy-three smaller ones as well. 'The largest shipyard in the river in 1815 employed only 400–500 shipwrights and 100 or so others . . . In 1818 the average number of hand-looms running, in the weavers' homes, for each of fifteen Spitalfields silk manufacturers, was only 58. These fifteen were the big employers.'[22] The typical Londoner worked either for himself or in a small business: only rarely in a really big workshop, and such big workshops were small by our standards.

This is the second point of importance—the meaning of the word 'factory' at this time. To us it signifies a large building, much machinery, many employees, and a somewhat impersonal and mechanical existence. It had a very different connotation in the early nineteenth century. The West London Lancasterian Association enquiry into the Drury Lane area records that there were in the district bounded by Bow Street and Long Acre: '5 day schools, 10 coffee houses, 11 public houses, 4 gin shops, 11 public brothels, 2 chapels, 1 theatre (Covent Garden), 1 public office (Bow Street) and 5 factories', as well as 254

[20] Clapham, op. cit., p. 70.
[21] Ibid. There were over 2,500 adult members of each of these trades in 1831.
[22] Clapham, op. cit., p. 69.

houses.[23] There would hardly be room for one modern factory in the whole area. It seems clear that the word 'factory' in Mill's day was used for any establishment where people assembled for the purposes of manufacture. Machinery there probably was—this was one of the raisons d'être of the factory. Much more important than this was the need for employer supervision of workers, for the domestic system of work allowed little check on labour time, and on materials used. So the factory was generally a small establishment with few employees. The largest in London at this time were those of the brewers— 'the eleven great brewers'. One of these—Barclays—still stood, until recently, in Southwark—a very modest building set amid its mighty neighbours up and down the banks of the twentieth century Thames. London was the home of small enterprises, and a major element in its life was the domestic system of industry, the craftsman's shop, and apprenticeship, with all its consequences for young children.

There were thus no clear-cut class divisions, nor was there any consciousness of one. On the contrary, the eighteenth century, writes Mrs George, 'was an age of minute social distinctions. Lines were drawn between artisan and labourer, the master and the journeyman as they were drawn between the lodger and the housekeeper. They were however drawn with difficulty.'[24] It was an age of 'clubs' in the general meaning of the term. Ashton writes 'every interest, tradition, or aspiration found expression in corporate form',[25] and the club might be social and pleasure-loving like the cock and hen club of the tavern, or occupational like the friendly society or early trade union. But whatever else they were, they were small, limited and local. England was not a nation of large clearly-defined classes but of a multitude of separate interests made even stronger by the club tendency. When James Mill recorded in his Commonplace Book 'sense of public interest—to create this sense and give it form is the ultimate point of good education' he was not commenting on the twentieth-century problem of capital and labour, employer and employee or even on diverse

[23] B.M. Place Collection, vol. 60.
[24] George, op. cit., pp. 156–7.
[25] Ashton, op. cit., p. 127.

aims of upper, middle and lower classes. His problem was the existence of a very large number of self-contained groups, each welded by its own limited interest or purpose, and none seeing any problems beyond.

There is one other fact about London life which is important. Hours were generally long, and leisure hard-earned and irregular. Whatever the trade, a twelve- or fourteen-hour day was general: the hours worked under the domestic system can of course hardly be assessed. With this went what Mrs George called the 'uncertainties of life'. She quotes Place, writing in 1837: 'In every London trade there is at least one period of the year when it is brisk, and another when it is slack: fluctuations at these times in the demand for labour are very great'.[26] His own account of his early career in tailoring bears eloquent testimony to this truth. Thus though hours were long, leisure when it came might also be long, and to some extent unforeseen. Wages might often be high: they were always uncertain. The security so valued in the twentieth century was almost entirely absent in Mill's day. It was not a state of things to encourage thrift and foresight among the people: on the contrary, it fostered the attitude of 'living for today'. It also had its influence on their leisure time pursuits.

What were the 'pleasures' of the Londoner at this time? The social historians of the period appear to be agreed that the three most frequent and regular constituents of the pleasures of the poor, and of the skilled workmen and tradesmen, were drink, gambling in some form or other, and what were termed 'Rough Sports'. 'At his work and in his amusements . . . it was difficult for the Londoner to escape the ever-present temptation to drink.'[27] Place records of his early life: 'It was the custom at this time, as it long had been, for almost every man who had the means to spend his evenings at some public house or tavern or other place of public entertainment.' All clubs whether social or friendly society met in the tavern. The tavern was the centre of lottery clubs, of punch clubs, the coach station, the place for the payment of wages, the recognized employment agency for a large number of trades—the more irregular the employment

26 George, op. cit., p. 270.
27 Ibid., p. 301.

the more frequently was the tavern haunted—and not infrequently the publican was the constable.[28] It would be difficult to overestimate the central importance of the tavern in the social life of the time.

With this went the kind of amusements and pleasure a tavern could provide. The evening might be spent in drinking as an ordinary customer in a bar—or if more respectable in the bar-parlour: it might be as a member of a drinking club, meeting in a private room, or as member of a lottery club, several of which might meet in one tavern. The state lotteries seem to have attracted most support, and they lured an alarmingly large number of tradesmen from good businesses to the debtors' prison. And no contest in sport or at cards was thought complete without a stake on the result.

'A ducking pond was the usual adjunct of taverns, especially in the vicinity of London.' Great cruelty was practised there: if no ducks were available, cats were thrown into the water and dogs set on them. Other sports not necessarily associated with taverns but which were popular amusements were cock-fighting, cock-throwing and bear- and bull-baiting. The keynote of all of them was a contest of some kind, accompanied by considerable brutality and cruelty, and what Place described as 'the most abominable scenes'.[29] Yet this was the third common 'pleasure' of the poor—in London, for instance, there were cockpits in Westminster, Drury Lane, Jermyn Street, Birdcage Walk, Pall Mall, Haymarket, and Covent Garden.[30] There were several ducking ponds on the east side of Tottenham Court Road.

Less regular entertainment came from the theatres with their satellite taverns and brothels—theatres were places of great disorder—and from the open market place for prostitutes. Still less regular were fairs like St Bartholomews, events like the Lord Mayor's show, and days of national festivity like the visit of the Czar of Russia after 1815—all made the occasion of drink, noise, and disorder. Boxing contests, also, were popular with both rich and poor.

[28] Ibid., p. 293.
[29] Ibid., p. 306.
[30] A. E. Richardson, *Georgian England: A Survey of Social Life*, London, 1931, pp. 89–90.

The pleasures of the rich bore something of the same hall-mark as those of the poor. Gambling was exceedingly common, and enormous sums were won and lost on the most trivial issues of chance. In the country, fox-hunting and other eques-trian sports predominated: in London, time was passed in clubs, card-playing, occasionally riding in Hyde Park, visits to Belsize House and the fashionable round. Boxing contests with attendant gambling were well attended and from a considerable distance. Drinking, it need hardly be said, was a constant accompaniment of most pleasures, but for the rich in the club in St James Street, or in the house, not in the tavern.[31]

The central themes of the pleasures of both rich and poor were three. First, there was a general absence of moderation in anything. 'To understand the value which the nineteenth cen-tury set on respectability', writes Mrs George, 'one should, like Place, have experienced the disastrous effects of the lack of it.'[32] Second, both rich and poor in their pleasures and amusements exemplified the philosophy of life of living for the day, not for the morrow. Foresight was difficult for the poor, and both uncongenial and unnecessary for the rich. All their pleasures were temporary and fleeting: all lived for the excitement of the moment, the day, or the evening. Third, neither rich nor poor cared for what might be called the 'intellectual pleasures' whether of literature, drama, reading, or conversation. There was generally an absence of any seeking after delight by the cultivation of the mind. The pleasures of the time arose largely from, exemplified and of course added to 'the uncertainties of life'. But these characteristic ways in which people enjoyed themselves must constantly be borne in mind when we come to consider Mill's philosophy with its accent on 'pleasure' as the end of human existence.

II

In addition to the London social scene before Mill's eyes, there were certain national problems which were his constant

[31] Cf. Richardson, chapter v, and A. Bryant, *Age of Elegance*, Collins, 1950.
[32] George, op. cit., p. 275.

preoccupation, which influenced his thought and which were indeed before the minds of many Londoners. These were the political system of the day, the national Press, the legal system, the established Church and its organization, and the state of education or the lack of it.

Perhaps the major point about the political system, to Mill and his friends, was that it was undemocratic, and failed to represent both all the people, and some of the newer interests. The cause of this was twofold. The right to vote varied considerably from place to place, but was generally considerably restricted—most of the population of England had no vote. Secondly, the constituency boundaries were completely out of date in that shifts of population during a century and a half had not resulted in corresponding changes in the boundaries. The consequence was well-known cases like Stockbridge with two voters and two members, and Old Sarum with no voters, and two members, and towns like Manchester and Birmingham with no members at all. The general effect of all this, together with the fact that voting was not secret was to place the power of electing members of Parliament squarely in the hands of the wealthy landowners, who could, by threatening eviction, easily control such votes as their tenants had. The fact that seats could be bought and sold, and were advertised in the press as such, did give the merchants a chance of purchasing representation, but the fact that they had to buy what the landowner possessed by right can hardly have been other than galling, though it did result in some merchant representation in the Commons, as, for instance, Mill's friend David Ricardo. Only the wealthy could do this and tradesmen, professional men and the large mass of the people were entirely unrepresented. 'Interests' or some of them, were represented, and such 'interests' were served; the community was not represented, and its needs were largely ignored.

With this went a considerable amount of patronage in the distribution of lesser offices, and of offices in the administrative machine. Just how widespread this was during Mill's time, it is difficult to say. Halévy argues that 'a great reform movement began about 1780, and although this movement undoubtedly died down during the anti-Jacobin reaction, during the last year of the war it was once more in full swing'. There was a reform movement, but it had, in the sphere of politics, so far effected little reform. England was in a stage of transition, but her political institutions showed little change. Whatever reform there had been was slight: it had certainly not gone far enough to be the rule in administrative matters. Halévy continues: 'by 1815, they [the Tories] were pledged to the defence of all the abuses employed by the 18th century Whigs to secure their power, for that power was now in Tory hands'. Halévy also comments: 'we cannot be surprised that public opinion watched with an ever-increasing scepticism a dispute in which both parties were obviously fighting for their own interests'.[33] One of these sceptical observers was James Mill, who recorded in his Commonplace Book: 'Under a bad government there is no common interest. Every man is governed by his private interest.'

This was to a large extent unfortunately true. Whatever the arguments advanced in favour of the Corn Laws, the modern historian is unlikely to feel that they would have been passed had not Parliament been dominated by landowners. The social conditions we have just described cried aloud for reform but Parliament, whose members can hardly have been ignorant of things in London, made little or no effort. The Industrial Revolution produced evils in the cotton mills which were the subject of an outcry before the turn of the century: not until 1833 was an effective measure passed. The chimney sweep's boys were a further abuse brought before Parliament shortly after 1815: the very modest bill to effect some reform was thrown out by the House of Lords. Brougham in 1817 demonstrated clearly the need for provision of education: 1833 was the time of the first government grant. These instances, most of them well known, could be multiplied. It would be foolish to offer one simple explanation for the inaction of Parliament and to suggest that it was the whole explanation. But it would be naive to ignore the pressure of private interest on government decisions or to deny that Mill's comment—'every man is governed by his private interest' appeared all too frequently true of the government of his day. By patronage men gained

[33] E. Halévy, *History of the English People in the Nineteenth Century*, i (Benn edn, 1961), pp. 18–20.

membership of Parliament or appointment to the administrative service: their primary preoccupation was to serve or at least to placate their patron. Other factors—the ignorance of Parliament of the extent of the social evils, the weakness of the administrative machine as a means of dealing with them, the identification of any reform movement as an incipient French Revolution—these were certainly there. But to the Radical, 'ignorance was no excuse', reform of the administrative machine had been pressed for years, and the fear of revolution was only too likely to produce it. Woodward's summing up may be quoted: 'a parliament of landowners, rich manufacturers and merchants was unlikely to look at industry, trade, or agriculture from the point of view of the labouring classes . . . Until parliamentary elections ceased to be a form of jobbery, there was no chance of breaking away from the tradition which gave official posts, active and sinecure, to the party in power as a means of rewarding followers and maintaining a majority . . . The "spoils system" was indeed at its worst in the last years of the unreformed parliament . . . Finally, reform in the other great institutions of the country, the church, the universities, the courts of law, was improbable until parliament, instead of providing specious arguments for the maintenance of abuses, set a standard by which laxity and corruption in other spheres could be judged and condemned.'[34] And he adds later, a confirmation of Mill's essential thesis: 'the main problem of government after the war may be expressed in terms of the defence of property'.[35] Not property as an institution, but their own property, with all its privileges and power. This was their problem, and their policy: to Mill both were the inevitable results of a bad system.

It is not so widely realized that the Church of England at this time suffered from very much the same defects, in part brought about by the same causes. Here, as in politics, there had been no re-adjustment of the number of churches, parishes, and livings to meet the shift in population from south to north and from country to town, especially to London. Halévy quotes

[34] E. L. Woodward, *Age of Reform*, Oxford History of England, O.U.P., 1939, pp. 26-7.
[35] Ibid., p. 56.

several instances of the consequences of this. The province of York, with rapidly growing new towns, 'counted but six bishops as against twenty in the province of Canterbury, and 2,000 parishes for 10,000 in the Southern Province. Bath, Chichester, Ely and Hereford possessed their bishops; Manchester, Birmingham, Leeds, and Liverpool had none. The total church accommodation of Liverpool amounted to but 21,000 seats. The population was 94,000. In Manchester there was accommodation for 11,000 of the 79,000 inhabitants. In London the Established Church provided about 150,000 seats for a population that exceeded a million.'[36] Earlier Halévy quotes: 'Cobbett, in the course of one of his rural rides, remarked a Wiltshire parish which was simply an ecclesiastical Old Sarum. The parson's income amounted to £300 a year. There was neither church nor parsonage.'[37]

This was the first of the factors which made the early nineteenth century perhaps the least creditable of all periods in the history of the Church of England. A second, and even more influential factor was the alliance between the church and the aristocracy. As far as the higher clergy went 'it was universally admitted that the choice of archbishops and bishops must be political'.[38] They were therefore, almost without exception, Tories. 'Eleven in 1815 were of noble birth, among them the Archbishop of Canterbury . . . a cousin of the Duke of Rutland, and the Archbishop of York, a brother of Lord Vernon. Ten had been tutors or schoolmasters of a prince, a duke or a statesman . . . the see of Sodor and Man was actually a benefice in the hereditary patronage of the Dukes of Athol. It was but the natural result that the present occupant, George Murray, should be a member of the family.'

Even more significant, however, was the state of things with the lower clergy. 'Out of the 11,700 benefices in England and Wales, the patronage of scarcely 1,500 belonged to the bishops or cathedral chapters . . . in one half of the parishes the appointment of the vicar was in the hands of the landlord, his legal and incontestable right . . . the landed gentry were

[36] Halévy, *History of the English People in* 1815, op. cit., p. 399.
[37] Ibid., p. 398.
[38] Ibid., p. 393.

masters equally of the ecclesiastical as of the civil administration.[39]

The combination of these two factors, failure to build churches
to meet shifts of population and aristocratic lay control of
appointment to livings, was a series of abuses. First, there was
little or no suggestion that the clerical body should have any
knowledge of or qualification in theology—'England was probably the sole country in Christendom where no proof of
theological knowledge was exacted from candidates for ordination.'[40] Second, so large a number of livings in the relatively
uninhabited south led to pluralism and absenteeism. 'One
incumbent could hold simultaneously two, three, four, or even
more benefices. There is an instance of a single ecclesiastic in
possession of eight.'[41] Where the population was small and the
living contiguous, the vicar could perform his duties perfunctorily without assistance. But a more common practice was to
employ curates at a miserably low wage—for instance 'Hesket
in the Carlisle diocese where the Dean and Chapter received
annually between £1,000 and £1,500 a year and paid their
curate £18-5 shillings a year'.[42] The result was that the incumbent of a living was more often than not non-resident: in 1806–7
there were over 6,000 non-resident incumbents, out of 11,000
livings.[43]

Such livings could be bestowed by patronage, usually on a
relative, or bought and sold, sometimes by auction. The price
depended on the age of the present holder, which determined
how soon the purchaser could enjoy the income from his
purchase. And the value of the livings was value to the landlord
whose interest it was to see that this value did not fall. Hence
the landlords were not merely indifferent to the shortage of
churches in the populated areas, they actively opposed any
increase for it would diminish the value of the existing churches
in their own possession. The 'Duke of Portland compelled the
parish of Marylebone, with a population of 40,000, to be content

[39] Ibid., p. 394.
[40] Ibid., p. 391.
[41] Ibid., p. 397.
[42] Ibid., p. 397.
[43] Ibid., p. 398.

with a village church with accommodation at the utmost for 200'.[44]

The picture is a lamentable one. It is a picture of a corrupt Church, indifferent to its spiritual duties, largely incapable of exercising them, hindering reform quite as actively as the political system in whose control it was. It was a situation calculated to rouse the anger of anyone seriously concerned to see an established church performing its proper function. It was a situation offering many and blatant examples of corruption, patronage and the preservation of privilege. Even more openly than in politics, 'men served only their private interest', and this in a calling which should have meant the abnegation of personal advantage. James Mill was an agnostic, but, as we shall see, he was by no means indifferent to these issues. And when we consider his doctrine of social education, that a bad society perverts the characters of its members by rewarding bad instead of good qualities, we shall do well to remember Dicey's moderate but measured condemnation of the whole system: 'In the service neither of the State nor of the Church was reward in any way proportioned to merit. A favoured few connected by relationship or interest with the rich and the powerful, received huge salaries for doing nothing, whilst the men who actually did the work were in many cases grossly underpaid.'[45]

The legal system of the country does not present so black a picture. The organization of the bar, the appointment of judges and their relationship with counsel, while doubtless open to criticism was certainly not so blatantly perverse as the system of Church and State. In the legal profession, the bar, at least at the top was well-paid, but the barristers worked for their money, and the same is true of the judges. There were of course abuses: judges were paid by fees for each case, instead of by annual salaries, and there were many sinecures. The time occupied in litigation was extraordinarily long. But the whole system was not bad, corrupt, and entirely inadequate to perform its function, as was the case with the Church and the State in both legislature and executive.

[44] Ibid., p. 400.
[45] A. V. Dicey, *Law and Public Opinion in England*, Macmillan, 1948, p. 87.

What was much less satisfactory was the local administration of justice. This was in the hands of magistrates, nominally appointed by the Crown, in fact always following the recommendation of the Lord Lieutenant of the County, who was in turn the largest landowner in the county. Thus the magistrates represented the landowning interests and, according to Halévy, more and more power was placed in their hands either at Petty or Quarter Sessions, and fewer and fewer were the cases allowed to go to Assize or to the Courts of Appeal in London. Their power, and their use of their power were certainly open to criticism.

But the main trouble was not the administration of the law but the law itself. Dicey comments: 'The immutability of the law during the earlier part of the 19th century may be regarded from different points of view. We may note the easy tolerance of large public abuses ... we may ... observe the general acquiescence in legal fictions and survivals, which, while they admitted no logical defence, constituted either the grave defects or the oddities of the law of England.'[46] There was, he continues, an 'indifference both of legislators and of the public to the maintenance of laws and customs which seriously affected private life, and might work obvious and palpable wrong and injustice'.[47] He cites as examples the game laws, by which landlords might set dangerous man-traps, to preserve their game 'at the cost of occasionally killing innocent trespassers', and by which men could be hanged for poaching. Prisoners on trial for felony were denied legal representation. And there were the many 'irrational restrictions placed by the Common Law upon the admissibility of evidence'.[48] There were, pervading the whole law, 'long labyrinths of judge-made fictions which ... seem to a lawyer of today as strange as the most fanciful dreams of Alice in Wonderland ... They were nevertheless tolerated ... by the public opinion of 1800 just as were other survivals or fictions which were as noxious as they were obviously ridiculous.'[49] The general point is clear: the law was

[46] Dicey, op. cit., p. 86.
[47] Ibid., p. 87.
[48] Ibid., p. 89.
[49] Ibid., p. 93.

irrational, and where it was not irrational it was repressive, unjust and served the interests of a group. On all these points the Utilitarian objected: Bentham and Mill perhaps to the first as much as to any. But the criminal law, with its long array of trivial offences punishable by death was a contradiction of the essence of the Utilitarian doctrine with its insistence that the punishment must be no more than is needed to provide adequate deterrence.

The Press at this time consisted of nine or ten London daily papers and approximately the same number appearing twice or three times a week. There were also newspapers in most provincial centres. Of these, the London papers appearing twice or thrice weekly circulated mainly in the country and the provincial papers were unknown outside their locality. Of the ten London papers, five were advertising journals. The circulation of all papers was small, and, since until 1814 they were printed by hand, production difficulties, as well as those of distribution and demand, set a limit to the number of copies.[50]

There were no 'national papers' in any real sense, owing to the difficulty of communication: London to Leeds in 1815 took 33 hours. 'Only a small proportion of the London papers was sent into the provinces, and a still smaller one to the colonies and to foreign countries.'[51] But even if there had been rapid communication, the illiteracy of the majority of the population set severe limits to the size of the circulation. Judging by the stamp duty returns, the total number of copies of London papers of all kinds in the year 1801 was about 7 million. By similar tests, 9 million provincial papers were sold during the year.[52] For 1836, these figures had risen to $19\frac{1}{4}$ millions for London, and 11 million for the provinces—an indication of the changes during the period, and of the gradual domination of the London papers.

The governments of the time, especially in the earlier period, disliked and feared the press, and by various measures confirmed and even reduced the already limited circulation of

[50] A. Aspinall, *Politics & the Press 1780-1805*, Home & Van Thal, 1949, pp. 6-7 (figures are for 1783).

[51] Ibid., p. 7.

[52] Ibid., p. 350. These figures are *not* circulation figures.

papers. The principal weapon was taxation. Others included the control of the Post Office facilities for distribution, and the legal prosecution for libel and other offences of editors and proprietors of certain periodicals. The latter measures were accentuated when, after 1819, people could be and were prosecuted for reading such periodicals as Cobbett's *Political Register.*

But the most onerous burden on the newspapers was taxation by stamp and advertisement duty. The stamp duty in 1780 was 1d per copy, by 1815 it had risen to 4d per copy. The advertisement duty was similarly increased from 2s 6d in 1780 to 3s 6d in 1815. The rates then remained virtually stationary for twenty years. The effect was that the price of the *Times* was 7d a copy after 1815, and this paper alone contributed £70,000 to revenue.[53] It reduced its price to 5d when the stamp duty fell to 1d in 1836, to 4d when the advertisement duty was abolished in 1853, and to 3d when the paper duty was repealed in 1861.[54] The tax was lucrative to the revenue: it totalled nearly half a million yearly. But it was crippling to the press and to the public, most of whom found newspapers a luxury far beyond their reach. Aspinall concludes: 'After 1815, right down to 1835, the last year of the 4d duty, the consumption of stamped newspapers was actually stationary per head of population. It was said in 1830 that heavy taxation was solely responsible for the recent disappearance of four newspapers ... The fact that heavy taxation was the most important cause of the restricted sales of newspapers was amply proved by statistics. Whereas the sale of stamped newspapers rose by only 33% in the twenty years ending 1836, it rose by over 70% from a larger initial figure as a result of the stamp duty reduction to 1d in 1836.'[55] Whether or not we accept Professor Aspinall's conclusions as strongly as he states them—there were other factors such as increased literacy and interest in public affairs—the figures are certainly highly suggestive, even if not 'ample proof', and they permit us to make a highly probable conjecture as to the dire effects of taxation on circulation.

[53] Ibid., p. 23. This was much the largest newspaper.
[54] Wickham Steed, *The Press*, Penguin Books, 1938, p. 124.
[55] Aspinall, op. cit., p. 23.

The consequences of these small circulations was very important. In the first place, newspapers were shared, and were read communally in taverns, coffee-houses and subscription reading-rooms. This was a significant social development when we compare it with the typical pleasures of the Londoner of the period.[56] After 1815 the government shewed its fear of this practice by attempting to suppress it, largely by threatening to remove the licenses of innkeepers whose rooms were used for reading dangerous newspapers.[57] The seditious meetings act of 1817 strengthened the hand of the magistrates by empowering them to remove the license of any public house where 'any meeting for any seditious purpose had been held'. The use of a room for reading a radical newspaper in common was all too easily brought under this head.

More important was the consequence of small circulation on the independence and freedom of the press. The small circulations made it difficult if not impossible for a newspaper to carry on without the aid of government subsidies and contracts for advertisements for government departments. These were the most overt ways in which the government exercised patronage over the press, and, in return, the government gained influence and some control over what the newspapers so befriended, published: only 'friendly' newspapers were favoured. The result of subsidies and judicious distribution of government advertisements was to weaken, and in some cases almost to destroy, the liberty and independence of the press. Yet taxation forced newspapers into an economic position where they were especially vulnerable to this temptation. Subsidies, during the French Revolutionary war, at least in the earlier part, amounted to nearly £5,000 a year—several papers received a regular income. The system continued well into the nineteenth century. Aspinall estimates that at least an equivalent sum was spent on advertising.[58] By 1814, the position had somewhat improved, in that there were some newspapers sufficiently independent of direct financial aid, to offer support to the government only as a return for less obvious bribes, such as priority of intelligence,

[56] Ibid., p. 44.
[57] Ibid., p. 24.
[58] Ibid., p. 133.

advertisements, and so on. Aspinall sums it up thus: 'A ministerial newspaper in 1814 was one which, in return for priority of intelligence, and departmental advertisements, gave the Government general support in its leading articles and undertook to publish officially inspired paragraphs. The freedom of the press was endangered just as much by the Government's efforts to control a newspaper's political opinions as by direct bribery.'[59]

Education in England at the turn of the century presented a picture of local, sporadic, unco-ordinated and totally inadequate facilities. Primary education, whether defined as elementary—meaning the three R's—or as the first few years of a child's school life, was variable: sometimes it existed in part, rarely were full facilities available, and what there was varied considerably in different parts of the country. There were three types of school: the endowed schools of private religious foundations which gave free education to poor children. According to Halévy, about 150,000 children attended these schools.[60] Here, as in other walks of life, the nominal schoolmaster often regarded his post as a sinecure and took the salary, leaving the work to a grossly underpaid subordinate. Secondly, there were the 'dames' schools where by the same calculation about 53,000 attended. Thirdly, there were schools of industry which provided some kind of elementary education, together with a training for a trade. Here, Halévy estimates that of nearly 200,000 Poor Law children between the ages of five and fourteen, only 20,000 gained this education. This was the state of things at the end of the eighteenth century: there was no national system of education, and what provision there was by private effort and inititative was largely distorted by the shift of population from south to north, and from country to town.

To this gloomy picture it is right to add some qualifications. First, we should not ignore the general system of apprenticeship which worked in the eighteenth century and continued in the first part of the nineteenth. Though this system was often abused, as by its nature it is easily open to abuse, it sometimes worked well, and even when it did not, it provided some

[59] Ibid., pp. 202–3.
[60] Halévy, op. cit., p. 526 (figures are for 1819).

vocational if not basic primary education.[61] Second, some good was done by Robert Raikes and his Sunday schools. Here, the children received elementary education as well as religious instruction. One factor aiding its success was that Sunday was the only day when most children were free for education. Third, and most important, was the monitorial system of Lancaster and Bell which started and expanded remarkably in the first quarter of the nineteenth century. This was the system whereby the master taught the senior or more advanced pupils, and they in turn taught their juniors. It was claimed that, in this way, one master could be responsible for several hundreds of boys. Educational benefits were also claimed for the system, but the principal reason for its widespread support and quite substantial private financial aid was the fact that it offered a rapid, cheap and apparently practicable solution to the very large national problem of primary education. With the rise in child population, the monitorial system had something of the attractions of an emergency training scheme for teachers, with its promise quickly to supply the national need.

For the problem was a considerable one, and once thoughtful people became aware of it, it seemed almost impossible to tackle. Halévy suggests quoting Colquhoun, that, in 1806, 2 million children in England and Wales received no education at all. The first official statistics in 1819 stated that only 674,803 children in England and Wales attended school, out of a total population of about 10 millions.[62] Place and the West London Lancasterian Association estimated that 30,000 children in London *west* of Temple Bar were without education.[63] What the position was like in the East End can only be guessed, but, as has been stated, in some of the areas round Long Acre, Place found more than half the children receiving no education. The problem was of a size that anything that individual enterprise could do seemed a mere drop in the ocean. The monitorial system offered a solution on a scale commensurate with the need, and of a kind within the financial limits of private philanthropy.

[61] Cf. George, op. cit.
[62] Cf. Halévy, op. cit., p. 532 n. 6.
[63] B.M. Place Collection, vol. 60.

2

It is difficult to generalize about secondary education. There were grammar schools—largely or entirely day schools—like the Royal Grammar School, Newcastle-on-Tyne, and there were also 'public schools' which were regarded as superior. But they were not 'public schools' as we understand the term today. Games, prefectorial rule and responsibility, the training of character as a major aim, even housemasters in charge of boarding houses—all these were later developments associated largely with the name of Thomas Arnold, and a kind of renaissance in the older public schools, together with the foundation of a large number of the present public schools of England, in the mid-nineteenth century.

There were therefore very few public schools in England in Mill's day—by some criteria as few as seven—and they were the preserve of the wealthy. The had become 'public' generally because they took boarders: other foundations, such as for example Witney, near Oxford, took no boarders and gradually declined. It was largely the accidents of history, the appointment of an enterprising headmaster and the vision of the governing body which decided whether these original grammar school foundations became boarding and therefore subsequently 'public' schools or remained day grammar schools. As day grammar schools, they were scattered up and down the country in a somewhat capricious fashion, according to their success in surviving the vicissitudes of history since their foundation, generally in Tudor times. As a result, they sometimes did, and sometimes did not, coincide with centres of population and their quality and size varied considerably.

Both grammar and public schools had two features in common: both were controlled by the Established Church and in almost every case the headmaster was in orders. All public schools and most grammar schools taught the same curriculum, namely a classical one. By a legal decision in 1805, re-iterated in 1826, both public schools and endowed grammar schools were held to be, in a very literal sense, 'grammar' schools, that is, schools devoted to an education in grammar, and this meant not only a classical curriculum but classics of a particular kind. Attention was concentrated on language rather than literature, on style and verses rather than classical history: the curriculum therefore prescribed a series of extracts rather than the study of any particular author. The classical languages were not regarded as a path of entry to the study of ancient civilizations: the prevailing belief was that classical languages could teach, as nothing else could, the basic elements of 'grammar' which would in turn lead to a mastery of correct English. There were some exceptions to this: Adamson notes that, despite the legal ruling, some of the less prosperous endowed schools provided some choice of curriculum. Of 500 schools at work in 1818, 120 taught 'every variety of study', some 56 offered 'English' subjects only and in 80, parents could choose between a classical and an 'English' curriculum.[64] This variety was however more marked in the private schools and the generality of public and grammar schools remained true to the classical tradition. This, and other features of the public schools, had been vigorously attacked by Sidney Smith and others in the *Edinburgh Review* from 1807 onwards: in 1830 the review commented that, with such a curriculum, 'attention is distracted from the really important lessons of history and philosophy to grammatical and metrical trifling'.

The state of the universities at Oxford and Cambridge was partly responsible for this situation. A contemporary writer, Vicesimus Knox, sometime Fellow of St John's, Oxford, and Headmaster of Tonbridge School, was unsparing in his strictures of Oxford and Cambridge, though a defender of the classical curriculum in the schools. He wrote of Oxford: 'I saw immorality, habitual drunkenness, idleness, ignorance, and vanity, openly and boastingly obtruding themselves on public view.'[65] In part this was due to the absence of any serious examination at the end of the course, and in part despite the 'opulence, buildings, libraries, professorships and scholarships' of Oxford and Cambridge, 'if there is an inferiority, it is in the persons, not in the places or their constitution. And here I cannot help confessing, that a desire to please the great and bring them to the universities, for the sake of honour and profit, and other political motives, causes a compliance with fashionable manners, a relaxation of discipline, and a connivance at

[64] J. W. Adamson, *English Education, 1789–1902*, C.U.P., 1964 edn, p. 47.
[65] Vicesimus Knox, *Liberal Education*, Works iv, p. 138.

ignorance and folly'.[66] Later, he goes into more detail. 'Few professors read lectures; very little literary emulation prevails; very little encouragement is given. Favour is chiefly shown to those whose parents will one day be able to assist the tutor or college officer by interest. Rank and riches engross the attention of those among the seniors who are aspiring to ecclesiastical preferment; and a modest and able young man, whose situation is obscure and circumstances narrow, may have the merit of an angel, and yet be totally disregarded; or, if he aspires to excelling others in solid merit, subject himself to all the mortification which envy and malice can inflict on a feeling mind.

'The tutors, it is true, give what are called lectures.[67] But they are often little more than the shadow of substantial forms: mere evasions, contrived to justify in appearance the acceptance of the scholar's money. The boys construe a classic, the jolly young tutor lolls in his elbow-chair, and seldom gives himself the trouble of interrupting the greatest dunce. But is the mere construing of an author a lecture? The truth is, as a very sensible author has observed, the tutor knowing himself to be secure in his office, independently of the pupils' or their parents' judgment, satisfies himself with performing the business in such a manner as most effectually to consult his own ease . . . In short, the foundation of fellowships has rendered colleges very different places from places of education. They are to many like alms-houses, where the bounty of the benefactors is to be plentifully enjoyed, their souls prayed for, and nothing done.'[68]

When, later, we find James Mill writing much the same thing, we should remember that others besides the Radicals condemned the English universities at this time.

In all these matters, in education at every stage, England stood in marked contrast to Scotland. In Scotland, a statute of 1696 amended in 1803, required every parish to maintain and lodge a schoolmaster. This did not mean free primary education for all, but it did mean that primary education was widely available, and pauper children could be educated at the expense

---

[66] Knox, op. cit., p. 145.

[67] The term 'lecture' means what is now called a tutorial in which the pupil gives the 'lecture', i.e. reads his essay.

[68] Knox, op. cit., pp. 199–200.

of the parish. In secondary education, the upper classes employed, at a low wage, a private tutor; the middle classes and others used the day-schools 'which existed in every town, large or small, throughout the kingdom [of Scotland]. Of these the most celebrated was the High School of Edinburgh.'[69] Competent if sometimes uninspired secondary education was widely available. Finally the four Scottish universities enjoyed a high intellectual reputation and in many ways they and their pupils were the core of the intellectual life of Britain at this time. Fees were low, classes were large, and students were young by English standards, and still more young by our standards today. But the professors of the time, especially at Edinburgh, were generally men of intellectual eminence. The same could be said of some of the students. The class list at Edinburgh in 1795 contains the names of James Mill, Jeffrey, to become editor of the *Edinburgh Review*, Brougham, a future Lord Chancellor, McVey Napier, a future editor of the *Encyclopedia Britannica*, McCulloch, a distinguished economist of the 1820s. Such was Edinburgh's reputation that many English noblemen sent their sons there, between leaving public school and going on to Oxford or Cambridge. These Scottish standards made the English deficiencies the more glaring by comparison. Where England had no system of primary education, Scotland had such schools available in every village. Where English secondary education was, to put it mildly, variable in both the place and the quality of its provision, Scotland had competent day schools in every town. Where English universities were centres of sloth, ease and religious intolerance, Scottish ones were genuine centres of education and, if not available to all, within reach of almost every able and hard-working aspirant, by means of a system of scholarships.

Education, then, in England was ripe for reform and change at all levels, and the debate as to what reforms were needed and in what direction they should be aimed was stimulated from many and varied quarters. First of all Rousseaus's ideas of 'education according to nature' had had considerable influence: it may be detected in, for example, Edgeworth's *Practical Education*, a book which was widely read at the time. Then

[69] Halévy, op. cit., p. 534.

there were those who, as in every age, demanded a 'relevant' education: this invariably took the form of condemning the classical curriculum, and substituting science and technology as more suited to the 'needs of society'. Of such critics, the most distinguished were Jeremy Bentham and his disciple in these matters, Dr Southwood Smith. But the movement for a 'relevant' curriculum was widely supported: in 1821 a bill was promoted for broadening the curriculum of the grammar schools by adding 'reading, writing and accounts' and freeing the schools from the restrictions of the Eldon judgment of 1805. Finally, there were those who sought to reform rather than remove the classical curriculum, by making it the vehicle of the study of ancient history and philosophy. This movement is generally held to have been started in the universities by the Noetics at Oriel College and in the schools by Thomas Arnold at Rugby. But the seeds of change were apparent before this. Vicesimus Knox attacked the bill of 1821 and wished to preserve the classical curriculum in the schools. None the less, we find him writing: 'In this point, then, consists one grand excellence of the old classic education established by our forefathers, and bequeathed, as an unalienable possession, to our country. The study of poetry, oratory, history, philosophy, particularly of moral philosophy, improves, refines, and liberalizes the sentiments of the human heart.'[70]

In all these ways and from many different quarters it would be right to say of education in England in the early nineteenth century that 'change was in the air': change prompted by the urgent need to extend the provision of education, change in methods of teaching and perhaps in curriculum as well, stemming from the notion of 'education according to nature', change stimulated by what were thought to be the needs of society and finally change in the classical tradition itself. It is within the context of the debate about education in these days, as well as in the context of his society in general, that James Mill's contribution must be seen.

---

[70] V. Knox, *Remarks on Grammar Schools*, Works iv, p. 352.

III

Mill's reaction to the various problems which have just been described in England and London of his day, was inevitably affected by one further factor to which we must now turn. This was the 'climate of opinion' of the day. This phrase which is often used needs some explanation. It means, first, the general background of philosophical thought which was current at the time—what did philosophers concern themselves with, what did they write about, and therefore what did those studying philosophy read? What were such students prompted to think about? Was it an age, like our own, pre-occupied with linguistic problems? Or was it more concerned with metaphysics? Second, a 'climate of opinion' refers not to what philosophers are thinking about but to the general framework of assumptions in which all men thought and acted at the time. Such assumptions were taken for granted unconsciously and therefore not examined at the time. The first kind of climate of opinion can appropriately be summarized in an opening chapter. The second is more difficult and must be established, not by assertions in advance, but by an examination of the political and social thinking of the time—it emerges, if at all, from the course of our examination of Mill's life and thought. But both kinds of climate of opinion are important: they form the framework of beliefs in which men reflected, they affect the manner of their reasoning, and, perhaps even more important, the questions they thought to ask.

The England of Mill's day was dominated by the strong philosophical tradition of the English empiricists whose general position has been succinctly stated by Bertrand Russell: 'Empiricism . . . is the doctrine that all our knowledge (with the possible exception of logic and mathematics) is derived from experience.'[71] By 'experience' is meant primarily, our knowledge of the external world through the five senses. The term can also cover our experience of ourselves, of our feelings, desires and emotions. Whether experience is restricted to

[71] B. Russell, *History of Western Philosophy*, Allen & Unwin, 1946, p. 633.

sense-experience of the external world, or whether it includes intro-spective experience, it is a denial of the rationalist thesis that knowledge consists of an apprehension of first principles, of categories of thought as a necessary preliminary to gaining any knowledge from experience. Plato's view, for instance, that the evidence of our senses gave us but the shadows on the wall of the cave, true reality being evident only to the mind—such a view stands at the farthest remove from empiricism. And the more extreme empiricists naturally tried to shew that even logic and mathematics could be shewn to be derived not from pure reason but from sense-experience. It followed from this that empiricism as a doctrine that all knowledge derived from experience also involved another and more common meaning of the word 'empiricism'. For such a view is not conducive to the formation of a complete, tidy and logical system of philosophy, with a final explanation of the universe. It proceeds step by step, depending on sense-experience at every stage, always conscious of what remains to be learnt and always therefore tending to meet problems as they arise. Of course, once the doctrine was accepted, it tended to lose these virtues and to be imposed, as a plan of its own, on experience, and on thinking about experience.

Historians of philosophy commonly associate the rise in English empiricism with the great development of scientific thought in the seventeenth and eighteenth centuries. Science concentrated attention upon the natural world in which man lived: it was an understandable reaction to this that philosophers should concentrate attention on man's observation or experience of this natural world, and should seek to explain man's knowledge in terms of his sense experience of this world of science. Just as science moved from pure observation to the establishment of laws governing the natural world, so did the philosophers in their turn seek laws governing man's knowledge or experience, and from Locke onwards, and even before, philosophers considered the laws of association of ideas as an important principle of explanation, sometimes allied, as with Hartley, to a physiological basis. English empiricism did not deny the need for laws of thought, or general principles of explanation, but it arrived at them inductively, as did science, by taking sense-experience in all its variety as its datum. And, as with Science, the method was the method of analysis and the philosophers sought always to reduce experience to its simplest terms. Just as Science sought the element and the atom, so did philosophy seek the smallest unit of sense-experience—the unit incapable of further division or analysis—and from this proceed to shew the laws by which these units became compounded into the ordinary phenomena of our experience.

In this development of British philosophy, John Locke is generally considered to be the founder. 'Locke is a sort of fundamental book', wrote James Mill. It gives 'what is necessary to be known as a key to all subsequent metaphysics which have been built upon his foundation.'[72] Locke was the basis in other matters besides the study of our knowledge of the external world in terms of sense-experience. When he turned to the psychology of conation and contemplated our own experience of our feelings and emotions he did so in terms of psychological hedonism—the theory that men inevitably pursue their own pleasure. When he turned to moral problems it was the problem of happiness which he was concerned with, as indeed were most philosophers in the eighteenth century.[73] And Locke thought that moral philosophy 'should be capable of becoming a demonstrative and exact science like mathematics'.[74] Finally Locke exampMind the tradition in that he was an individualist: it was the good of the individual which should be the object of state policy. Again we see the contrast with Plato who sought first the ideal community.

This is not to suggest that Locke was at all points the source of the Utilitarian philosophy. His individualism for instance, led him to insist on certain inalienable rights of man. Such a theory is incompatible with Utilitarianism which asserts that no right of man is valid except if and in so far as it promotes the general happiness. But Locke did lay the foundations of eighteenth-century philosophy and he did cause subsequent philosophers to be preoccupied with certain questions to the

[72] B.M. Add. MSS. 35152, f. 160, Mill to Place, 6 September, 1815.

[73] There is preserved in the University of Edinburgh a set of students' notes of the Moral Philosophy course of lectures attended by James Mill. Nearly a term is devoted to the problem of happiness.

[74] C. R. Morris, *Locke, Berkeley and Hume*, O.U.P., 1930, p. 56.

2*

exclusion of others. In theory of knowledge it was accepted that the central problem was the problem of sense-experience—its analysis and the discovery of the laws which governed its explanation. The question was not whether sense-experience was important—that was accepted—but how much of our knowledge it could explain, and whether it could be shewn to explain everything. And it was generally accepted that the analysis of sense-experience was the starting point of this problem: up to a point philosophers assumed their answer and were really concerned not so much to discover it as to demonstrate it. All that claimed to be knowledge was subjected to the test of sense-experience: if it could not pass the test, it was suspect as personal, subjective and unscientific impression. On the other side, philosophers laboured unceasingly to shew that even knowledge which was thus suspect could in fact be reduced to the evidence and experience of the five senses. In psychology, the problem of will, of emotions and of feeling became a problem of analysing the nature of 'pleasure'. In ethics, it was the meaning of happiness which dominated attention. That there could be duties not leading to happiness was unbelievable, or at most, an eccentric exception to the general rule. We can see the confines of the tradition if we mention some of the questions which were *not* asked. Whether truth consisted in correspondence with external reality or in coherence with total experience was unimportant, and, generally, not an issue. Whether desire for the good was the same thing as desire for ordinary pleasures was rarely questioned. Whether sense-experience really gave any sure knowledge at all was not in question, as it certainly was to Plato. Whether the community had a common welfare distinct from that of the individuals composing it, was also not debated, despite the apparent implications of the term 'Social Contract'.

When James Mill came to England from Scotland in 1802, it would be too much to say that he was steeped in the tradition of the English empiricists. Other thinkers, as we shall see, helped to form his mind, and to influence his outlook, notably the Greek philosophers on the one hand, and the contemporary Scottish ones on the other. But the tradition which Mill seems to have adopted most whole-heartedly in philosophy was that of the English empiricists, though he came to it gradually during his time in England, rather than as a direct result of his university training. But, when he came to England in 1802, the England he saw was the one described in this chapter, and this, too, was a potent factor in determining his thinking, first on political matters, and later in philosophy. To understand the influence and interaction of these various factors we must turn to a more detailed study of Mill's life and career, and of what he did in practice in trying to solve the problems of England in the first quarter of the nineteenth century.

Life and Career of James Mill

James Mill's father was a shoemaker (at Logie Pert, in Forfar-shire, Scotland) who employed two or three assistants in his business. Although this might seem to us a 'humble parentage', it was not so in the circumstances of the time, for, by reason of being both a craftsman and an employer, the elder Mill was regarded as superior to many of those living in his village. No-one was more convinced of this than his wife, and she took full advantage of the possibilities of the situation, and worked unceasingly to raise her own social position and that of her son. She mixed little with her neighbours, but cultivated, with some success, the friendship of a wealthy and influential family in the district, the Barclays. She also sedulously shielded her son from all contact with his father's trade, and, from the start, he was brought up to believe that he was destined for higher things. It would be erroneous to describe anything as 'middle class' at this period when such class divisions were unknown, and when people thought rather in terms of an infinite number of small gradations from the agricultural labourer to the craftsman's apprentice, and from the master-craftsman to the squire. But Mill's upbringing did have many of the characteristics later described as 'middle class'. There was the code of personal con-duct by which Mrs Mill and her son distinguished themselves from the rest of the village. There was, for Mill junior, unremit-ting industry, and for his mother, thrift. Finally there was a faith that those who cultivated their talents would not go unrewarded—that industry and ability would open the gate to higher things.

Even in the village school, James Mill was recognized as a pupil of exceptional ability, and he rapidly moved from there to Montrose Academy. In the meantime, he had the good fortune to meet Sir John and Lady Stuart whose estate and residence was near his home. Mill writes of this friendship: 'At an early age I was taken notice of by him and Lady Stuart— when the time came for my going to college it was my father's intention to send me to Aberdeen, as both nearer and less expensive than Edinburgh. Sir John and Lady Stuart insisted that he should let them take me to Edinburgh which was the more celebrated university, that they would look after me, and take care that the expenses to my father should not be greater than at Aberdeen—I went to Edinburgh, and from that time lived as much in their house as in my father's, and there had many advantages, saw the best company, and had an educated man to direct my education—and who paid for several expensive branches of education which but for him I must have gone without and above all had unlimited access in both town and country to well-chosen libraries. So you see, I owe much to Sir John Stuart, who had a daughter—an only child about the same age as myself—who besides being a beautiful person was in point of intellect and disposition one of the most perfect human beings I have ever known—we grew up together and studied together and were about the best friends that either of us ever had.'[1]

At the University of Edinburgh, Mill studied first a basic course in Classics and Philosophy. He has left us his own account of his education there: 'The days of study are five in the week, and the months in the year rather less than six. First year Latin, two hours a day, Greek, two hours a day, Maths, two hours a day. Second year: Latin, one hour, Greek, two hours, Logic, one hour. Third year: Moral Philosophy, one hour, with a repetition of the second Maths and Greek classes as often as the student desires. Fourth year: Natural philosophy, or rather mechanical philosophy, one hour, with a repetition of any of the preceding classes the student chooses. This is the regular course of preparatory discipline for the two professions of Law and Divinity—after which they ascend to the classes appropriated to the teaching of Law and Divinity.'[2] Mill's course in Divinity also included much philosophy, especially

[1] B.M. Add. MSS. 35153, Mill to Place, 26 October 1817.
[2] Bentham MSS., University College London, Mill to Allen, Box 165, f. 1.

the philosophy of Plato: his whole career at Edinburgh lasted eight years, and in 1798, at the end of it, he was licensed as a preacher.

This education was primarily a training in philosophy, with a special emphasis on Greek philosophy. Greek philosophy remained with Mill throughout his life as a major inspiration to his thought. It was the centre of the curriculum which he prescribed for the education of his son, John Stuart Mill. 'There was no author', writes the latter, 'to whom my father thought himself more indebted for his own mental culture, than Plato, or whom he more frequently recommended to young students.'[3] And again, 'my father's moral convictions, wholly dissevered from religion, were very much of the character of those of the Greek philosophers'.[4] Many references to Plato and Aristotle in James Mill's Commonplace Book bear out these statements. He also favoured the Socratic method of teaching: he used it in teaching his son, and also attempted one or two dialogues, only one of which, so far as we know, was published.[5]

His training in theology affords a contrast to this: it left no enduring mark on Mill's thought. By 1808 he was an agnostic, and from that time onwards uninterested in theological matters. But it is important to remember these Edinburgh days, when we come to consider Mill's writings. He did not start as an ethical naturalist, as a hedonist and as an agnostic. On the contrary, the prevailing philosophical tradition at Edinburgh favoured none of these things, and Mill's approach to moral and religious problems was that of a believer rather than that of a sceptic. But Edinburgh, like other centres of thought at this time was affected by the spirit of scientific analysis. Finlayson's course of Logic attempted to view all objects of human thought as a unity, to classify them and to explain the laws of human understanding. Dugald Stewart's course in Ethics contained a long preamble on Association Psychology, in which Stewart did not entirely believe.[6] So Mill was provided not only with the

---

[3] J. S. Mill, *An Autobiography*, ed. H. J. Laski, World's Classics, O.U.P., p. 18.
[4] Ibid., p. 39.
[5] Cf. John Mill's autobiography, and James Mill's dialogue *On the Ballot*, London Review, 1835.
[6] From notes taken by John Lee, 1796–7, and preserved in the library of the University of Edinburgh.

inspiration of the Greeks, and a Presbyterian training: he acquired also the destructive weapons of criticism from the scientific spirit of the age.

We know little of Mill's life between 1798 and 1802. He did not succeed as a preacher, and turned instead to private tutoring—he is reported as being the tutor to the family of a Scottish nobleman in East Lothian, and he may well have done similar work during his association with the Stuarts. Be that as it may, in 1802 he set forth for London, by coach, in the company of Sir John Stuart.

He arrived in London armed with a number of introductions, and with their aid rapidly obtained work in journalism, with the *Anti-Jacobin Review* from 1802, and with the *Literary Journal* as editor, from 1803. He was keenly interested in politics, and often attended the debates of the House of Commons. He was also, in 1803, a volunteer in a force of men recruited to repel Napoleon's threatened invasion of England.

In 1804 he became engaged, and in 1805 married Miss Harriet Burrow, and they went to live in Rodney Street, Pentonville, where, in the following year, the first son was born, named after Sir John Stuart. At this time Mill was still a regular attendant at Church, and his son was duly baptized. Meantime, the *Literary Journal* ceased publication, and Mill was left with the *St James' Chronicle* which had given him some employment since 1805. His income dropped as a result of these changes, and he now in 1806 reduced it still further by embarking upon the enterprise of writing the *History of British India*, a task which he expected to complete in three or four years but which in fact took twelve.[7] His original calculation must have been that, with some occasional journalistic work, he could keep going with his savings during these few years, until his book set him on the road to higher earnings. We shall see that in fact he was faced with much graver financial difficulties and a rapidly growing family, for a much longer period than he contemplated.

1808 is a convenient date at which to pause and take stock.

[7] Cf. A. Bain, *James Mill: A Biography*, Longmans, 1882, ch. 11. This is the main source of information about Mill's life: it has the advantage of having been written by a friend of the family, who during the writing of it was able to consult John Stuart Mill and other contemporaries of James Mill. It has the corresponding disadvantage of being too close to its subject to permit impartial appraisal.

In his opinions, Mill was still a Christian in religion, and not yet a Radical in politics. He had started indeed, on the other side, during his association with the *Anti-Jacobin Review*. But there is some evidence in his writings in 1806 of that severe rationalism which he was later to apply to political questions. He had acquired a considerable knowledge of contemporary political and economic affairs—one of his earliest large articles was written during this period in defence of merchants, against those who held that only industry and agriculture were really productive in the true economic sense of the term.[8] He also read and reviewed several histories. English politics must, however, be regarded as his main pre-occupation during this early period in London, and politics was the main influence at this time on the development of his thought.

II

Most authorities date Mill's meeting with Bentham in 1808. It speedily became a warm personal friendship and every week James Mill walked from Pentonville to Queen's Square Place, Westminster, where Bentham resided, to dine and talk with him. In 1809, they spent the first of many summers together: Bentham rented Barrow Green House at Oxted as a summer residence, and the Mill family joined him there for quite extended periods every summer until 1814.[9] This generous hospitality to Mill came at a useful time when, as we have seen, his earnings were diminished and his responsibilities increased. But he repaid Bentham by giving him considerable secretarial assistance in editing the latter's work on *Evidence* for the press. At the same time, the association between Mill and Bentham became not only a friendship but a union of minds. Mill became a whole-hearted Utilitarian and an agnostic, and he was a loyal and fervent disciple in support of Bentham. But it

---

[8] James Mill, *Commerce Defended*, 1807, pamphlet, 154 pages.

[9] Bowring asserts, quoting Bentham, that these visits were as long as six months each year, but he was a prejudiced observer. John Stuart Mill denies this, and says that the holidays were about a month each year. His version seems to be nearer the truth.

should be noticed that Utilitarianism for Bentham was primarily a programme and criterion for political and legal reform,
not a complete philosophical system. And it was as a political
creed that Mill first adopted it, as is shewn by his writings
during this period.

The year 1808 also marked the first of Mill's articles for the
Edinburgh Review. This connexion is said to be due to the good
offices of Henry Brougham who urged Francis Jeffery, the
editor, to employ Mill as much as possible. Both Brougham and
Jeffery had been contemporaries of Mill's at Edinburgh, though
Brougham was the person with whom he was most friendly.
Not for the last time in his life, was Mill to be indebted to his
old university, not merely for the excellence of its education,
but also for the privilege of studying with men who were later
to become eminent in the intellectual and political life of
England and who, it appears, had strong feelings of loyalty to
their former fellow-students. The rates of payment for the
Edinburgh Review articles were generous and for the next five
years Mill contributed about three long articles per year to the
review, on subjects ranging from Economics, Law and Religion
to Liberty of the Press and the Education of the Poor.[10] On
this last subject he took a more practical interest as well, for he

---

[10] Bain, op. cit., p. 75, is the authority for saying that Brougham urged Jeffery
to employ Mill. But Jeffery wrote to Brougham, 25 November, 1809: 'Granted—
Mill must write no more about law and I must tell him so explicitly & at once
... for I am as much annoyed as you can be at the badness of this article. Indeed
I see clearly the necessity of keeping him to lower ground—for there is a vulgarity
in his arrogance & in his Jacobinism that not only does us discredit but puts me
out of humour with the decidedness I have of liberty.' (Brougham MSS., University
College.) This must be the article on Bexon: Code de la Législation Penale, which
Mill reviewed in the October 1809 number, and complained to Bentham that
his review had been 'sadly mangled. The mention of you [Bentham] struck out
in all but one place, and there my words, every one of them, removed, and those
of Jeffrey put in their place.' (Bain, op. cit., p. 103.) The incident is interesting in
shewing how far Mill had advanced in his views, from being 'anti-Jacobin' in
1802, to being so Radical a Utilitarian with regard to the law, that to the Whig
Edinburgh Review he was a 'Jacobin'. Brougham, as a professional lawyer who had
studied law unlike Mill, no doubt had other reasons for disapproving Mill's legal
theories. But although Mill wrote no more on law for the *Edinburgh Review*, he
contributed articles in the field to the *Encyclopedia Britannica* in 1818, notably one
on Jurisprudence. So his abilities in legal matters must not be judged by Jeffrey's
comment. And the Utilitarian theories of law dominated all legal thinking in the
nineteenth century, and are still the basis of our law.

joined, in 1809, the Royal Lancasterian Association for the founding of non-denominational primary schools on the monitorial system. He remained a subscriber to this throughout his life, and in the early days was a member of its committee.

In 1810, Bentham offered Mill the tenancy of Milton's house, in the garden of his own at Westminster. After several months' trial, Mrs Mill found it unsuitable, and the Mills moved to Newington Green, then a detached village to the north of London. Despite the enormous distance involved, James Mill still kept up his weekly walks and visits to Bentham, and his family still spent their summer holidays at Barrow Green. In the meantime, his work with the Lancasterian Schools Association brought him new friends: William Allen, the Quaker chemist, Francis Place, the Radical tailor of Charing Cross Road, Edward Wakefield, and David Ricardo, a stockbroker, later to become one of the ablest economists of the day, and perhaps Mill's closest friend. But with all these, Mill's friendship was steady and lasting, and many were the causes—political and educational—which this little group served together. It is especially to be noted that Allen found Mill a congenial partner, despite his agnosticism, both in the affairs of the Lancasterian schools, and in running Allen's journal the *Philanthropist*, to which Mill contributed generously with his pen, and behind the scenes with his advice.

In 1814, two changes took place, both indicating Bentham's desire to have Mill as his constant companion. Bentham leased the house next door to his own in Westminster to Mill at £50 a year—a very low rent; the Mills thus left Newington Green and came to live at No. 1 Queen's Square Place, Westminster (now No. 40 Queen Anne's Gate). Secondly, Bentham gave up the tenancy of Barrow Green House, and became the tenant of a much larger and more remote establishment, Ford Abbey, near Chard in Somerset. For the next four years, the Mill family, which now contained five children, spent half of each year with Bentham at Ford Abbey.

Ford Abbey had been founded in 1136, and some parts of the original building remained. A good deal was added or renovated in the seventeenth century, however, and in a letter to David Ricardo, Mill describes his first sight of the place: 'It is an irregular pile of building, of large extent, and still retains a large share of its monkish appearance, the inside however made into rooms which have comforts, and some of them no little magnificence for the taste of people of a more mundane description than monks. It is one of the places which travellers come to see; and we have many visitors . . . It stands upon the river Axe, at the very bottom of a tolerably pretty valley, surrounded by hills of the Devonshire breed, of gentle ascent, and moderate altitude, and rather too much than too little covered with wood. There is cloisters in the house, a piece of very beautiful Gothic architecture, which acts as a long wide passage in summer . . . there is also in it an ancient Gothic hall which looks like a church; there is an apartment called the saloon, built by Inigo Jones, on express purpose to receive some beautiful tapestry which still adorns its walls, and of this room the dimensions are 50' x 25' with correspondent height . . . The grounds about are far from ugly—but not much has lately been done to improve them by art. There is a deer park, containing 140 head of deer of which we have already killed a few.'[11]

In this isolated spot in the west country, James Mill completed his history of India, educated his children entirely without outside help, wrote his articles for the *Encyclopedia Britannica*, and in innumerable ways assisted Bentham, generally in the work of preparing the latter's often illegible notes into a form suitable to go to the printer. Hard work was the keynote of these four years in the west: in 1817 Francis Place wrote his wife a detailed account of life down there: 'All our days are alike so an account of one may do for all. Mill is up, between five and six; he and John compare his proofs, John reading the copy and his father the proof. Willie and Clara are in the saloon before seven, and as soon as the proofs are done with, John goes to the farther end of the room to teach his sisters. When this has been done, and part of the time while it is doing, he learns geometry: this continues until nine o'clock when breakfast is ready . . .

'Breakfast ended, Mill hears Willie and Clara, and then

11 Mill to Ricardo, 1814, *Letters of David Ricardo*, ed. Sraffa, C.U.P., vi, no. 37. The saloon, where Bentham and Mill worked, was mostly constructed after the death of Inigo Jones.

John. Lessons are heard under a broad balcony, walking from end to end, the breakfast parlour on the one hand and pots of flowers rising one above another as high as your head on the other; this place is in the front of the Abbey. All the lessons and readings are performed aloud, and occupy full three hours, say till one o'clock . . .

'At one we all three walk in the lanes and fields for an hour. At two all go to work again till dinner at six, when Mrs Mill, Mill, Bentham, I and Colls dine together . . . The first day I came wine was put upon the table: but as I took none, none has since made its appearance. After dinner Mill and I take a sharp walk for two hours, say till a quarter past eight, then one of us alternately walks with Mr Bentham for an hour; then comes tea, at which we read the periodical publications; and eleven o'clock comes but too soon, and we all go to bed.

'Mrs Mill marches in great style round the green in front of the house for about half an hour before breakfast and again after dinner with all the children, till their bed-time.'[12]

We can only conjecture what financial arrangements lay behind these extended periods of hospitality for the Mill family. Heavily occupied as he was, with the *History of British India*, and with the education of his children, Mill was earning little. The *Edinburgh Review* articles had ceased in 1813: Mill wrote subsequently for the *Philanthropist*, but this journal could not afford much payment, and it is doubtful whether Mill received anything. His work was done out of friendship for William Allen, the editor, and because he supported the causes, such as the education of the poor, on which he wrote. In 1814, Mill was invited to write some articles for the *Encyclopedia Britannica*: he records that the payment was generous, but both the work and the payment were spread over several years until 1823. We learn from Bain that 'Francis Place made him advances while he was writing his history. These, of course, were all repaid'.[13] During the absences at Ford Abbey, Mill sublet the house in Westminster, no doubt at a profit. But when all is

---

[12] Place to Mrs Place, 17 August 1817, quoted in G. Wallas, *Life of Francis Place*, Allen & Unwin, 1925, pp. 75–7. Willie and Clara were John Mill's younger sisters, Colls was Bentham's amanuensis.

[13] Bain, op. cit., p. 163.

taken into account, these years must have been a period of considerable financial stringency when Bentham's hospitality was the basic factor in enabling Mill to carry on.

On the other hand, the arrangement with Bentham was by no means one-sided: Mill undertook definite obligations in return. He records, during his first year: 'The duration of my stay here of course does not altogether depend upon myself. I hold myself engaged to remain with Bentham, who will soon have nobody with him except myself and appendages, and who would not stay a day alone, as long as he finds it agreeable to remain. The present intention is not to return to London much before Christmas, but whether the pleasure of remaining here will not be exhausted a good deal before that time, I hold very doubtful.'[14] Two years later, he writes in the same strain: 'Could I have got away I should have found infinite pleasure in spending . . . a week with you at Gatcombe; but Koe, upon whom I counted to relieve me here, has been uncertain in his motions and I could not prevail upon Mr B. to part with me.'[15] During this time Mill edited, and assisted considerably in the writing of, Bentham's *Table of the Springs of Action*: this and *Chrestomathia*, Bentham's one published work on education, were prepared for the press by Mill. And Bentham's methods of writing his thoughts on separate sheets of paper, leaving their arrangement to his assistant, meant that preparing his books for the press was an onerous task. How much else Mill did we do not know, but it is clear enough that he regarded himself as under an obligation to Bentham to be present as a companion and as an assistant, and the visits to Ford Abbey grew longer and longer until Bentham gave up the lease in 1818.

Down in Somerset, Bentham and Mill were isolated from much that went on in the life of the nation. There are no references shewing any awareness of industrial evils—naturally enough since Mill's life was bounded by London, not yet touched by the Industrial Revolution, and the heart of the country near Chard. But the voluminous Place correspondence shews an active interest throughout this time in political developments, ranging from national affairs to detailed comments on

[14] *Ricardo's Letters*, op. cit., Mill to Ricardo, 30 September 1814.
[15] Ibid., Mill to Ricardo, 10 October 1816.

the affairs of the Westminster constituency—the one constituency in England where something like a democratic election could take place. Various political figures visited Ford Abbey from time to time: Mill and Bentham were also on good terms with their neighbours, including the local cleric.[16] If unaware of the cotton towns and their problems, Mill was acutely aware of a more primitive one—the destitution and famine caused to country folk by a failure in the harvest. He wrote to Ricardo: 'I have been so much a hermit since I came here that I can tell you little of the actual measure of distress which is felt in this country. But does not this weather frighten you? The corn here is absolutely green, nothing whatsoever in the ear and a perfect continuance of rain and cold. There must now be of necessity a very deficient crop, and very high prices—and therewith an unexampled scarcity of work will produce a degree of misery, the thought of which makes the flesh creep on one's bones—one third of the people must die.'[17] Two months later, he returns to the same topic: 'The corn here is mostly got in. For want of a sun to ripen it, a great deal of it however will not be productive —and prices will be high. Is there much suffering about you? I do not mean of the farmers, at present, whose suffering is only that of comparative poverty—but of the people who live by the daily work of their hands; and whose suffering means starvation and death. Here the quantity is great—and our clergyman, who is also a magistrate and a good man tells me that the decisions which as a magistrate he is obliged to make in the case of applications for parochial aid, render his life a burthen to him —as it is giving to a man who is starving, by taking from others, the mass of the parishioners, who are but one degree removed from the starving condition.'[18] These passages underline the truth that England was still, in the main, an agricultural country, and that her people thought in these terms: a failure of the harvest was a vital matter to all. But they also shew something of Mill's personal attitudes—although denouncing the Church of England with vigour, he could still praise its

---

[16] Also we hear that the Bishop of Gloucester paid them a visit and 'left us all very much in love with him'. *Ricardo's Letters*, op. cit., 10 October 1815.

[17] *Ricardo's Letters*, op. cit., Mill to Ricardo, 14 August 1816.

[18] Ibid., Mill to Ricardo, 25 October 1816.

local representative. Place lamented once: 'He cared nothing for the individual, only for the mass.'[19] This may be true, but so was the reverse: Mill did not hate the people in control in Church and State—it was the system which he condemned.

Apart from the completion of his history, and the education of his children, the most important development in Mill's career at Ford Abbey was the invitation to write for the *Encyclopedia Britannica*. The editor of this was MacVey Napier, who had been a fellow-student at Edinburgh. Mill was first asked to write in May 1814[20] and he wrote in all ten articles over a period lasting till 1823. Most of the articles were on topics in the field of Politics, Economics, and Law, and Mill had been thinking and writing on all these topics for some years.[21] But the article on Education was different. Mill's writings on this theme had been confined to what may be called the politics of education—who shall be educated, how much and by whom? He had not hitherto reflected on the theory of education, though his experience in educating his son was an advantage, and his assistance to Bentham in editing *Chrestomathia* must have been useful to his thinking. Unlike *Chrestomathia*, Mill's *Essay on Education* covers the whole theory of education, in philosophical manner, and its preparation caused him to return to his early interests and to read extensively in philosophy. This was a turning point in his intellectual life: up till then, he had supported Utilitarianism as a political creed—he was now to develop and expound it as a philosophy, and this was his own distinctive contribution to the Benthamite school. It is the article on Education which, so far as we can judge, starts Mill thinking on the philosophy of Utilitarianism. It is during this period that we find him asking Place to obtain philosophical works, and to despatch them to Ford Abbey. It is in 1816 that Mill wrote that he had 'begun to read the *Critique of Pure Reason*', and adds, 'I see well enough what poor Kant is about but it would require no little time to give an account

---

[19] B.M. Add. MSS. 35144, Place Diary.
[20] B.M. Add. MSS. 34611, f. 55, Mill to Napier.
[21] The ten articles were: Government, Jurisprudence, Liberty of the Press, Prisons, Colony, Law of Nations, Education, Beggar, Benefit Societies, and Banks for Savings.

of him. I have given a hasty reading to Hartley since I came
here. Hartley's is the true scent, but his book is obscurely
written: and it will require no little persevering reflection to
render the application of his theory perfectly familiar to one's
mind, in every part of the field of thought. This I shall be going
on doing, doing—but how long it will take to the being done
depends upon many circumstances.'[22] Hartley's book was a full
exposition of Association Psychology, which Mill used in his
theory of education. Although he subsequently wrote a large
treatise on Psychology, there is no evidence that this project
was contemplated as early as this, and the reference here to
Mill's writing on the subject must refer to the article on Education for the Encyclopedia. And this article sets out his first
original thinking in the sphere of philosophy, though, as with
his political writing, we should not forget that Mill wrote from
some practical experience before evolving a theory.

We have little information as to the exact date of the different
articles.[23] In 1817 we find him thanking Napier for cheques for
some of the articles and adding that 'the articles were got up
without much labour from the materials which were nearest to
hand; and assuredly I expected no fame from them so that I am
agreeably surprised to hear from you, that they receive some
approbation'.[24] In August of the same year he writes again,
thanking Napier for payment and praise, and saying: 'I
tremble to undertake colonies.' In May 1820, he refers to
writing the articles on *Government* and *Jurisprudence*, and in
September of the same year thanks Napier for a 'liberal enclo-
sure for the article *Government*'.[25] In 1821 there is a reference to
Liberty of the Press, which was his own suggestion: 'I believe I
have now fulfilled all the obligations in the way of articles which
I am under to you. There is one article more, however, which,
if you have not otherwise provided for it, I shall be very glad
to undertake. That is *Liberty of the Press*.'[26] A letter in the following year refers to *Prisons* and finds him still hard at work on

[22] B.M. Add. MSS. 35152, no. 221, Mill to Place, October 1816.
[23] Bain dates the Education article 1818: this would be a likely date, cf. Bain,
op. cit., p. 247.
[24] B.M. Add. MSS. 34612, no. 70, Mill to Napier, April 1817.
[25] B.M. Add. MSS. 34611, Mill to Napier, 28 September 1820.
[26] Ibid., Mill to Napier, 3 January 1821.

Law of Nations, a subject he is unfamiliar with. The Supplement to the Encyclopedia was completed and published in 1824.

A year or two before this, several people had come forward with a proposal to reprint a thousand copies of the article *Government*.[27] Permission was granted for this, and was later extended to most of Mill's other articles. The result was the appearance of a series of volumes, some containing four articles, and some as many as eight, reprinted many times as late as 1828. These essays were regarded as the bible of the Philosophical Radicals, and many was the study group of young intellectuals who made them the basis of their discussion. To such people Mill's clear and succinct summary of Utilitarianism, in its applications in the fields of Law, Politics, Economics, and Education, seemed to hold the key to the future, and provided them with the intellectual armoury they needed to convince the thinking mind of the justice of their cause, if not to convert the general public. When we remember how dominant an influence Utilitarianism was, at least in developments in Law, Politics, and Economics, throughout the nineteenth century, these young reformers were perhaps not so far wrong in their conviction.

III

We have noticed the years 1816–18 as marking a turning point in Mill's intellectual life, when he prepared and completed the *Essay on Education*: the year 1819 marks just as decisive a stage in his material fortunes. As a result of the publication of his *History of British India*, and some energetic canvassing by his friends, Mill was appointed as assistant to the examiner of India correspondence at India House, at a salary of £800 a year. This meant an end to financial worry, secure but not onerous employment, freedom from the need to write articles for a living—freedom, that is, to develop the philosophy of Utilitarianism. Though his interest in politics and the provision of better educational facilities never flagged, and though he contributed several articles on political matters, from now on his major work was philosophical.

[27] Ibid., Mill to Napier, 28 September 1820.

The immediate period after his appointment, however, found him quite heavily occupied, by the standards of the time, with official duties. The hours were 10 to 4, and he observed them strictly, unlike most of his colleagues. In 1819 he wrote to Napier, declining to undertake further articles because 'I am afraid of overloading my time. I am preparing a second edition of my *History of British India*, and I have loads of East India despatches with their enclosures to read, of a size which would frighten you. When I have got up the arrears, which had accumulated in this department before my admission, I shall be more at my ease.'[28] Actually, the work proved much less heavy than he feared, and, as we have seen, he did in fact write further articles for the Encyclopedia; he also found that he had plenty of leisure, for a man of his energy, for writing books, public work, and the education of his children. Meanwhile, in the office, he gained rapid promotion. In 1821, his salary was raised to £1,000 a year, and in 1823, to £1,200. This made him second in command in the office, and his promotion coincides with the admission of John Stuart Mill as his subordinate in the same office.[29]

James Mill had been a close friend of David Ricardo for some years, and had been primarily responsible for persuading Ricardo to write his *Principles of Political Economy*, and later to become a member of Parliament. They had also co-operated over a plan to establish a secondary school in London, on the monitorial plan. Partly as a result of this friendship, and partly arising out of his course of training for his son in Economics, James Mill now wrote an elementary text-book in Economics. This has its immediate origins in the lessons to John Stuart Mill. 'My father', writes J. S. Mill, 'commenced instructing me in the science by a sort of lectures, which he delivered to me on our walks. He expounded each day a portion of the subject and I gave him next day a written account of it.'[30] This was re-written again and again until it was 'clear, precise, and tolerably complete', and it served his father afterwards as notes from which to write his *Elements of Political Economy*. He reports to

[28] Mill to Napier, 10 September 1819, quoted in Bain, op. cit., pp. 187–8.
[29] Bain, op. cit., p. 205.
[30] *Autobiography*, op. cit., pp. 23–4.

Ricardo that he is 'making good progress' with his 'school book of Political Economy', in 1820, and adds that the 'diffusing of Knowledge is now the work of greatest importance'.[31] The manuscript was submitted to Ricardo for comment but he asks also for 'unlearned opinion' of it, as it is intended to make the science of Economics clear to the ordinary man. It was published in 1822.

Meanwhile, a group of political economists including Mill, Ricardo, and Malthus formed the Political Economy Club, the foremost object of which was the furtherance of Free Trade. But Mill was asked to draft the Rules of the club, and he concluded his draft with some paragraphs giving the club a wider function:

'The Members of this Society will regard their mutual instruction, and the diffusion amongst others of the first principles of Political Economy, as a real and important obligation.

'As the Press is the grand instrument for the diffusion of knowledge or of error, all the Members of this Society will regard it as incumbent upon them to watch closely the proceedings of the Press, and to ascertain if any doctrines hostile to sound views on Political Economy have been propagated; to contribute whatever may be in their power to refute such erroneous doctrines, and controvert their influence; and to avail themselves of every favourable opportunity for the publication of seasonable truths within the province of this Science.

'It shall be considered the duty of the Society, individually and collectively, to aid the circulation of all publications which they deem useful to the Science, by making the merits of them known as widely as possible, and to limit the influence of hurtful publications by the same means.'[32]

Here we see clearly the faith that reason and argument will solve all problems, and lead to a rational community, granted only a free press, a literate population and prompt refutation of fallacious or interested argument. The Club grew rapidly in

[31] *Ricardo's Letters*, op. cit., viii, no. 413, Mill to Ricardo, 12 December 1820. Mill later was on the Committee of the Society for the Diffusion of Useful Knowledge, 1827.
[32] Bain, op. cit., pp. 198-9.

size, and most leading politicians became members, thus illustrating another characteristic of Utilitarian activity: the marriage of discussion and reflection in the pure light of reason to the practical problems of the day, and to the politicians responsible for these developments.

The same purpose of disseminating truth and exposing fallacy in the realms of politics and economics, and indeed of thought in general, gave birth to another important development: the founding of a new Radical quarterly, the *Westminster Review*, in 1823. This had been a project of Mill and Bentham for some years past and Bentham had hoped that Mill would become its editor. But Mill's appointment to India House reduced his time, and, moreover, the post which he held was not compatible with assuming the editorship of this new and controversial review.[33] So Bentham put up the money, and his secretary Bowring became the editor. The opening number contained a long review of existing reviews, by James Mill, in the course of which he made a strong attack on the *Edinburgh Review*. The gist of his argument is useful as shewing a number of Mill's strongest convictions. Any periodical is under an economic incentive to produce knowledge and argument palatable to its readers. Where a periodical is Whig it panders not to the majority but to the minority—the Whig aristocracy—a term used in a broad sense to include the Whig landowners who controlled the composition of Parliament. Where the reading public is limited to this minority the loyalty and the interests of such a periodical unite to drive it in one direction, and that a mischievous one—to suppress all inimical to the interests of the Whig aristocracy and to disseminate by all means all doctrines true or false which favour them. For this purpose 'it is essential to deal as much as possible in vague language and to cultivate the skilful use of it'. Armed with this preamble, Mill examined every number of the *Edinburgh Review* since its foundation at the turn of the century, finding numerous illustrations of his thesis. And this thesis was not only that in fact the *Edinburgh Review* propagated false opinions and arguments, but that, in the circumstances of the time and its own domination by the Whigs, it could do no other. This is a clear expression of one of Mill's

[33] Cf. Bain, op. cit., pp. 260-1.

most cherished convictions, that, as he had noted early in his life 'all men are governed by their interests—judgment of good and evil almost wholly depend upon interest'. This doctrine was derived from various sources. Mill thought himself in line with Plato who had made special and extensive arrangements to ensure that his rulers had no private interest to divert them from the public good. But Mill was also making an empirical observation on the England of his day, and, as we have seen, it offered extensive illustration of the thesis that 'men served only their private interest'. Since the basis of reform was a literate population, with power over the government, it can be seen how fatal, in Mill's eyes, was the situation if a periodical publication, on which the public relied for fair and disinterested argument, was corrupted as much as those in political and ecclesiastical power.

During these first five years at the India Office Mill maintained his old friendships. We hear of weekly dinners with Bentham, of regular breakfasts with Brougham, and, at times, of daily walks with Ricardo in the London parks.[34] But Mill continued the habit of a country week-end, and repaired to Dorking most week-ends, and for his six weeks summer vacation. He suffered a great shock in 1823 with the unexpected and untimely death of David Ricardo: with no-one else, not even Francis Place, had his friendship been so warm, so far as his correspondence reveals, and Mrs Grote wrote of the funeral: 'Mill was terribly affected—far more so than you would have supposed likely. The heart of him was touched, and his nature revealed more tenderness on this occasion than I have believed to reside within his philosophic frame.'[35]

A year earlier, in 1822, Mill had commenced work on his first large treatise in philosophy, the *Analysis of the Phenomena of the Human Mind*. His first interest in this, as we have seen, goes back to the time when he was writing his article on Education for the Encyclopedia, and in 1817 he wrote to Place: 'If I had the time to write a book I would make the human mind as plain as the road from Charing Cross to St Paul's.'[36] The next

[34] Ibid., p. 189.
[35] Ibid., p. 211.
[36] B.M. Add. MSS. 35153, Mill to Place, 6 December 1817.

we hear of this subject is in 1822, when, as a final stage in John Stuart Mill's education, he read under his father's direction the higher branches of analytical psychology. Much the same method was used as with the study of Economics: John Stuart Mill made summaries or abstracts of his reading, and discussed them fully with his father until they attained final precision. The main authors studied in this way were Locke, Helvétius, and Hartley. J. S. Mill reports that his father started writing his *Analysis of the Human Mind* in his summer vacations at Dorking in 1822, and worked on it 'during several successive vacations' until its publication in 1829. Each chapter and section was passed to John to read, as it was completed. James Mill's own account of his progress is contained in a letter to Ricardo in 1823: 'Last year I did something considerable towards the exposition of all the phenomena classed under the title of Thought. I have pushed the subject during the last few weeks; and all the phenomena called the intellectual (still leaving the moral) have undergone investigation. You know my opinion was that they might all be expounded up on the principles of Hartley, and might be satisfactorily shewn to be nothing but sensation, and the ideas, the copies of these sensations, combined in groups by association. I think I have now made this satisfactory exposition ... After explaining in an elementary manner the phenomena of sensation and the representation of sensations, the ideas and also the laws of association, and the artifice of naming, I proceed to apply these elements, and examine how far they go in accounting for all the complicated phenomena included under the titles, Imagination, Memory, Belief, Judgment, Ratiocination, Abstraction, and so on. Nobody has seen the papers but John, whose mind however is perfectly ripe to judge of them; and to him the expositions appear easy of comprehension and perfectly satisfactory ... I confess that the evidence has turned out to be shorter, more simple, and conclusive, so far, than I had dared to anticipate ... I mean to go on, next, to the exposition of the *Will*, and the different phenomena commonly classed under it, the desires, passions, etc., called the "active Powers of the Mind" by the Scotch and other philosophers ... when this is done the whole of what we call mind will be explained ... I got so full of my

subject that I could not tear myself away from Dorking.'[37] Most
of this letter needs no comment but two points may be noted.
First is James Mill's confidence in the independent judgment
of his son: to some extent this was justified but there have been
some commentators who have insisted that he was a pale
imitation of his father's thinking. This is hardly justified, when
we think of John Stuart Mill's later and substantial contribu-
tions to thought. A more important limitation, however, is that
it is unlikely that John Mill, at the age of seventeen, offered
very frank and open criticism to his father. Roebuck records:
'John Mill was ... armed at all points. At that time the mere
creation of his father's teaching with nothing original, yet
being endowed with great intellectual powers, he was a wonderful product of factitious training ... John Mill took especial
care to confine his criticisms to Bentham, and always avoided
calling in question the views of his father.'[38] The second point
of interest in the letter is that it refutes any suggestion that
James Mill took over Association Psychology uncritically from
the tradition of his day. Although they are set forth in outline
in the *Essay on Education*, alternative views are also mentioned,
and Mill's own views at that time must have been tentative.

In 1828 Mill took as his country week-end retreat the house
at Mickleham where he was to remain till his death in 1836. It
gave him a countryside which he loved, though the house, at
first, lacked much in the way of comfort. Most week-ends he
went there on Fridays, was joined the next day by John, whose
junior status required him to be at India House on Saturdays,
and by the week-end guests. During the week he remained at
Queen Square Place, Westminster until 1831, and then moved
to a large house in Vicarage Place, off Church Street, Kensington. This move may have reflected his improved finances—in
1830 he was appointed head of his office at a salary of £1,900 a
year. It may also have been connected with the age of Bentham,
the owner of the Westminster house, then in his 83rd year; he
died in 1832.

During these years Mill had been concerned since 1825 with
the project to set up University College, London, and was a

---

[37] *Ricardo's Letters*, op. cit., ix, no. 539, Mill to Ricardo, 8 August 1823.
[38] *Life and Letters of J. A. Roebuck*, ed. R. E. Leader, 1897, p. 36.

member of its council. He also completed his work on the human mind which was published in 1828. He contributed some articles to the *Westminster Review* until 1826, when he had a disagreement with Bowring, the editor. After a four years' gap, his articles re-appear in the *London Review*[39] and continue up to the year of his death. They cover most of Mill's favourite subjects—the Church and its Reform (1825, 1826, and 1835) the State of the Nation (1826, 1827, and 1835)—being surveys of contemporary issues which he thought important and demanding reform, two important and timely articles *On the Ballot* (1830 and 1836) and others on *Aristocracy, Formation of Opinions*, and *Law Reform*. They reflect Mill's constant pre-occupation with the immediate problems of his day and also his desire to promote practical reform in his own lifetime.

Of these articles those on political subjects follow the general line of thought set out in the *Essay on Government*. Representative Government was a new device of major importance since it solved the problem which had perplexed political theorists since Plato's day, how to stop rulers ruling in their own interests, and how to ensure that they ruled for the good of the whole community. If everyone had a vote then the rulers would have to rule in the interests of all or lose their power. That people should know their own interests was essential, but it could be assured by universal education and a free press in which errors, fallacies, and interested argument would be remorselessly exposed. From this general standpoint, Mill considered the legislation of the day, in his articles on the state of the nation, and various proposals for political reform, in his studies of the Ballot.

The articles on the Church and its reform are interesting since they reveal the root of his objection to the existing church. Although Mill himself was an agnostic, the root of his disagreement with the Church of England was much more political than religious. In his 1826 article on *Ecclesiastical Establishments* he opens with a statement of his opinion 'that an ecclesiastical establishment is essentially anti-Christian; that religion can never be safe or sound, unless where it is left free to every man's choice ... wholly uninfluenced by the operation either of

---

[39] The *London Review* later amalgamated with the *Westminster Review*.

punishment or reward on the part of the magistrate. We think it proper to go even further and declare that it is not religion only to which an ecclesiastical establishment is hostile: in our opinion, there is not one of the great interests of humanity, on which it does not exercise a baleful influence'. The general argument in support of this is that organized religion soon gains power and privilege and becomes pre-occupied with its preservation. When, in addition to being organized it is 'established' and 'aided by the magistrate' it becomes almost wholly concerned to increase its powers without limit.[40] The argument is profusely illustrated from the history of the Church of England—more especially during its periods of intolerance and persecution. The basis of the argument is the same as in Mill's political articles—that men in power and privilege inevitably serve their own interests. But it is interesting to observe Mill's extreme individualism in religious matters coming out: partly, no doubt, due to his Presbyterian training, but partly, as we shall see, due to more profound causes.

Mill gave his positive proposals for reform in his 1835 article. Here he was more extreme in his objections to the existing system, and, many would say, in his objection to all religion. His proposals virtually sweep away all traditionally religious functions from the Church, leaving to it the general duty of moral education. All collective prayer was denounced as mere ceremony, and the work of the clergy should consist of promoting good conduct: their success should be judged by the standard of conduct in their parishes.[41] Mill's views in private, and when a practical outcome seemed possible, were not quite so extreme as this, as is seen in a letter to Brougham: 'To be acceptable to those whom he has to instruct and persuade I think an essential condition in the qualifications of a clergyman. I would sacrifice a good deal of the securities I might desire for a high degree of intellect, in order to secure that one great requisite. I think, however, it would lower the character of the kirk to make the choice popular; and therefore I wish some middle way could be found by which we might both have an intellectual clergy and a clergy acceptable to the people. After

[40] Bain, op. cit., pp. 295–7.
[41] Ibid., pp. 381–9.

3

all when we look at the people's choice it is not so much amiss. The Scots have Dr. McCorr, Dr. Wardlaw and many others who would be sure of eminence in any church. How many men of eminence among the dissenting clergy of England? It is only in those sects where religion is made to consist of heated feelings, that mere ranters have the lead; and of that tribe of Saints there are very few in Scotland. However, do what we will we are now come to that state in which the people consider their religion to be their own concern; and when they will have it shaped to their own taste. The established sects must either conform to that taste or few will conform to them.'[42]

When we remember the deplorable state of the Church of England at this time, Mill's writings and views can be seen more as a commentary on the Church of his day than as a system of reform based on his agnosticism. The latter indeed never intruded: he was in fact an agnostic in a literal sense—not opposed to belief in God but believing that nothing could be known of it. Hence religious belief as such roused no strong emotions in him. But the Church of England, with its many abuses, its unholy alliance with the aristocracy, and its opposition to so many reforms—all this was calculated to arouse Mill's most bitter condemnation, the more so when he contrasted it, as he does in his letter to Brougham, with his native Scotland. But his main thesis is the same with the Church as with the State: men serve only their interests, and until the system is altered to make those interests coincide with the public benefit, no real reform was possible.

All these articles were, of course, written anonymously, for Mill's position at India House did not permit him openly to engage in such controversial matters. He was an active correspondent with Lord Brougham on the subject of Parliamentary Reform, however. But, during the period 1830–5 he was quite heavily occupied at the India Office. The renewal of the charter of the East India Company fell due at this time, and a select committee of the House of Commons was set up to consider the matter. Mill was a key witness on whom much of the

---

[42] Mill to Brougham, April 1834, University College London, Brougham MSS. It should be noted that the date of this letter is very close to that at which the article must have been written.

burden lay; far from resenting the work he rejoiced in it for he regarded his work for India as a really practicable attempt to increase the happiness of large numbers of people.

The other task which occupied these last few years of Mill's life was the writing of what proved to be a full statement of his moral philosophy—the *Fragment on Mackintosh*, a title which is somewhat misleading, for it is a volume of some 400 pages. The genesis of this book is given in a letter to Brougham: 'I am amusing myself during these holidays with looking over a thing which, if I can get it put in order while here, you may hear something more of. When Mackintosh's *Dissertations* first appeared, indeed before it was published, I had prepared some strictures upon it, chiefly with a view to expose his perversions of the principle of utility, and indeed the manner in which he had smattered with ethical science to evil purpose altogether. But I had written it in the form of letters to him; which would not do when he was dead; and with an asperity, which I could not find it in my heart to use of a man who was just dead, and who could not stand up in his own defence. The papers thereupon lay by till now. But I could not help feeling that something useful might be done in removing confusion from men's minds on that important subject, of which Sir James's book is a wonderful example, and in shewing the misfortune of men's deluding themselves with unmeaning words of which Sir James's book is not less an example.'[43] Mill may have softened his original asperity but the book is still, in places, exceedingly caustic. None the less, for the most part it goes in some detail into the main problems of moral philosophy and it is a valuable source of information of Mill's views, especially in interpreting his other writings.

In 1835 Mill was taken seriously ill with a lung complaint, and although he returned to London in late autumn of that year, he was unable to resume active work. In a letter to his son, James Bentham Mill, he says: 'My complaint is not removed. The lungs are clear but the cough remains . . . However I must take all the care I can.'[44] The illness was the beginning of the end, though it was much protracted, and as

---

[43] Mill to Brougham, 27 August 1834, quoted in Bain, op. cit., pp. 372–4.
[44] Bain, op. cit., pp. 397–8. Written from Mickleham, 18 October 1835.

late as March 1836 Mill seems to have believed in his recovery, for he wrote to James, then in Calcutta: 'As soon as I get a little strength (for I am so weak that everything is still a burthen to me) I shall set seriously to work on Logic with Derry. I think he will penetrate it rapidly; and it will be of immense importance to him: it will give clearness and force to his intellect to a wonderful degree.' He adds: 'The lessons go well on. I have not yet resumed my hearing of them; but John hears them and gives me a highly favourable account.'[45] Right through this period since 1820, Mill had continued the personal education of his children, hearing their lessons each day himself. From these letters it is clear that he regarded this aspect of his activities as among the most important. He died on 23 June 1836. His last thoughts are recorded by another son, Henry: 'When he thought he should not recover, he used to say to me or George that he would willingly die, if it were not that he left us too young to be sure how we should turn out.'[46]

James Mill had lived a life of extraordinary energy and unremitting endeavour in the service of a cause—the cause of the greatest happiness of the greatest number of people. In a moment of pique, when Mill declined to do him a personal favour, Francis Place lamented that 'he cared nothing for the individual, only for the mass'. This was hardly a fair judgment, as the warmth of Mill's writings to Ricardo testifies. But Mill was not a man who readily displayed his feelings and in all his long correspondence with Francis Place little real affection is shewn; it could well be argued that he regarded his friendship with Place not mainly as a personal matter but as an association with someone who would aid the cause. This thesis breaks down when we hear of Mill's extensive efforts to aid Place in the education of his daughter. But Mill was certainly not a demonstrative man, and if he did not display his affections openly himself, there is little doubt as to the warmth of affection he inspired in others throughout his life. McCulloch found him 'extremely kind and friendly',[47] Mrs Grote on the other hand

---

45 Ibid., p. 406, Mill to James Bentham Mill, 9 March 1836. Derry was Henry, born 1820, and then 16 years old.
46 Ibid., p. 408, letter by Henry Mill, July 1836.
47 Correspondence of MacVey Napier, McCulloch to Napier, 2 May 1824.

would not have endorsed this. To her he was 'a propagandist of a high order, equally master of the pen and of speech. Moreover he possessed the faculty of kindling in his auditors the generous impulses towards the popular side, both in politics and social theories: leading them at the same time to regard the cultivation of individual affections and sympathies as destructive of lofty aims, and indubitably hurtful to the mental character'.[48] Henry Solly gives an impression with which many would have agreed: 'His manner to me and other visitors was usually stately, simple and courteous, and not unkind to his children, though he seemed to take very little notice of them except John; but accustomed as I was to my father's behaviour to my mother, and that of other gentlemen whom I had observed in similar relations, I could not help being rather pained at his manner occasionally to Mrs. Mill. She was a tall handsome lady, sweet-tempered, with pleasant manners, fond of her children: but I think not much interested in what the elder ones and their father talked about.'[49] There seems to be wide agreement that Mill's marriage was not a success: James Mill largely ignored his wife, intent as he was on two things, the public cause, and the education of his children.

The public cause was the Utilitarian ideal; it was adopted first as a practical criterion of legal reform, then as a political creed, and lastly as a philosophy. It is important to remember the development of Mill's thought, and especially two influences or factors in this development which are usually overlooked. The first of these is the influence of the Greeks. There is, as we have seen, much evidence both direct, in Mill's correspondence, and indirect, in his thought, to suggest that Mill found Greek philosophy a lasting inspiration to his own philosophical thinking. The second, is the intense and constant pre-occupation Mill had with the practical issues of his day; this factor means that in interpreting his thought we must always seek how far he was writing for his own day, instead of, or as well as, for posterity. Both these factors emphasise that it would be an error to regard Mill, as superficially he can be regarded, as part of a continuous line of development in thought

[48] *Personal Life of George Grote*, by Mrs Grote, 1873, pp. 22f.
[49] Henry Solly, *These Eighty Years*, vi, p. 147.

through the eighteenth-century tradition of association psychology, hedonism and various forms of Utilitarianism. Our account of Mill's career suggests that we are more likely to arrive at a true interpretation of his thought if we consider him strictly in his historical context—the context of the times in which he lived, and of the particular influences on his own thought.

III

Practical Work in Education

In Education as in Politics, Mill's theoretical writings followed a considerable amount of practical experience. In considering this experience we may ignore his brief employment as a tutor, before leaving Scotland, and concentrate on two main themes. The first is Mill's connexion with various schemes to establish and expand provision for public education. This commences with his support for the Royal Lancasterian Society in 1809, and ends with his participation in the founding of University College, London in 1826. The second is his education of his son John Stuart Mill, and thereafter successively of his other eight children.

Joseph Lancaster, in 1798, had started a school in a back-room or outhouse of his father's house in Borough Road, Waterloo, London. He adopted, and indeed claimed to have invented, the monitorial system of teaching, by which he taught the ablest and eldest pupils, and they in turn taught the rest who were divided according to their abilities and progress into small groups for that purpose. By 1805 his methods had attracted royal attention, and Lancaster himself turned from teaching to propaganda and lecturing in favour of his method. In 1810 The Royal Lancasterian Association was formed to popularize the method and encourage the establishment of schools on the monitorial system up and down the country. The society was backed financially by a number of wealthy Quakers, and Lancaster was given a generous allowance while he divided his time between lecturing and teaching a small number of pupils in the original Borough Road school, who were expected to become, at the age of eighteen, schoolmasters equipped to take charge of new schools in various parts of the country. In this way, the Borough Road school became an embryonic training college, or at least, this was the intention of the Society.

The monitorial system has, on the whole, been roundly condemned by subsequent educationalists as mechanical, and as ignoring the special skills required in teaching. So it is desirable to start by noting some aspects of the system which were thought important at the time. First, it was clearly cheaper than any system hitherto envisaged, and it could quickly be put into operation. By having an efficient group of older boys, the monitors, it was thought that one master could be responsible for as many as a thousand pupils. No complicated building was required—one large room was the usual design suggested—and the whole enterprise reduced initial capital outlay to a minimum. It must be mentioned at once that although the schools were clearly cheap, they were not nearly so cheap as their protagonists claimed. The Society claimed that, in a large school, the cost of educating a child 'need not exceed five or six shillings' a year.[1] But when Francis Place made a careful investigation of the accounts of several schools, he found the cost nearer a guinea a head, partly because none of the schools were as large as they were advertised to be, and partly because no proper accounting was done. In his diary he concludes: 'the public were imposed upon and made to believe that the expense per head in these schools was much smaller than it really was'.[2] Amongst other complications in assessing the true cost was the fact that the normal, and recommended method of starting a school was to raise a public subscription: every subscriber of one guinea had the right to have one child free at the school.

Second, the Lancasterian schools were, from the start, undenominational. This appealed to the non-conformists, who were thereby freed from Church control and domination, and it appealed to the Utilitarians as eminently practical. If there were to be denominational schools then each town or village would need one for each denomination, and the result would

[1] *Manual of the System of Primary Instruction in Model Schools of the British & Foreign Schools Society*, London, 1831, ch. 1, p. 1.

[2] B.M. Add. MSS. 27823, Place Diary, pp. 111ff. Borough Road, for instance, the parent school, cost at least a guinea a head, was advertised as a school for 1,000 pupils, and in fact could hold only 400. Much the same was true of the Horseferry Road school. Cf. also B.M. Place Collection, vol. 60.

be, at best, a large number of small schools, hopelessly uneconomic to run, or, much more likely, no schools at all, because so many would need to be established. Denominational schools would rob the monitorial system of its cheapness and of its immediate practicability.

Third, it was claimed that the monitorial system, as a method of teaching, was not merely cheap, but good in itself. It was argued that boys understood their comrades much better than any adult could hope to do, and that, knowing their own difficulties in learning, they were more capable of smoothing the path of younger boys than an adult whose learning period was many years behind him. This line of argument finds some echoes in those later to be used in favour of prefectorial rule in the public schools. It was also held that schoolmasters had little incentive to do their work well, but that monitors had. Under the monitorial system, a monitor only held his place so long as he deserved it; at any weekly test he might be displaced. And under James Mill's interpretation of the monitorial system, the monitor was held responsible for faults and failings in his pupils.[3]

Fourthly, the system made possible the division of pupils into small groups of approximately the same standard and ability. This was a considerable advantage over the usual conditions obtaining at that time. Schools in general were either very small, as in England, and containing a wide range of age and ability, or very large, as in Scotland, where in Edinburgh High School the Latin class was 100 strong, and in Glasgow 200. In either case, the Lancasterian system represented a great advance. In the small school, with say ninety pupils ranging in age from say six to fifteen years, and widely varying in ability, it offered one or two masters a practicable method of coping with the almost impossible teaching situation presented by the school taken as a whole. Such schools abounded in London.[4] In a large class where hitherto the method had been to hear each boy in turn, while the rest of the class was idle, or at least unsupervised and untaught, it offered the prospect of continuous employment and supervision of the whole class. In its day,

[3] Cf. J. S. Mill, *Autobiography*, p. 8; also Wallas, *Life of Francis Place*, op. cit., pp. 74–5.

[4] Cf. Wakefield's report, already quoted, of the Drury Lane district of London.

3*

the Lancasterian system was progressive and valuable. It marks, in reality, not so much monitorial instruction, though it rested on this, as the beginning of class teaching—that is, the teaching of a group as a unit. In order to do this the units had to be, and still have to be, homogeneous in ability and attainment. This meant breaking the small school into very small groups of the same age, and the large class, in the large school, into many small groups, each under the instruction of a monitor. In either case, progress would be infinitely improved by adopting the monitorial system. With the small school, it was the only hope. With the large class, it was equally the most economic method, unless the teaching staff were to be expanded, and this was certainly alien to traditions, even in Scotland, at that time.

James Mill supported the Lancasterian movement on all four counts. He believed strongly in universal primary education. It was an essential pre-requisite to his device of representative government resting on universal male suffrage, and enlightened by a free press. And he also felt, as did many at the time, that what would now be called 'juvenile delinquency' would be sensibly reduced by an expansion of primary education. His belief in undenominational schools was purely a practical one: it was the only way to establish universal primary education for all. But it was strengthened with dark suspicions as to the motives of the Church of England in resisting the Lancasterian movement. In actual fact, there was some explanation, though not justification, of the attitude of the Church of England. Shortly after the West London Lancasterian Association took over the school in Horseferry Road, Westminster, its pupils consisted of 195 members of the Church of England, and some thirty-seven Dissenters of all kinds. In the Lancasterian school in City Road, about half the pupils were members of the Church of England. To the Church this must have looked like poaching; it was, in fact, losing its pupils owing to its own lethargy, the Lancasterian movement's energy, and the intense public demand for education. The Church fought back by setting up its own monitorial schools, under the auspices of the British National Society, founded in 1811. But there is probably a good deal of truth in Mill's comment that the Church was only active as a direct result of Lancasterian competition, and only in the areas where the Lancasterian movement established schools. To the practical Utilitarians, this produced the absurd situation that, at a time when a majority of the population was receiving no education, the establishment of a Lancasterian school in a locality was likely to produce a second school to serve the same district under the auspices of the Church, instead of a school for another district that was without any education at all.

Mill was a member of the committee of the Royal Lancasterian Society and appears to have been active at many of its meetings. The most powerful support for it came from some wealthy Quakers, notably Joseph Fox, and the committee contained all shades of religious opinion at least on the Dissenting side. But from the start there was the possibility that the more strongly religious, or more bigoted, of the Quakers might resent the presence of 'infidels' and suspect their advice. On Mill's side, his attitude was clear: all should co-operate for the cause and such suspicions should be patiently borne. This attitude was reciprocated by most of the Quakers, but not by the most powerful: Joseph Fox. And Place found the suspicions of Fox much more difficult to bear than did Mill. A second latent cause of the split which ultimately came, was the business-like attitude which Place and Mill wished to take towards financial matters, contrasted with the vague and sentimental, though extremely generous, philanthropy of Fox. Lancaster himself was exceedingly extravagant, and there were continual financial crises; the need for proper accounting grew more clear with every year that passed. But in the meantime, an offshoot of the main society was formed, largely at the instigation of Place, Mill, and Wakefield, called the West London Lancasterian Association. It had the design of surveying London west of Temple Bar, and north of the river, to discover just how many schools were needed to give this area primary education for all, and then to set to work on an impressive scale, and with proper organization, to meet this need.

Mill was a member of this association and of its committee. And the latter was very widely representative of different opinions. Place records that it contained Unitarians, Methodists, 'several Churchmen', Scotch Presbyterians, Baptists,

Roman Catholics, and 'four Infidels'[5] two of whom were himself and Mill. After preliminary private meetings, a public meeting to launch the Association was held on 2 August 1813. The address to the public, according to Place 'had been previously settled between Mr Mill, Mr Wakefield and myself',[6] and it is worth quoting because it expresses accurately, and probably in his own prose,[7] Mill's view on the need for popular education:

'In whatever degree happiness depends upon good conduct, and in whatever degree good conduct depends upon good understanding and good habits, in that same degree do happiness and good conduct depend upon training or education.

'That the happiness of the great majority is not the second but the first of national objects, no Englishman will controvert.

'That the happiness of the nation, all orders included, depends upon the good conduct of the majority, all men are forward to proclaim.

'It is impossible to train the young to good habits and good inclinations by leaving them in idleness. The ground work of our training must be employment . . .'

The full title of the association was 'West London Lancasterian Association for teaching Reading, Writing, Arithmetic and Good Morals'.[8]

The association founded no schools and did not complete its survey of educational needs. The survey was undertaken by groups of three, who made house-to-house visits. Its efficacy varied with the different groups and the persistence they shewed in getting the information they wanted—in some areas the constantly shifting population made it difficult. Parts of the area were successfully surveyed and the information proved of great value to Brougham's Royal Commission a few years later. Mill's part in the association was largely behind the scenes, for he was so often and so long at Ford Abbey. But he emerges on important occasions, for instance, as the author of a letter on behalf of the association to Earl Stanhope, who had wondered

[5] B.M. Add. MSS. 27823, Place Collection, pp. 98ff.
[6] Ibid., p. 88.
[7] Cf. Bain, op. cit., p. 86.
[8] B.M. Add. MSS. 27823.

at the absence of progress, and had asked where the money subscribed had gone. Mill assured him that the most strict accountancy was observed, but that money was short: 'Up to the period of the general meeting, a few weeks ago, the whole of the sum subscribed did not amount to £300 . . . No efforts have since that time been spared to find a proper place for the erection of a school. But the difficulty has been found to be great to find a place which united all the requisites—one reason is that it is highly necessary to have the school in a populous neighbourhood, and that in such a situation ground is more valuable than suits the condition of their funds—they have now, however, one or two places in view, one of which it is their intention to chuse. It is necessary however to state, that the whole sum as yet subscribed is not adequate to the erecting and fitting up of one school, that no person has yet been called for the money subscribed at the general meeting, nor will be until the building of the school is begun, and that no expense since that meeting except the current expenses has been incurred.'[9] It was not only lack of funds which caused the West London Association to fail; they fell out with the parent body, now renamed the British and Foreign Schools Society. The latter insisted under the influence of Fox that the Bible should be the only book read in Lancasterian schools, and it wanted a regulation enforced that children who did not attend a place of worship on Sundays should be banned from the schools. The West London Association refused to enforce either rule; a fatal split occurred, and from 1816 the West London Association was virtually dead.

Meanwhile Mill and Place had become active in a project more peculiarly their own: that of founding a secondary or superior day school in London, run on the monitorial system. The idea may well have been prompted by the contrast between London and Edinburgh in this matter. The main sponsors, in addition to Place and Mill, were Bentham, Edward Wakefield, and David Ricardo. 'Mill', says Place, 'became an active promoter of the necessary steps for the establishment of a school',[10] and certainly, in day-to-day service to the cause, Mill gave

---

[9] Mill to Stanhope, 28 June 1814, B.M. Place Collection, vol. 60.
[10] B.M. Add. MSS. 27823, Place Diary, p. 144.

more time to this than to any other project for public education. He appeared regularly at the meeting of the small committee, which met weekly, and sometimes more often. He was ever-zealous in raising funds and, with Place, drew up the 'Proposals' which were the basis of the appeal to the public. While at Ford Abbey, he was the principal liaison officer between Bentham and the London protagonists of the scheme.

This project was much more under the control and guidance of the Utilitarians than either of their previous ventures in public education, and from the start it was handled with caution, prudence, and a keen sense of what was practicable. Bentham's contribution was a book called *Chrestomathia* setting out the syllabus and methods of instruction to be used. It was a theoretical justification of the monitorial system, and it is interesting to note that, in the preface, Bentham acknowledges the assistance not of Lancaster, but of Bell, the Church of England protagonist of this system of education, who had set forth his views in a book entitled *Elements of Tuition*. Both Mill and Place read and commented on *Chrestomathia* in draft form, and Mill prepared it for the press—a task which, as we have already noticed, was considerable in the case of Bentham's writings. There is little doubt that he endorsed all that was said on method, though not the suggestions for syllabus. Mill also was in the forefront in advising on the free distribution of the book in quarters most influential and likely to secure financial support for the scheme.

Before endorsing the monitorial system, the committee had made careful enquiries in one or two schools where it had been already used,[11] and they received detailed comments from the High School, Edinburgh. Gray, of Edinburgh, wrote enthusiastically: 'The system has been fully tried in our school in the teaching of Latin and Greek and with the most distinguished effect . . . In my own case it has converted a laborious and often irksome profession into the most easy and most delightful employment possible . . . not one of my boys has failed . . . Instead of that inattention, drowsiness, and even insubordination, which too frequently prevail at the bottom of all large classes, all is activity, cheerfulness and prompt obedience.' In a

[11] Charterhouse School used the monitorial system, apparently successfully.

further letter he expands: 'On this [the earlier system of teach-ing] I have experienced two unavoidable evils: 1. that the upper boys gain a knowledge of the lesson soon after they enter the class-room cannot be kept still while the master is employed in teaching the under boys: and as the example is contagious, the restlessness soon becomes universal, and 2. ... while the upper boys are construing, the lower ones are generally trifling and when the lesson comes round to them are totally ignorant of it ... on the new system, every boy is employed every minute of time he is in school, either in the acquisition or communica-tion of knowledge ... It seems indeed that boys are better qualified to teach boys than men. They enter more readily into their feelings: they are more sensible of the difficulties which they themselves have just mastered: and will adopt more simple and familiar modes of illustration ... The superiority of this mode over the other is incalculable, as it tends to store the mind with useful knowledge—to infuse a love of learning—to form habits of industry—and to render the whole economy of a school delightful both to scholars and master.'[12] This letter, says Place, 'produced the very best effects on the many persons to whom it was shewn. Mr. Mill who from the first moment the plan was mentioned heartily concurred in it became an active promoter of the necessary steps to the establishment of a school'.[13]

Bentham originally offered his garden as a site for the school. But as early as 1814 Mill wrote to Place: 'Mr. Bentham's eagerness to have it in his garden was originally very great ... he is still quite keen ... but Mr. Koe who knows him and all his circumstances better than anybody, says that he is per-suaded that Mr. Bentham will not continue to like it, that there are a multitude of disagreeables connected with it of which he will not at present allow himself to think, but which will swell into great objections hereafter.' Mill continues: 'I could wish you at any rate to take note in the meantime of any spot of ground which may appear fit for the purpose. The money for this object I am persuaded would not be difficult to obtain. We

[12] B.M. Place Collection, vol. 60, letters from James Gray, High School Edinburgh, 17 and 18 December 1813. Similar testimony was received from Pillans, Rector of Glasgow Academy.
[13] Place Collection, vol. 60.

shall circulate a prospectus as soon as the town is full, that is, after Xmas, and shall build, I hope, early in the spring.'[14]

These high hopes must have been based on the fact that the school would cater largely for the sons of tradesmen, and that it would be demonstrably useful to them. But despite Mill's confidence, no school was ever built. Money was raised, and promised, and an architect named Beavans designed a schoolroom. But Bentham reacted as anticipated, and made so many difficulties that the committee looked for other sites. These proved unexpectedly difficult; those available were in poor localities and likely to repel tradesmen parents, and others were more expensive than the funds of the committee permitted them to contemplate. At one point Ricardo was prepared to purchase a site in Leicester Square, but the threat of legal action by other owners to prevent any building in the square, deterred him. The committee then returned perforce to Bentham's garden, but the difficulties made by the owner proved insuperable and by 1822 the project was abandoned, and funds subscribed returned.[15] 'The immediate cause of our failure', wrote Place, 'was want of money . . . There were no sectarian doctrines to be inculcated . . . there were no party politics to be made . . . There was no particular present eminence to be obtained. There was nothing but good to be done, almost solely for its own sake, and the number of persons willing to assist in so very novel a project being few, neither money nor assistance of any kind beyond a very small amount could be obtained.'[16]

[14] B.M. Add. MSS. 27823, p. 181, Mill to Place, 14 October 1814.

[15] But two letters are given in the Place MSS. in which the Chrestomathic proposals are circulated as late as April 1825, with the comment that 'the school was to have been built by subscription . . . but . . . the money subscribed was returned. It is now to be built at the cost of about half a dozen gentlemen only . . . we want a square or nearly square piece of ground of 100ft diameter on which to build the schoolroom' (Place to Clarke, B.M. Place Collection, vol. 60). Some authors have regarded University College as the final realisation of the Chrestomathic idea (e.g. Halévy *Growth of Philosophical Radicalism*, p. 296). I can find no evidence to support this. And a letter from James Mill to Dumont speaks first of the difficulties of raising money for the University College project, and then adds: 'I am happy however to tell you that I think we see our way to a Chrestomathic School'. From this it is clear that, at this time, they were two separate projects. Mill to Dumont, 5 February 1825 (Dumont MSS, Box 76 ff. 21–31).

[16] B.M. Add. MSS. 27823, Place Diary, p. 124.

Mill and Place, with others, were now connected, in 1825, with another, and this time successful, project for the advancement of public education: the founding of University College, London. Thomas Campbell, the poet, was an enthusiast in this cause and had written to the *Times* in February, advocating it. Place sounded Mill, whose first reaction was discouraging, not surprisingly, in view of the fate of earlier schemes. But Brougham gave a dinner at which Campbell and Mill were present, Mill was converted and was among the most active in securing subscriptions for the new university. At the end of the year Mill was elected to the first council of the University College, and in 1827 the foundation stone was laid.

Meantime Mill had been active in the academic affairs of the new university. He tried to persuade his friend Dr Thompson to take the chair of Chemistry.[17] He was unsuccessful in this, but University College opened with an able and eminent jurist in John Austin, who, says Bain, 'had the most distinguished attendance that ever honoured any lecturer'.[18] James Mill concerned himself not only with appointments but also with curriculum, and drafted *Outlines of the Course of Lectures*. This consisted of Logic, Moral Philosophy, and History—the 'highest part of a complete education and the last in order among the subjects of tuition'. Logic included a good deal on Association Psychology, and a section on logical fallacies. History was to be the study not of the facts, but of 'the mode of studying History and of deriving from it the lessons it affords'. Part of this consisted in analysing historical evidence, and part in drawing inferences from historical events—this smacked of sociology, as does Mill's view of History in general. We do not know for whom this course was intended, but it would accord with other evidence of Mill's views on education, that it was intended for all, as part of a general education.[19]

Mill set forth his defence of the founding of University College in London in the course of a 'State of the Nation' article in 1826. He praises greater general literacy, the

17 A fellow student of Mill's at Edinburgh, at this time professor of Chemistry at Glasgow.
18 Bain, op. cit., p. 329.
19 Preserved in University of London Library, Senate House.

Mechanics Institute, to which he was a subscriber though he had taken little active part, and regards the next step as a greater supply of good books for the general population. For the middle class Londoner, a great step forward was the establishment of University College. The Londoners had hitherto had a poor education and the competition the new university would offer to Oxford and Cambridge would be good for both of them for 'monopolies of influence over the mind are not favourable soil for the higher moralities'. It is essential that the new university should have no religious ties.[20] Mill was, in practice, prepared to compromise on this latter principle for the sake of getting full co-operation from religious supporters. Halévy records that 'the Protestant Dissenters . . . dreamt of using the new institution for the instruction of their ministers. They succeeded in turning aside the candidature for the chair of philosophy of Charles Hay Cameron, who was supported by James Mill: James Mill was more conciliatory than George Grote who for reasons of principle did not want an ecclesiastic, and gave way and accepted the nomination of a clergyman, on condition that he should teach Hartley's psychology'.[21]

The religious opposition on the part of the Church of England was considerable, and led to the founding of King's College. Meantime, University College had plenty of internal trouble of its own. This arose primarily from differences between the Warden—Leonard Horner, a brother of Francis who had been at Edinburgh with Mill—and his professors. Mill wrote to Napier, after a meeting of Council that 'it has left us in the same perplexities in which it found us . . . The Warden (though personally far more sinned against than sinning) is the grand source of difficulty; for in the state of hostile feeling among them [the professors] it is vain to expect that the machine will work well—and there is the less hope of it, that it is the rooted opinion of the Warden, that there is but one cure for all the evil, and that is, giving plenty of power to him. Brougham, with sincere friendship for him, did not conceal from me his wish and his hope, that his friends would prevail upon him to resign. This I can mention to you in confidence because I know

---

[20] *Westminster Review*, October 1826.
[21] Halévy, op. cit., pp. 482–3.

that the same is to a great degree your opinion as well as mine. And yet I should dislike to give any appearance of victory to those professors who have carried on a disreputable war against him: and in this respect differ from him radically—that he has the interest of the university deeply at heart—they have shewn that they have not. I do believe (and I am grieved to say it) there is not a man among them who, if his own interests were perfectly detached, would care if it were burned to the ground tomorrow.'[22] In 1831, Mill repeats: 'You will find our poor University in a melancholy way . . . Matters began well at the beginning of the session—I had been absent for some time from illness . . . and having heard nothing to the contrary believed that all was still going well—but presently there was a breaking-out which proved that all the old sources of evil were in strong operation.'[23] The Warden had voluntarily sacrificed part of his salary in view of the state of the college funds, and of his enemies among the professors. Mill comments: 'I confess I think this hard.'[24] Horner resigned in 1831.

University College School was founded in 1830, also in Gower Street. Mill was a subscriber. We may suppose that the primary object of the school was to give students the necessary preliminary training before they went on to University College. It is interesting to notice that, despite the fact that Mill and other Utilitarians were decidedly influential in appointments to this school, the first headmaster was a cleric, the Rev. Browne.[25] Much of his policy appears to contradict the principle of religious neutrality and Francis Place was outraged at the appointment. None the less it stood, and Mill was clearly one of those responsible. It is an indication of the extent of his tolerance in practical matters, and of his willingness and ability to work with all who served the same earthly cause.

This completes an account of the main schemes for furthering public education in which James Mill took an active practical part. In each of them he had shewn an ability and a desire to work with anyone, whatever his religion or politics, who would

[22] Mill to Napier, 8 July 1830, B.M. Add. MSS. 34611.
[23] Mill to Napier, 1 June 1831.
[24] Mill to Napier, 21 February 1831.
[25] The responsible appointing body was the Council of University College; Bain, op. cit., p. 354.

further the cause of public education. In the event, it was the scheme sponsored mainly by the Philosophical Radicals themselves—University College—which was the only one to succeed, and one can hardly fail to remark that the Utilitarians shewed themselves to be more business-like and more practical than some of their associates. Yet their early ventures with the Quakers ought not to be written off as abortive. The Lancasterian movement founded many schools, if not so many as the Society was wont to claim. The West London Association brought home to many the extent of the need. This, with Mill's ever-active pen in support of the cause,[26] did much to prepare the ground for ultimate success later on. Another factor which must be borne in mind is that these different campaigns were not for the same kind of public education. The Lancasterian schools were designed to give primary education to the poor—as far as Mill and Place were concerned in West London, for all. But both the Chrestomathic school and the new university met a different need, that for relevant higher education for the sons of the 'middling ranks' whose example Mill thought was vital in shewing the mass of the people good habits, and where their true happiness lay. It may well be argued that this higher education was, from the start, more likely to command financial support, and of course, it was only the building of one school, as against the large number of primary schools contemplated by the West London Lancasterian Association. It is more likely that practical considerations of this kind turned Mill from primary to secondary and university education; there is no evidence that he ever lost his conviction of the urgent need for primary education for all.

---

[26] Mill wrote articles in the *Edinburgh Review* (1813) and in the *Philanthropist* (1812)—this latter was reprinted as a pamphlet: *Schools for all not Schools for Churchmen only*. Mill had also tried to interest Ricardo in an experimental nursery school, in co-operation with Robert Owen. Ricardo objected that, if the children were fed at school, it would lead to an excess of population. Mill to Ricardo, December 1818, *Ricardo's Letters*, op. cit.

II

The second kind of practical experience of education which Mill had was his personal, single-handed education first of his eldest son, John Stuart Mill, and thereafter of each of his other eight children. While at Ford Abbey, at the most difficult period of his life when engaged on his history, on the occasional article, and on helping Bentham, Mill yet devoted several hours daily to John's education. And this educational work lasted, as we have seen, to the end of his life.

It is convenient to start by considering that aspect of Mill's education of his children most clearly connected with his outside educational work—his use of the monitorial system within his own family. We have noticed that practising schoolmasters had found the greatest advantage of this in that it made possible the splitting of a large class into small homogeneous units, each of which could be simultaneously instructed at a pace appropriate to its ability. On the face of it, these advantages could scarcely be expected to accrue with home instruction of a family. Yet in fact the same problem existed—that each child was at a different stage in learning and achievement, and therefore the same solution was appropriate—to teach the ablest, and let him transmit the learning to the next and so on. The monitorial system made possible the same economy of a parent's time, in James Mill's hands, as it had done for the schoolmasters in Edinburgh and Glasgow. And in addition, Bentham in his book had made it clear that he approved of scholar teaching scholar as a principle—on the grounds that the young understood one another's difficulties better. Mill appears to have been of the same belief. His system was to teach John, and then to set John to teach his sisters, and later his brothers. Then James Mill would hear the lessons of all of them: if they were unsatisfactory, all, including John, were sent back to do them again. Place was very impressed, but he thought Mill too severe: 'His method is by far the best that I have ever witnessed, and is infinitely precise; but he is excessively severe. No fault, however trivial, escapes his notice, and

none goes without reprehension and punishment of some sort.'[27]
John Stuart Mill, on the other hand, while acknowledging the
excellence of his own education, did not praise the monitorial
system: 'In my eighth year I commenced learning Latin, in
conjunction with a younger sister, to whom I taught it as I
went on, and who afterwards repeated the lessons to my father:
and from this time, sisters and brothers being successively
added as pupils, a considerable part of my day's work consisted
of this preparatory teaching. It was a part which I greatly disliked; the more so as I was held responsible for the lessons of
my pupils, in almost as full a sense as for my own: I, however,
derived from this discipline the great advantage of learning
more thoroughly and retaining more lastingly the things which
I was set to teach . . . In other respects, however, the experience
of boyhood is not favourable to the plan of teaching children
by means of one another. The teaching, I am sure, is very
inefficient as teaching, and I well know that the relation
between teacher and taught is not a good discipline for either.'[28]
One or two points may be noted. John was only eight, when he
became a 'monitor': this was surely much younger than
Lancaster had envisaged. On the other hand children of this
age do in fact teach each other a good deal in play, if not in
work. Secondly, John is set to teach his sister in 1814: this was
the date of Bentham's *Chrestomathia*, and is also about the time
when Mill read, and was impressed by, the experience of
Edinburgh High School in using the monitorial system for the
teaching of Latin. These factors may be connected: at all events,
the evidence suggests that Mill believed in the monitorial
system as an educational principle. The only adverse comment
he ever made was an obvious one, that John would make more
rapid progress in Latin 'but he is kept back by Billie'[29] (his
sister).

John Stuart Mill was brought up on a classical curriculum,
later extended to classical philosophy, and there is little doubt

[27] Place to Mrs Place, from Ford Abbey, 17 August 1817. Quoted in Wallas,
Life of Francis Place, pp. 74–5.

[28] J. S. Mill, *An Autobiography*, ed. Laski, World's Classics, O.U.P., p. 8. John
Mill 'often acted the part of mediator' between his elder sisters and their severe
father; Bain, op. cit., pp. 334–5.

[29] B.M. Add. MSS. 35152, f. 92, Mill to Place, 14 October 1814.

that his father regarded this as the best of all educations. John started Greek at the age of three, and he had read a large number of standard authors in both Greek and Latin by the time he was twelve. 'During the same years', he writes, 'I learnt elementary geometry and algebra thoroughly, and other portions of the higher mathematics far from thoroughly: for my father, not having kept up this part of his early acquired knowledge, could not spare time to qualify himself for the removal of my difficulties.'[30] History was private reading and much enjoyed; the writing of English verses was compulsory, and much disliked. At the age of twelve more advanced study took place, commencing with Logic, a subject which James Mill thought fundamental in education.[31] A little later he undertook more serious study of Plato—James Mill's favourite philosophical author—and finally he was given a complete course in Political Economy.[32]

This was John Stuart Mill's education, entirely devised and supervised by his father. It bore at least a family relationship to the father's own education in Scotland. But all depended on an early start with the classical languages, and the object of studying these was to obtain an entry into the minds of those whom James Mill regarded as the greatest of all philosophers—Plato and Aristotle. The real centre of this curriculum was philosophy, and especially Logic—the 'method of analysis' as the Benthamite circle called it. The curriculum was well in advance of Mill's day, especially by comparison with Oxford and Cambridge, where Classics meant not the 'Greats' of the end of the century, but an arid and generally fruitless study of niceties of style, syntax, and language. Where a pupil had no knowledge of the classical languages, Mill none the less prescribed philosophy as the main diet, thus emphasising his view that the languages were a means to the study of philosophy, and not an end in themselves. Thus he counselled Place, in regard to his daughter Annie for whom Mill had a great regard: 'You should at this moment institute a course of study in company with

---

[30] *Autobiography*, op. cit., p. 10.

[31] Cf. Bain, op. cit., p. 406.

[32] *Autobiography*, op. cit., p. 23. His first study of Plato was at the age of eight but he comments that 'It would have been better omitted, as it was totally impossible that I should understand it'.

your daughter. And it should be on the abstruser subjects. Of languages, unless for the purposes of show as a governess, she has quite enough. As to *belles lettres*, any of the best books which analyse well the principles of fine writing she might read with advantage. The fact, however, is that none of the books I know, analyse these principles well. Dr. Campbell's philosophy of rhetoric is perhaps the best. It is in many respects a good book. You will find a copy of it among my books, if she is inclined to take it . . . The benefit of such works is that they will give her a view of the whole field of criticism at once; and give her some practice in the important operation of taking in a great whole as a whole and contemplating the relation and bearing of its parts. This is one of the leading functions of a great intellect and one to which the present pitiful education enables very few persons to rise. After this she might read along with you Horne Tooke's work, which is the best introduction we yet have—though most objectionable in its form and manner—to all the logical studies . . . After Horne Tooke, Locke is a sort of fundamental book and much there is in it of use to the youthful mind. The account of complex and abstract ideas is altogether wrong—and the chapters on that subject are puzzling and vexatious—but if she is told to read it, not as to what she is to believe, but as what gives her the history of Locke's speculations, and what is necessary to be known as a key to all subsequent metaphysics which have been built upon his foundation, she will get on with more delight. Before she has digested all this I shall be in London to give her mind a bit of a scrutiny.'[33] James Mill thought highly of Locke, especially as a book for beginners in philosophy, for he also advised Ricardo: 'If you have not read, or read lately, Locke's *Essay on the Human Understanding*, I think you should do so; both because it is perpetually referred to in all books, and in all speculative conversation, and also because it really is an excellent introduction to intellectual matters in general. Locke's mode of proceeding trains the mind into paths of right enquiry; it gives you the end of the clue and tells you how you may explore by yourself the labyrinth.'[34] It should be noted that James Mill made no

[33] B.M. Add. MSS. 35152, f. 160, Mill to Place, 6 September 1815.
[34] *Ricardo's Letters*, op. cit., vi, no. 232, Mill to Ricardo, 10 October 1817.

distinction between girls and boys in the intellectual education
he recommended. The only difference was that if, unlike his
own daughters, they had not learnt the classical languages,
English philosophy rather than Plato and Aristotle must be the
basis. But the real core was philosophy, and especially Logic—
the 'method of analysis', and clear thinking which would be
valuable not only in philosophical problems, but also in, for
instance, reflecting on problems of government.

If the content of John Stuart Mill's education was liberal and
enlightened, the same can hardly be said of the age at which he
took the various courses. By our standards the most striking
thing about this education is the extraordinarily young age at
which it commenced, and the amount of progress which James
Mill expected by the age of twelve, when John Mill started on
Plato's philosophical dialogues. Two factors need to be remembered before condemning this rapid and early education out of
hand. First, the customs of the time, certainly in Scotland,
differed from ours: James Mill himself had started at the
University of Edinburgh at the age of seventeen, much later
than most:[35] many went to Oxford or Edinburgh at the age of
fifteen. Second, John Stuart Mill, who does not hesitate to
criticize parts of his education, bestows unqualified approval
on this aspect of it: 'In the course of instruction which I have
partly retraced, the point most superficially apparent is the
great effort to give, during the years of childhood an amount of
knowledge in what are considered to be the higher branches of
education, which is seldom acquired (if acquired at all) until
the age of manhood. The result of the experiment shews the
ease with which this may be done ... what I could do, could
assuredly be done by any boy or girl of average capacity and
healthy physical constitution: and if I have accomplished anything, I owe it, among other fortunate circumstances, to the
fact that through the early training bestowed on me by my
father, I started, I may fairly say, with an advantage of a
quarter of a century over my contemporaries.'[36] This is presumably a comparison with England where standards were
low: and John Mill is obviously overmodest. His father was

35 Bain comments 'unusually advanced age', p. 13.
36 *Autobiography*, op. cit., pp. 25–6.

also, as we shall see, in many ways an exceptionally able teacher.[37]

John Mill comments that his father was a stern and exacting task-master who 'in all his teaching, demanded of me not only the utmost I could do, but much that I could by no possibility have done'.[38] He refers, too, to his father's impatient temper: when John performed ill at the art of elocution, his father 'perpetually lost his temper with me'.[39] On the other hand, despite his impatient temper, he suffered the incessant interruption, without shewing his irritation, of giving John the meaning of every word in Greek or Latin which he did not know, while at the same time hard at work on his *History of British India*. In mathematics, John found his father most unreasonable: 'I was constantly incurring his displeasure by my inability to solve difficult problems for which he did not see that I had not the necessary previous knowledge.'[40] It is only fair to add to these strictures that John approved a high standard being demanded of him: 'a child from whom nothing is demanded' will attain little: his criticism is that, especially in those fields of knowledge in which James Mill himself was not well-versed, the standard demanded was unreasonably high.[41]

In his actual methods of teaching, there is much to praise in James Mill's conduct of his son's education. All observers agree that it was not an education of 'cram'. His son endorses this: 'Mine was not an education of cram. My father never permitted anything which I learnt to degenerate into a mere exercise of memory. He strove to make the understanding not

[37] Although there is no direct evidence, the early start of John Stuart Mill's education may well have been due to the influence of Bentham. Among his manuscripts there are two early drafts on Pauper Education, written in 1795, both of which emphasise repeatedly the waste of the period from four to fourteen years in a child's life, which might be put to useful and educative purposes. And he speaks of a child being able to learn letters before he can speak. (Bentham MSS. U.C.L. Boxes 149, 153A.) Mill met Bentham in 1808, when John Stuart Mill was two years old.

[38] *Autobiography*, op. cit., p. 25.

[39] Ibid., p. 19.

[40] Cf. *Autobiography*, p. 27. 'A pupil from whom nothing is demanded which he cannot do, never does all he can.'

[41] Ibid., pp. 26–7.

only go along with every step of the teaching, but, if possible, precede it. Anything which could be found out by thinking, I was never told until I had exhausted my efforts to find it out for myself.' He commends especially his father's method of teaching him Economics and Logic: 'I do not believe that any scientific teaching ever was more thorough or better fitted for training the faculties than the mode by which Logic and Political Economy were taught me by my father. Striving, even in an exaggerated degree, to call forth the activity of my faculties, by making me find out everything for myself, he gave his explanations not before but after I had felt the full force of the difficulties . . . he made me a thinker in both subjects . . . At a later period I even occasionally convinced him and altered his opinion on some points of detail; which I state to his honour, not to my own. It at once exemplifies his perfect candour, and the real worth of his method of teaching.'[42] School logic was a subject in which John was most 'perseveringly drilled': it was also the subject he found most valuable of all. Much of his education in its later stages took place informally on long walks with his father: these were the occasions for all kinds of discussions in history, political theory, logic and economics. Each day the son was required to explain to the father what had been explained to him the day before. Another voluntary part of his education was 'what I called writing historics'—summaries of existing books he had read. 'My father encouraged me in this useful amusement, though, as I think judiciously, he never asked to see what I wrote: so that I did not feel that in writing it I was accountable to anyone, nor had the chilling sensation of being under a critical eye.'[43] Stern and formidable as James Mill was, he seems to have had some insight into youthful feelings, perhaps because he knew so well the lack of confidence which can so easily assail the writer.

According to John, his education was 'much more fitted for training me to know than to do'.[44] Yet the non-academic side of his education was, in his father's eyes, an essential element in the whole, and just as carefully planned. James Mill was

[42] Ibid., pp. 24-5.
[43] Ibid., p. 12.
[44] Ibid., p. 31.

'very earnestly bent upon my escaping not only the corrupting influence which boys exercise over boys, but the contagion of vulgar modes of thought and feeling; and for this he was willing to pay the price of inferiority in accomplishments which school-boys in all countries chiefly cultivate . . . From temperance and much walking, I grew up healthy and hardy . . . It was not that play or the time for it was refused me. Though no holidays were allowed, lest the habit of work should be broken and a taste for idleness acquired, I had ample leisure each day to amuse myself; but I had no boy companions, and the animal need for physical activity was satisfied by walking . . . my amusements were mostly solitary . . . I consequently remained long inexpert at anything requiring manual dexterity'.[45] His father was aware of his deficiences and admonished him, but 'while he saved me from the demoralizing effects of school life, he made no effort to provide me with any sufficient substitute for its practicalizing influences . . . here, as well as in some other points of my tuition, he seems to have expected effects without causes'.[46] The essence of the matter was that James Mill saw the necessity for controlling the whole environment of his pupil, if his education was to have maximum effect and be conducted with maximum efficiency, and if suitable moral training were to result. But in the process something was lost; boys may be demoralizing influences but their companionship is essential and so also, perhaps, is an element of 'living' as against perpetual education. There is something of the ultra-planner in this side of James Mill's plans, especially when we read of the employ-ment of an army drill sergeant to give the children physical training.[47]

The moral education of John Stuart Mill had no religious basis. By this time his father was an agnostic, and held that nothing could be known on metaphysical problems. Despite his father's enlightened methods of teaching, John Mill neces-sarily grew up with a strong Benthamite background,[48] owing

[45] Ibid., pp. 30–1.
[46] Ibid., pp. 30–1.
[47] Bain, op. cit., p. 333. But this too may be Bentham's influence: he regarded all sports except swimming as inferior forms of exercise (Bentham MSS. U.C.L. Box 153A.)
[48] *Autobiography*, op. cit., p. 54.

probably to his father's strong personality and the system of ideas within which he reasoned. Mrs Grote had remarked James Mill's great power to convert the younger generation to his views. But this Benthamite training was anything but a training in love of 'pleasure' as we should understand the word. Temperance, in the sense of 'moderation', 'was with my father the central point of educational precept' wrote John.

When the parent is also the schoolmaster there are bound to be difficulties, for the parent must, in such circumstances, strive to provide both the sympathy and love of a father, and the discipline, rigour, and less personal routine of the schoolmaster. To his son, James Mill was more the schoolmaster than the parent: 'The element which was chiefly deficient in his moral relation to his children was that of tenderness ... This was no longer the case later in life and with his younger children. They loved him tenderly: and if I cannot say so much of myself, I was always loyally devoted to him. As regards my own education, I hesitate to pronounce whether I was more the gainer or the loser by his severity ... I do not ... believe that fear, as an element in education can be dispensed with; but ... when it predominates so much as to preclude love and confidence on the part of the child to those who should be the unreservedly trusted advisers of after years, and perhaps to seal up the fountains of frank and spontaneous communicativeness in the child's nature, it is an evil for which a large abatement must be made from the benefits, moral and intellectual which may flow from any other part of the education.'[49]

This passage is quoted in isolation, and John Mill's verdict on his own education taken as a whole is a favourable one. But bearing in mind the measured terms in which all his comments are framed, and remembering, too, that the general tendency is for adults to respect and be grateful for a disciplined childhood, and to regard it in recollection as much less onerous than it appeared at the time, I think this comment should be regarded as strong condemnation. This view is supported by a section of the original manuscript of the *Autobiography* which John Stuart Mill subsequently cut out, and refused to have published. Here he in part blames his mother for not softening his father. He

[49] Ibid., pp. 44–5.

writes: 'But in respect to what I am here concerned with—the moral agencies which acted on myself—It must be mentioned as a most shameful one that my father's older children neither loved him, nor with any warmth of affection, anybody else . . . I thus grew up in the absence of love and in the presence of fear; and many and indelible are the effects of this bringing-up in the stunting of my moral growth. I grew up with an instinct of closeness. I had no-one to whom I desired to express everything which I felt—the only person I was in communication with to whom I looked up, I had too much fear of to make the communication to him of any act or feeling ever a matter of frank impulse or spontaneous inclination. Another evil I shared with many of the sons of energetic fathers. To have been through childhood under the constant rule of a strong will certainly is not favourable to strength of will. I was so much accustomed to be told what to do either in the form of direct command or of rebuke for not doing it that I acquired a habit of leaving my responsibility as a moral agent to rest on my father and my conscience never speaking to me except by his voice.'[50]

We must assess this evidence with care. The fact that it is secret and that the author prohibited its publication does not give it special authority, and make it a passage which must be literally accepted without critical judgment. On the contrary, the fact that John Stuart Mill declined to publish it means more probably that he felt that it was unfair, or incorrect as a record of his childhood experiences. But what it does mean, at the minimum, is that those passages in the published text, which hint at or state much the same thing, ought to be given due weight. In a letter in 1836, a sentence by James Mill to his son James Bentham, is perhaps a commentary on John Stuart Mill's comment: 'John is still in rather a pining way; though, as he does not choose to tell the cause of his pining, he leaves other people to their conjectures.'[51] This seems to speak for itself, though it was written when James Mill was suffering from the illness from which he was to die, and John might well have thought it unfair to worry a sick man.

[50] A. W. Levi, 'Mental Crisis of John Stuart Mill', *Psycho-analytical Review*, vol. 32, 1945. The manuscript is in Baltimore, and is quoted in this article.

[51] Bain, op. cit., p. 408, Mill to J. B. Mill, 9 March 1836.

But Mill's daughters had less appreciation of their education, and endorsed John's verdict on their father's irascibility. Harriet wrote: 'His great want was temper, though I quite believe circumstances had made it what it was in our childhood, both because of the warm affection of his early friends, and because in the later years of his life he became much softened and treated the younger children very differently ... After he was at India House, we could only see him in an evening, when we were always in disgrace over the hated Latin. We were never shewn how to learn, but had difficult books given us in which we were ordered to translate! He [John] ... wrote and pinned on the walls the way in which the hours of the day were to be passed by the four of us ... Any regular teaching we had was from him, and he carried some of us very far in mathematics and algebra. Indeed I have been told that he said I could have taken the Senior Wrangler's degree at Cambridge, I believe that mathematical training has been very useful to me.'[52]

There is abundant evidence that James Mill himself was exceedingly pleased and proud of John Stuart Mill's progress. He apologized to Place in 1814: 'This looks like bragging, but as I tell you the untoward part of my circumstances it is but right you should hear that which gives me pleasure also—there are few to whom I talk of either.'[53] He had been extolling John's progress. In 1818 he was delighted when some Oxford and Cambridge dons—'very accomplished scholars' met John and expressed 'extravagant admiration' for him. He was at that time at Bagshot, near a military college, where some lectures in chemistry were being given, and 'the great authorities of the place united in an invitation to John to attend them, and the opportunity of some importance, as now the time was come when I wished him to see a course of chemical experiments'. John acquired the invitation as a result of some of the professors casually meeting him and being most impressed by his intellectual powers, and 'he began to be taken too much notice of; the governor begged that he might be allowed to go to his house as much as possible, and make friendship with his boys,

[52] Harriet Mill to Rev. J. Crompton, 26 October 1873, in King's College Cambridge MSS. collection. Quoted in M. St J. Packe, *John Stuart Mill*, p. 47.
[53] B.M. Add. MSS. 35144, Mill to Place, December 1814.

and so the thing has gone on. I was anxious he should hear the lectures, and I was unwilling to appear to slight the compliments which had been paid him, by taking him away: and I was still more unwilling to leave him to the spoiling of the notice he is receiving. I have arranged matters accordingly thus. This week and next will finish the said lectures, all but a few on geology which he can learn from books'[54] and John could hear those and then depart. Ricardo's reply is significant: 'At any rate it will be of great advantage to him [John] if it introduces him into such society as you approve, for from the very retired and private manner in which he has been educated he stands in need of that collision which is obtained only in society and by which a knowledge of the world and its manners is best acquired.'[55] Both letters are significant as to the kind of education John received from his father, and shew both its undoubted excellence as an education of the mind, and its shortcomings as an education of the character. But the education of his son was the cause of all causes nearest to James Mill's heart. When seriously ill, many years before, he had written to Bentham, his chosen leader in public causes, 'if I were to die any time before the poor boy is a man, one of the things that would pinch me most sorely, would be the being obliged to leave his mind unmade to the degree of excellence I hope to make it'.[56] And, as we have seen, almost his last thought when his time to die came in 1836 was a similar anxiety with regard to his younger children.

John Stuart Mill's education continued with a fourteen-month visit to France in 1820, lasting until midsummer of the following year. This came about by the generosity of Sir Samuel Bentham, brother of Jeremy, who invited John first for six months and then for a further eight to his home in the South of France. Although the occasion was fortuitous, there is plenty of evidence that James Mill strongly favoured a period of living abroad as part of an education, In 1815 when he thought of moving to France to live, he spoke of the educational advantages:

[54] *Ricardo's Letters*, op. cit., vi, no. 278, Mill to Ricardo, 26 October 1818.
[55] Ibid., no. 280, Ricardo to Mill, 11 November 1818.
[56] Bowring, *Memoirs and Correspondence of Bentham*, x, p. 472, Mill to Bentham, 28 July 1812.

'My children will acquire a familiarity with the language and with the manners and character of a new people. When they have enough of this we shall remove into Germany till the same effects are accomplished.' After that, Italy, and 'we shall then return accomplished people'.[57] This project came to nothing but John Stuart Mill, when he went to France, paid glowing tribute to the educational value of his year abroad, and especially to the 'benefit of having breathed for a whole year, the free and genial'[58] atmosphere of France.

James Mill characteristically expected a year abroad to be spent in systematic study of the foreign country. We have no record of any instructions to John Mill, but there exists a long letter to Francis Place, containing detailed advice to a young protégé of his, Thomas Hodgskin, entitled *Instructions to Thomas Hodgskin on his Travels*.[59] This document really throws more light on Mill's political theory than on his educational philosophy; Hodgskin was instructed to study the political, social, and economic structure of Germany, where the nominal power lay, where the real power and influence lay and so on. Particular attention should be paid to education, 'of the higher orders and 2ndly and more important, that of the lower', also to the education of the women; 1st of the higher ranks and 2ndly of the lower'. Mill advises Hodgskin to 'board himself in the houses of' peasants, schoolmaster, a priest, a poor student, and so on, by turn, and in this manner 'get the greater of the knowledge, independently of introductions to men of consequence'. Finally he is recommended to keep a daily journal—two copies—'one to be sent to Mill and Bentham that they may suggest supplementary lines of enquiry'. Mill concludes: 'This is prescribing hard labour. But we here are not afraid of hard labour.' Except that John Mill's residence abroad was fixed in the family of Sir Samuel Bentham, he no doubt received similar instructions verbally.[60] He seems to have had a pleasant time, and rather easier than these instructions suggest, and James

[57] B.M. Add. MSS. 35152, f. 160, Mill to Place, 6 September 1815.
[58] *Autobiography*, op. cit., pp. 48–9ff.
[59] B.M. Add. MSS. 35153. See Appendix for full document. Although in Mill's hand, it may have been written by Bentham.
[60] He certainly kept a journal. Cf. *John Mill's Boyhood Visit to France*, ed. A. J. Mill, Toronto, 1960.

4

was well pleased with him on his return: 'John is returned much grown; looking almost a man; in other respects not much different from when he went. He has got the French language—but almost forgot his own—and is nearly as shy and awkward as before. His love of study, however, remains, and he shews tractability and good sense. I have no doubt he will make what the English call an amiable and a useful one.'[61] At any rate, apart from the course in Economics we have already noticed, and which was undertaken partly to assist James Mill to write his book, John's education was now complete. In 1823 he was appointed to India House; shortly before, in the same year, James Mill had refused a pressing invitation from Professor Townshend of Cambridge University to send John there, to 'form acquaintance with his contemporaries'.[62] This was the last of several attempts by different people to persuade James Mill to let John mix with others of his own age.

Mill, in later life, seems to have lost some of his antipathy to educational institutions, or perhaps it would be more accurate to say that his antipathy was not to institutions as such, but to Oxford and Cambridge. At all events, James Bentham Mill received his early education from Mill, by the monitorial system, and then went first to University College, and later to the East India Company's training establishment at Hailey-bury. His whole education is admirably summarized in a testimonial with which his father supported his application in 1835 for a post in the East India Company's overseas service: 'I certify that my son, James Bentham Mill, received the early part of his education, corresponding to what is usually received at school, in my house, and under my eye, myself being his principal teacher, and that it comprehended the usual subjects, Latin, Greek, Mathematics, Geography, and History—that he afterwards entered the University of London, in which he studied during the whole of four years, attending the Latin, Greek, and Mathematical classes, and for two years, the class of Natural Philosophy, the class of Chemistry, the class of Logic and the class of Jurisprudence; and that since he left the University the whole of his time, an interval of about two years,

---

[61] *Ricardo's Letters*, op. cit., ix, no. 438, Mill to Ricardo, 5 July 1821.
[62] Bain, op. cit., p. 205.

has been employed in prosecuting his studies at home, under my superintendence, improving himself in his knowledge of Latin, Greek, and Mathematics, and reading such books as I recommended him, giving me regularly an account of what he read, sometimes orally, sometimes in writing. I add the expression of my belief that he will be found a well-educated youth. And I cannot be mistaken in affirming that all his habits at present are good; that he is laborious and steady, of a calm and considerate disposition, and free from vice, as far as I know, of every kind.'[63]

There are some points of interest in this. There is relatively little philosophy, though, since we don't know what the advanced study of Greek consisted of, we cannot tell quite how much. There are History and Geography as formal subjects, and there is Science and Mathematics, the latter carried to an advanced stage, possibly for vocational reasons. It was a good balanced general education shewing ideas of curriculum considerably in advance of the time. It would appear that Classics was given the greatest weight, and, on a testimonial, John Stuart Mill's curriculum would not have looked so very different. There is no reason to suppose that James Mill had changed his view that Classics were mainly useful as an entry into Greek philosophy.

A letter from James Mill to James Bentham Mill while the latter was at Haileybury is characteristic of the father, and illustrates some of the precepts he observed in his children's education. He writes: 'I am much pleased to see you had the highest mark in everything last month. You must strive hard to have the same in the remainder . . . He who works more than all the others will in the end excel all others. Difficulties are made to be overcome. Life consists in a succession of them. And he gets best through them, who has best made up his mind to contend with them. I do not like to give you any instruction about your essay, both because it would not be fair towards those with whom you have to contend, and because I am desirous to see what you yourself make of it.'[64] Mill was truly a

---

[63] Bain, op. cit., p. 376. J. B. Mill was then 21: he had been at University College from 15 to 19 years old.

[64] Ibid., pp. 397–8. From Mickleham, 18 October 1835.

schoolmaster first and a parent second. But, after reading this letter, no-one could seriously have any doubts that his educational methods were the reverse of cramming, and that the emphasis throughout was on the need for his sons to think for themselves.

This completes an account of James Mill's practical experience in education. In both his activity for public education, and as a personal teacher, it was an unusually wide one, and there can be very little doubt, that in a wide meaning of the term, he would have regarded himself first and foremost as an educationist—as he wrote to Ricardo –the 'diffusion of Knowledge' is the most important thing now. But he also considered himself, and was considered by his friends to be an expert of high standing on every aspect of the theory and practice of education, and we have now to turn to the theory which he evolved in 1818, after his work with the Lancasterian and Chrestomathic schools, and after much of John Stuart Mill's education was complete.

APPENDIX

Instructions to Thomas Hodgskin on his Travels

by James Mill

(Ford Abbey, Chard.)

1. All the political power is possessed by, and shared among, the Elector (or King) the nobles and clergy. — His first inquiry is, in what portions it is shared amongst them: what powers the nobles have over the king; what the clergy have over both; and that either in the legislature, judicative or executive branches. In particular, (which is the main exercise of the legislative power) how the power of taxation in the hands of the king, is restrained by the power of the nobles or the clergy.

2. The indirect power of the king, viz, by influence. What is the extent of the offices and sinecures, civil or military, of which he has the gift. How the church patronage is lodged and who has the bestowing of ecclesiastical good things. All this in detail.

3. The state of taxation—from what sources—how great the amount—how collected—Also the different heads of disbursement and the amount under each.

4. The administration of justice. What are the courts of justice? How are they constituted: i.e. who are the judges and by whom appointed? What is the medium cost of a law suit? What is the medium length? Are law-suits numerous? Are the practicing lawyers numerous? Or rich? Is the profession of barrister and attorney, separate, or united? In what books are the laws contained?
   How do they classify crimes? Are crimes numerous? What

are the principal punishments they employ and for what offences? Is torture still practised? If not, when did it begin to be disused? If not used whether abolished by law or still revivable.

5. How is landed property distributed? Is it all in the hands of great owners? Or have they a proportion of small proprietors? If so, what is that proportion?

The next inquiry under that head is of the highest importance —What is the nature of the possession given to the cultivator who holds under these proprietors? Is it wholly dependent on the will of the proprietor; or have cultivators leases? If they have leases, what are the ordinary conditions of those leases? And are the cultivators in a condition to enforce the observance of them?

What is the condition of the cultivators? Affluent, or indigent? What sort of food, houses, furniture and clothing have they? What is the state of the agricultural art?

6. Religion. What is the clerical establishment, viz. the orders of the priests: and the revenues of the church? How is religion taught to the people? That is, what is the character and behaviour of the parish priests? And how do the people seem to be governed by their doctrines? Little or much? What toleration is there, by law or in practice? And what diversity of religious profession?

7. Education—1st that of the higher orders—2ndly and more especially, that of the lower. Are the body of the people taught to read and write? What ideas and intelligence do they display? Are they full of credulity and superstition?

As the education of the higher orders, a good thing would be, to give a description of the course of study at the University of Göttingen—to suppose a young man just entered and then to tell us everything that he does, what the first year, what the second, and so on, till he leaves the university, with what is reckoned a complete education. Also, he should ascertain what proportion of the upper ranks get this education; and what substitute is used for those who do not get it.

Ascertain as much as possible of the education of the women; 1st of the higher ranks 2ndly of the lower.

8. What is the state of wages, and the condition of the labouring classes, in respect of food, clothing, lodging, and morals?

Such are the principal heads of inquiry. Round each of the questions I have put down, a number of related ones will easily be seen to range themselves, so as to make out the full, *minute* picture.

As advice for the mode of collecting: were I in his situation, I would do this. In order to get, for example, a knowledge of the state of the cultivators of the ground, I would go and board myself in the house of a farmer, live in the family, see everything, and ask explanations of everything, and remain there till I had the information I was in quest of.

Next I would try to board myself in the house of a schoolmaster, till I had learned all that I could from him.

Next I would board myself in the house of some parish priest, who was poor enough to board me for such a sum as I could afford. And then I would learn all that was to be learned about the clergy and religion.

As to the University, if not able to board myself with a professor, I would go to some of the boarding or lodging houses of the poorer students, and by conversation with them, acquire the knowledge of which I was in quest.

In this manner I should get the greater part of the knowledge I wanted independently of introductions to men of consequence. And I would take that which could only be got at by such introduction last.

Another recommendation to Mr. Hodgskin should be, to write down every day what occurs every day, and to trust nothing to memory. What is written fresh at the moment, has a zest, which is often lost in one day. His first writing should be remarkably full, and notice every circumstance down to the most minute. Every interesting conversation, even with a peasant, should be written in full and in dialogue, just as it took place.

With respect to one important head of enquiry, the relation

between this country and Hanover; what Hanover gets by this country, and what our royal personages get by Hanover, the newspaper articles which Mr. Bentham has had copied will suggest useful topics of inquiry.

He should send over his journals here as fast as he writes them, reserving to himself a copy, in case of miscarriage. This will both ensure the preservation of them; and will enable us, upon reading to suggest fresh inquiries upon every subject on which additional information may be required.

This is prescribing hard labour. But we here are not afraid of hard labour.

(B.M. Add. MSS. 35153)

IV

The Aims of Education

From the account we have given in the preceding chapters of James Mill's life and career, it is clear that he was neither the philosopher meditating alone upon the mountain-top, nor the practical reformer uninterested in speculation. He was both philosopher and reformer—in its most general sense, 'political' reformer—and none more than he deserved the title 'philosophical radical'. In considering his statement of the aims of education, therefore, we must remember, first, his background of a training in philosophy, especially Greek philosophy, and of an early training of high and rigid standards of personal conduct. Second, and just as important, we must never forget the contemporary scene from which his eye was never far removed: if we are to understand his educational thought it must be considered in relation to his political theory, and to what he said on the practical problems of his day. If this approach is adopted, the first thing to notice is that he defined 'education' very widely, so as to include family influence as well as schooling, and later, to cover the influence of society and the state which he considered fundamental. It is within this context that we should consider our first problem: his statement of the aims of education. This is contained in a single sentence: 'The end of education is to render the individual, as much as possible, an instrument of happiness, first to himself, and next to other beings.'[1] In this statement there are really two aims and it will be convenient to follow Mill's order, and to discuss, first, the ideal of personal happiness, and second, the ideal of the happiness of others.

---

[1] 'Essay on Education' in *James Mill on Education*, ed. W. H. Burston, C.U.P., 1969, p. 41.

I

The fullest statement of Mill's conception of personal happiness appears in the *Essay on Education*. Here we are told that personal happiness does not mean pursuing every pleasure or gratifying every fleeting desire that presents itself. On the contrary, it means resisting some desires, abnegating some pleasures, in order to pursue others which will yield us a greater satisfaction, and 'the greatest possible quantity of happiness'. To do this, we must cultivate the virtue of Temperance, which Mill defines as the power of resisting appetite and passion, and the virtue of Fortitude—the capacity to endure pain. The relevant passage is as follows: 'If he [man] has any appetite in his nature which leads him to pursue certain things with which the most effective pursuit of happiness is inconsistent . . . evil is incurred. A perfect command, then, over a man's appetites and desires . . . which insures him against the illusions of the passions, and enables him to pursue constantly what he deliberately approves, is indispensably requisite to enable him to produce the greatest possible quantity of happiness. This is what the ancient philosophers called Temperance . . . and consisted in the power of resisting the immediate propensity, if yielding to it would lead to an overbalance of evil, or prevent the enjoyment of a superior good, in whatever the good or evil of the present life consists.'[2] Now, it is arguable that in stipulating this, Mill is demanding a special *quality* of pleasure—what we 'deliberately approve', and is thus introducing a new principle other than happiness as such, into his ideal. But he would not have admitted this. He means that only in this way shall we gain the greatest possible *quantity* of pleasure, because, he would argue that it is a matter of common experience that gratifying fleeting desires brings no lasting pleasure, and inhibits the pursuit of lasting pleasure. Whether we think his argument sound or not, there is no doubt that he did stipulate the pursuit of lasting pleasures if happiness was to be gained, and he stresses this point whenever he writes on education. In a letter to his friend Francis Place regarding

[2] Ibid., p. 63.

the education of Place's daughter Annie, he writes: 'Think of her happiness solely, and what will increase or diminish it, without one jot of passion allowed to step into the scale.'[3] This is a curious adjuration to a fond and proud parent: it can only be explained if it is paraphrased as: 'Think always of what is good for her, and steel yourself against granting all her desires without regard to her ultimate happiness.'

Mill was not, I think, unaware of the difficulty he was creating for himself by stipulating that men should cultivate Temperance in order to pursue only what they 'deliberately approved'. In his Commonplace Book, there is a draft of a dialogue on Drama which contains some remarks relevant to this point. In this dialogue, Mill attacks the drama, and argues that the fact that it gives people pleasure affords us no ground for bestowing on it our approbation. He goes on to argue the general principle: 'Mr. X. distributes his approbation in proportion as people give him pleasure. Are you prepared to defend this proposition, or will you confess that you are reduced to an untenable proposition? . . . Will you not allow that there are certain sorts of people to whom this does not apply? Bandits, —the commodities which they keep yield pleasure. Ought we to bestow our esteem upon these bandits and their commodities? To the receivers of stolen goods nobody yields more pleasure than thieves and robbers. Ought these to be the objects of our esteem? . . . It is not the givers of any kind of pleasure that should have our esteem, but the givers of *certain kinds of pleasure*. [My italics] . . . There is then a gradation of pleasures and according as the pleasure is more noble is the artificer more entitled to our esteem.' Mill goes on to discuss the theatre in particular and to say that the actor 'is the slave of the most irregular appetites and passions of his species'. Most of this dialogue is negative—it criticises strongly the idea that mere pleasure, even if given to others, can be a good thing, and many pleasures are referred to by Mill as 'mere appetite'. But Mill never comes to any positive conclusion save that one big objection to theatrical pleasure is that it involves the prostitution of the actor—'the man whose profession it is to assume false appearances . . . cannot easily be a man of direct, true,

[3] B.M. Add. MSS. 35152.

undisguised, simple and sincere mind ... Does this habit of violating the truth not corrupt all principles of honour in a man's breast?' In the course of his argument, however, he does make the highly significant comment that pleasures must therefore differ in quality, and that this means that we are 'taking a different ground for our approbation'.

This dialogue was never published, as far as I know, and therefore it may represent views which Mill rapidly discarded. It clearly shews the influence both of Plato and of the contemporary climate of opinion among middle-class people of the early nineteenth century. Its date must be a matter of conjecture, for neither the Commonplace Book nor any of its entries are dated. We do not know whether Mill continued to make entries throughout his life, or only during his early journalistic career in London. Judging by most of the entries, the latter seems the more probable conclusion. The dialogue on drama is an early entry, and its argument suggests that it was written at an early stage in Mill's thought. It could hardly have been written after 1816— the approximate time of commencing the Encyclopedia articles, for it is entirely inconsistent with, for instance, both the article on Government and that on Education, and there is no other evidence, either printed or in Mill's letters, to suggest that he changed his views so decisively. It is just conceivable that it could have been written after he met Bentham—about 1808— and after he had espoused Utilitarianism as a working creed for political reform. For a man of Mill's education and philosophical ability this seems most unlikely. The weight of the evidence therefore favours the view that it was written soon after he came to London in 1802, and before 1808.

It is an important piece of evidence. It shews that Mill started his reflections on moral philosophy by considering his own moral experience and by considering it in terms of non-naturalist moral philosophy. It is clear that it is most misleading to think of James Mill as the apostle of pleasure as opposed to duty, although, in the end, his philosophy seems to reduce morals to an illusion. But he did not think he was doing this: the last thing he wished to do was to deny the fact of moral experience—he thought he was explaining it without altering its nature, or reducing its strength as a motive to action. Late in his life, when he was accused of reducing morals to personal advantage, he angrily protested: 'This is to affirm that he who analyses any of the complicated phenomena of human nature, and points out the circumstances of their formation puts an end to them ... Gratitude remains gratitude, resentment remains resentment, generosity, generosity, in the mind of him who feels them, after analysis, the same as before.'[4] It is essential to a correct understanding of Mill that we should realize that he thought, rightly or wrongly, that he was founding, not liquidating, moral philosophy. And the essence of what he says in the essay on Education, regarding Temperance, is now clearer. We are told that we should resist some pleasures and cultivate others. This is a familiar part of moral experience—the fact of moral conflict between duty and desire. At first, Mill thought that the conflict was correctly described as between duty and desire. But later, in the essay on Education, he is saying that, although cultivating some pleasures and resisting others seems like 'taking another ground for our approbation', on careful analysis it can be shewn that this is not so, for 'what we deliberately approve' will in fact bring us the greatest possible *quantity* of pleasure. And this carries with it the important implication that it is not pleasure only which should be our aim, but the greatest possible quantity of pleasure.

Before we arrive at a final conclusion on this point, there is one further question to ask, and that is: 'What did Mill mean by "pleasure"?' It seems clear that he did not mean what we should understand today by that term. In one place he asserts that 'desire' can be defined as the 'idea of a pleasure'—he writes: 'The terms, therefore, "idea of pleasure" and "desire" are but two names; the thing named, the state of consciousness, is one and the same.'[5] From this, 'pleasure' is equated with 'object of desire' and it is at least as likely that Mill was analysing the nature of desire when he talks of 'pleasure' as that he was asserting that desire had no other object than 'pleasure'. He is using words in a different sense from our modern usage of them. The problem is this: granted that Mill regards the two terms 'object of desire' and 'pleasure' as two names for the

---

[4] James Mill, *Fragment on Mackintosh*, 1835, p. 51.
[5] James Mill, *Analysis of the Human Mind*, 2nd edn, 1878, ii, p. 192.

same thing, what is he really describing, when he talks of 'pleasure'? Is he reflecting on human experience of 'desire', or upon human experience of 'pleasure' in our sense of the term? Is he reducing all desire to pleasure, or is he expanding the term pleasure to include all forms of desire and its satisfaction?

It seems to me probable that Mill is really analysing the nature of desire and its satisfaction when he talks of 'pleasure'. Elsewhere he writes: 'Pleasure is an end, and *generically speaking*, the only end.'[6] (My italics.) And later: 'A man acts for the sake of something agreeable to him, either proximately or remotely ... So that pleasure, in a general way or speaking generically: that is in a way to include all the species of pleasure ... is the end of action.'[7] The only part of human experience that really fits this description is not 'pleasure' in our sense of the term, but 'satisfactions' of desires. When he insists that the 'sensation of an object or a situation, and the pleasure it brings'[8] are the same thing—that the two are inseparable he is surely referring to the object of desire, for it is a matter of common experience that we can distinguish between the fact of attaining our objective, and the accompanying pleasure. Thus when he speaks of 'what we deliberately approve' he is thinking of desire —not momentary or fleeting wants, but rational desire. If this is true, then one obvious criticism of Mill cannot be sustained: we cannot argue that we often desire things which bring us no pleasure, for he says that 'pleasure' is the generic term for all the objects of desire.

If this is applied to Mill's aim of personal happiness, then it comes to this: some desires—'what we deliberately approve'— should dominate our lives, and education should be designed to fit us so that those desires are in fact our strongest desires, and so that we are best able to satisfy them. This implies an education of which important elements must be authoritarian so that the child is taught to forgo some desires and to concentrate on others. In the immediate political situation, too, it would mean that the State would have to be authoritarian, for the majority of the people had not had the education which Mill prescribed,

[6] *Fragment on Mackintosh*, op. cit., p. 360.
[7] Ibid., p. 389.
[8] *Analysis of the Human Mind*, op. cit., ii, pp. 184–5.

and so would desire the wrong things. The political problem is, however, a complicated one, and is obviously more intimately connected with Mill's second aim—the happiness of others. At this stage, we can only make the general point that, granted that men do not naturally desire the greatest pleasures, and that, ideally they should desire the greatest pleasures, the conclusion is ineluctable that sanctions are needed, from parents in the case of children, and from the state in the case of contemporary society, in order to restrain people from following the wrong desires.

If Mill's first ideal is then not merely that man should seek pleasure, but the greatest quantity of pleasure, then it lends powerful support to the interpretation I have suggested here, that by 'pleasure' Mill meant 'satisfactions of desires'. For it is hard to maintain that it is my duty to seek my own pleasure: still less can it be held that I am failing in my duty if I seek or gain anything less than my maximum pleasure. If we look at it from the point of view of desire, the situation is different. Mill is then saying that mere satisfaction of desire is not enough: it is our duty to cultivate certain desires, and they are of such a nature that they will bring us a greater satisfaction than any others. It seems to me clear that what Mill is thinking of is the cultivation or realization or fulfilment of the highest part of our natures—his doctrine of personal happiness is a doctrine of self-realization. At the end of the essay on Government, he uses language that seems to make it clear that he was thinking on these lines: 'The Middle rank', he says, 'is the chief source of all that has exalted and refined human nature'—it is 'that most intelligent and virtuous rank.'[9] Leaving aside for the moment the stress on the importance of the middle classes, the really significant point in these words is the idea of an 'exalted and refined' man.

This is but the first part of Mill's ideal, but already we can detect two important influences on his thought. The first of these is the climate of opinion of his time—his ideal is a 'respectable' middle class gentleman of early nineteenth-century England: one who likes the right things and sternly eschews the wrong ones. It is an attempt to adapt Hedonism to an age which

[9] James Mill, *An Essay on Government*, ed. Ernest Barker, C.U.P., 1939, p. 72.

was the reverse of pleasure-loving. But, with Mill, there is a second influence—that of the Greek philosophers to whom there are many references in the Commonplace Book. Mill had a great and lasting admiration for Greek philosophy[10]—it was, for instance, the main constituent in the education he prescribed for his son, John Stuart Mill. We see the influence of the Greeks, especially of Aristotle, in the whole idea of self-realization. Though Mill differs on fundamental points from Aristotle, there are none the less striking similarities. Like Aristotle Mill seeks a final end or purpose; like Aristotle he seeks it in terms of rational desire; finally, like Aristotle, he finds at least part of his ideal in a state or condition of ourselves.

II

The second part of Mill's statement of the aims of education brings us at once to the familiar Utilitarian ideal—the greatest happiness of the greatest number of people. In the *Essay on Education*, Mill specifies the qualities needed to make man 'the best possible artificer of happiness to others'. He writes: 'A man can affect the happiness of others, either by abstaining from doing them harm, or by doing them positive good. To abstain from doing them harm, receives the name of Justice; to do positive good receives that of Generosity. Justice and Generosity, then, are the two qualities by which a man is fitted to promote the happiness of his fellow-creatures. And it thus appears that the four cardinal virtues of the ancients do pretty completely include all the qualities to the possession of which it is desirable that the human mind should be trained.'[11]

Mill elaborates this second aim in the *Fragment of Mackintosh*: 'To make an act moral, it is farther necessary that he [the agent] have a conviction of its general utility (i.e. of its pleasureable effects on others).'[12] This process of giving pleasure to others involves what Mill calls the 'moral calculation'—'the question

[10] Cf. for examples, John Stuart Mill, *An Autobiography*, ed. Laski, O.U.P., World's Classics, pp. 39–40.
[11] Op. cit., pp. 64–5. The other two qualities are those of Temperance, which includes Fortitude, and Intelligence.
[12] Op. cit., p. 321.

ought, or ought not an action to be performed is evidently a question of comparison'.[13] About this, there are a number of points to notice. What Mill wants is that the agent should always balance his own pleasure against any pleasure or pain resulting to others from his action. He should then act always so as to produce the greatest total pleasure irrespective of by whom it is enjoyed. In this calculation, everyone must count for one, and none for more than one, and this includes the doer of the action. Further, a vital part of this calculation is a correct anticipation of the consequences on one's actions, and especially an ability to imagine the painful or pleasurable effects on others. Thus stated it is clear that this second aim involves not only the ideal of general happiness but also the principle of equality— the principle that every human being is equally entitled to our consideration—happiness must not merely be maximized, it must be justly distributed.

Now, the first question we have to consider is whether Mill is still using 'happiness' in the same sense as he did when he was speaking of education for personal happiness. The evidence on the whole suggests that he was, and that, when he speaks of the happiness of others, he means that we should give them 'what we deliberately approve'. Thus he says: 'Acts are virtuous if *good* to others is intended' (my italics), and again: 'If along with the idea of pleasure to the agents, the dispositions include the idea of *good* to some other person or persons we call them, and the actions they produce good' (my italics).[14] And Mill's advice to Place upon the education of his daughter counselled him to think of her happiness, not of her immediate desires. All these examples refer to the happiness we should bring to others, and they suggest that Mill regarded his first aim—education for personal happiness—not only as an end but also as a means. It was a necessary preliminary to his second and greatest ideal, for unless we had first experienced true happiness we should not know what to bring to others.

There is really no doubt about James Mill's personal view on the matter, which is well-stated by his son in his *Autobiography*: 'His standard of morals was Epicurean, in-as-much

---

[13] Ibid., p. 162.
[14] Ibid., pp. 394 ff.

as it was utilitarian, taking as the exclusive test of right and wrong, the tendency of actions to produce pleasure or pain. But he had . . . scarcely any belief in pleasure . . . The greater number of miscarriages in life he considered to be attributable to the overvaluing of pleasures. Accordingly, temperance, in the large sense intended by the Greek philosophers—stopping short at the point of moderation in all indulgences—was with him, as with them, almost the central point of educational precept.'[15] And this only confirms what we know from other sources of James Mill's character, of his personal life and of the times in which he lived. His greatest personal efforts at distributing happiness were in the field of education, and here he was giving the poor not merely pleasure, but what he 'deliberately approved'. It would be hard to imagine him approving a gift to enable theatrical performances to be seen at cheaper prices, or supporting an extension and cheapening of the facilities for the consumption of alcohol.

It is true that Mill is not always consistent in this, and that, when he is writing of the happiness of others he frequently identifies the word with 'pleasure', any kind of pleasure, and not 'what we deliberately approve'. This is especially true of his political articles. And, in the *Fragment on Mackintosh*, he says in one place: 'When the consequences of the act are *pleasureable* to other persons . . . the intention . . . is good' (my italics). The essential point about this is that Mill is clearly not prescribing the greatest possible quantity of pleasure, as he did when he was talking of personal happiness. He is mainly concerned that some pleasure should be given to others, and that it should be equally distributed.

It is most important to remember, however, that his inconsistency is between two conceptions of pleasure both of which are hedonistic. Mill was a hedonist and an ethical naturalist. The only evidence which casts any doubt on this statement is the fact that, in two places, he declares that he does not know 'wherein Happiness consists', and it might be argued that he would not have said this if he had identified happiness with pleasure. The first of these occurs in the short section III of the *Essay on Education* (pp. 24–5), and the second, at the end of his

---

[15] Op. cit., p. 40.

life, in the *Fragment on Mackintosh*, where he wrote: 'When we found that good to mankind gives their moral quality to actions, one thing remains, namely, where in that good consists . . . This is an important part of the investigation, but not necessary to our present enquiry.' (p. 394, Appendix A.) But there is a possible interpretation of these words which is consistent with ethical naturalism. Mill may have had in mind a kind of sociological analysis which would classify the objects and situations which in fact brought pleasure to people. If so, a concrete situation could be stated, analogous to the concept of economic welfare where as many people as possible enjoyed the maximum material welfare. Mill would not have confined himself to material things, for he would have wanted all to savour the pleasures of the middle classes. But he might well have thought that these pleasures, like those arising from the satisfaction of material needs, could be classified and measured, so that eventually one could reach a precise and objective situation which could be described as the greatest happiness of the greatest number of people.

Whether this conjecture is sound or not, it is clear that on Mill's view of happiness the principle of equality must be regarded as additional and extraneous: it cannot be inferred from the ideal of general happiness. For it is possible to imagine a situation of the greatest happiness in a community where happiness is not equally distributed. We can think of occasions where insistence on equal distribution of welfare has brought little advantage to the many, at the cost of great disadvantage to the few. And there is the situation, not entirely fictional, of the lifeboat crew who have enough food to keep half only of their number alive.

Mill seems to have been quite unaware of this discrepancy, and the most probable explanation of this serious flaw in his thinking lies in the social and economic conditions of England in his day. For at that time, it was hard to imagine any greater step forward towards greater happiness than the more equal distribution of it: no-one doubted that the Golden Age had begun, that indefinite progress was not only possible but inevitable, and that an unlimited expansion of material welfare was at hand. But there was a striking maldistribution of material welfare, and, in fact, the ideal of the greatest happiness could best be realized by more equitable distribution. The problem was not one of greater production, but of just distribution.

This is an explanation of Mill's view: it is not a justification of it. The flaw in his argument arises, however, not from postulating happiness as an ideal, but from his particular interpretation of happiness in hedonistic terms. If happiness is thought of as a state or attitude of mind of ourselves towards other people, then it can quite consistently be argued that an essential feature of this ideal state of mind would be that we should treat all other human beings equally—as individual personalities. The final ideal—the ultimate good—would then be not the happiness of the recipients of our benevolence, but the happiness in ourselves produced by the fact that we desired the happiness of others. This would be a self-realization theory, and it would follow Greek thought, especially that of Aristotle, very closely.

Now, although we know that Mill was influenced by the Greeks, and, indeed thought he was developing their philosophy, there has so far been no evidence that he thought on these lines when dealing with the happiness of others. We shall gain more light on this question if we examine Mill's statements on the subject of the motives to right action. Are the motives from which we do good actions important? And if so, what motives ought we to cultivate?

Mill insists several times, and quite explicitly, in the *Fragment on Mackintosh*, that 'morality is an attribute of intention'. When we give pleasure to others, 'the case is simple, the intention has in it nothing but what is good'.[16] He expands this: 'Without an immoral intention there is no immoral act. An intention is immoral in two cases: first, when a man acts with a foreknowledge of the preponderance of evil consequences, secondly, when he acts without enquiring, that is without caring, whether there will be a preponderance of evil consequences or not . . . Morality is an attribute of intention, and an intention is only good when the act intended has in the sum of its *ascertainable* consequences a superiority of good over evil . . . To act without regard to consequences is the property of an irrational

16 Op. cit., p. 162.

nature. But to act without calculation is to act without regard to consequences.'[17]

But Mill distinguishes 'intention' from 'motive', for he writes: 'Can there be any greater degree of social love required than that the good of others should cause us pleasure: in other words that their good should be ours? . . . Acts are virtuous if good to others is intended, though it be not the motive to the act. They are virtuous in a still higher degree if good to others is also the motive.'[18] 'Motive' is elsewhere defined as the association of desire with an action which will satisfy the desire —'the idea of every pleasure associated with that of an action of ours as the cause, is a motive: that is, leads to the action. But every motive does not produce the action. The reason is the existence of other motives which prevent it.'[19] But 'intention' has no necessary connexion with desire, for it consists in having 'certain consequences of an act in view',[20] whether or not they are desired. What Mill is saying therefore is that actions are good, if, among the foreseeable consequences, there is pleasure to others, though this is not our motive, i.e. we derive no pleasure from this particular result. But actions are still better if we gain pleasure from this result, i.e. if our motive for doing the action is to bring pleasure to others.

So far, this is explicit enough: motives are important, some are better than others, we can do the same action from good or evil motives, and if we cultivate the right motives, actions producing identical results become morally better. In short, Mill is nearer the Greek philosophers than he is usually credited with being. For if morality is an 'attribute of intention' then surely the final *summum bonum* lies not in the external results of an action, but in the state or attitude of mind that willed the action. But, although this is a much more tenable theory of the ideal than hedonistic Utilitarianism, Mill clings to the latter in two fundamental respects. First, he rules out of account those results of actions which are neither pleasurable nor painful— such results have no moral significance for Mill. Second, and

[17] Ibid., p. 163.
[18] Ibid., p. 394.
[19] *Analysis of the Human Mind*, ii, p. 258.
[20] Ibid., p. 400.

even more important, he declares that the pleasure the agent derives from giving pleasure to others is only one of the relevant results of good actions—not even a *primus inter pares*, for it is a by-product. True, it is not part of the moral calculation, for it results from the act of making the calculation. But Mill insists: 'The value to mankind of having the feeling of benevolence is one thing; the value to them of the good things which spring from benevolence as effects, is another. The first value is not lessened by the magnitude of the second. The sum of the ingredients of Happiness is only so much the greater . . . What is the good of bringing the pleasure of having goodwill toward other men into comparison, either with the delight of being the object of their good will, or that of being the object of their good acts, the effect of their good will?'[21] It is the effects of actions that Mill emphasizes, and he is quite logical in including the effects of an action upon the agent, for to ignore this is to fail to consider all the relevant results of an action. Thus the final position is that, despite his assertion that morality is an 'attribute of intention', he in fact makes it an attribute of the consequences of actions.

If this is so, he has still not explained why it is more virtuous to enjoy the pleasure of others than to enjoy some other consequence of an action with the same results, and we must therefore look more closely at Mill's account of the motives to right action. He was aware that this was a major problem, for he wrote: 'There has never been any question about the state of mind in which a man seeks his own gratification: what is in doubt is the state of mind in which he seeks the gratification of others.'[22] In general, his explanation is in terms of an association of our own pleasure with other people's happiness: thus we may not only know the ideal, but feel impelled to seek it. He does not deny that feelings like benevolence and generosity exist, nor that they are genuine and effective springs of action. But his hedonism compels him to explain the origins of these feelings in terms of selfish pleasure, and association of this with other people's pleasure. But, if he does this, what becomes of his protest that 'gratitude remains gratitude, generosity, generosity,

---

[21] *Fragment on Mackintosh*, op. cit., p. 191.
[22] Ibid., p. 73.

after analysis, the same as before'? His theory requires him to
shew an effective motive to right action. Either the origins
persist, or the motive is unselfish, and if the motive is unselfish,
man cannot be explained in terms of hedonism. If Mill insists
on his hedonism, and he does do so, then his account of the
motives to good action is not in terms of a moral motive, but in
terms of hitching ordinary desires to a moral star.

Thus, Mill's statement that though to do good is virtuous, to
like doing good is still more virtuous, cannot be explained in
terms of liking to do good for its own sake, for hedonistic man
cannot like good for any other reason than his own pleasure,
and he cannot therefore pursue the ideal unless artificial ties are
formed between his own pleasure and the happiness of others.
But it is not Mill's account of the ideal which is the difficulty: it
is his psychological hedonism which makes it impossible for
man ever to want, for its own sake, the greatest happiness of the
greatest number of people.

Within the terms of his own philosophy, Mill cannot then
justify his assertion that to like giving pleasure increases our
virtue. But there is an explanation of his view, if we consider
the dual purpose he wanted Utilitarianism to serve—to be at
once both a statement of the ideal, and a practical criterion for
immediate reform in his own day. The latter was a transition
stage, and at this stage motives—the wrong motives—were
already formed by defective education and still more defective
society. As an extreme environmentalist, Mill held that society
and education could never be neutral inactive forces: if they
did not do good, they did harm. All one could hope for in the
transition stage was to use existing bad motives to produce good
results, by so arranging society that men gained the common
good by seeking their private interest—it is a concept analagous
to the economic theory of the natural harmony of interest
where, by seeking private profit, men produce the maximum
and thus bring about general economic welfare. In Mill's view,
Representative Government was a device of this kind: if all
were represented the selfish interests of none could be disregarded. Mill's democracy is not, at least in its first stages, the
working of a General Will for the good of the community: it is
the Will of All—the agglomeration of the selfish desires of

everyone. But a government forced to take notice of all these interests would have to rule for the whole community and so reform would come, and perhaps, if the rulers found pleasure in the proceedings, their motives might in time become transformed and they would seek the greatest happiness of the greatest number of people not because they had to, but because they wanted to.

Mill's inconsistencies on the subject of motives and consequences can be explained in the same way, for, granted that motives in existing society were necessarily bad, moral judgment in the transition stage must perforce concentrate upon the consequences of actions. The motives could be taken for granted, and in any case could not be changed overnight. But, ideally, good intentions and perfect foresight should be formed by education and men would seek the pleasure of others not as a by-product resulting from the pursuit of private interest, but because their own greatest pleasure had been from childhood associated with the general happiness. Intention was relevant when considering the ideal, but not when considering the immediate present. The educationist must seek to form good intentions: the contemporary politician could not, and must concentrate on beneficial consequences.

This dualism in Mill's Utilitarianism has shewn itself at every stage in our consideration of his second aim in education. When he is considering educational aims, he is talking of the ideal society, and he emphasizes the importance of good intentions, and of seeking 'what we deliberately approve'. All this is consistent with Greek philosophy, and with a self-realization theory, and, as we saw, if Mill had carried it to its logical conclusion, it could have contained the principle of equality. But his argument is wrecked by his insistence on psychological hedonism. By contrast, when he is speaking of the transition stage he ignores intention and concentrates on consequences, he evades 'what we deliberately approve' and stresses the just distribution of any pleasure, and is so immersed in the social evils of his day that he fails to perceive equality as a separate principle at all. But this principle of equality is very much bound up with a third element in Mill's thought—his individualism—which we must now examine.

III

Although Mill's individualism is implied rather than expressly stated, there can be no doubt that it is there. He means not only that men should seek the greatest happiness of the greatest number of people, but also that each man should judge for himself where his happiness lies. This is most clearly seen if we look at the political implications of Mill's theory. Utilitarianism as such could easily be the basis of a benevolent despotism: indeed, many would say that this is the only form of government with which it is consistent. But this is not Mill's conception. In the *Essay on Government* he demands universal male suffrage so that each may protect his interests and happiness. It is true that he has great faith that the masses will be led and advised by the middle classes, but he gives each man the power to accept or reject that advice for himself, thus implying that each man must be the final judge of where his own happiness lies. As we have suggested, he was in part thinking of a transitional period, but there is no evidence that Mill thought that representative government was only suitable for a transitional period. On the contrary, he regarded it as a new device comparable in importance with the form of government sketched in Plato's *Republic*.[23]

The addition of individualism to Mill's Utilitarianism has far-reaching consequences upon the theory. The first of these, as we have seen, is that it implies democratic and not despotic government. The second is that it means that everyone must be capable of being educated—at least as far as moral education is concerned—to the same standard. To an extreme environmentalist like Mill, this presented no theoretical difficulty. In the *Essay on Education* he expounds his view that different kinds and degrees of education are the main causes of differences in ability between men: thus he concludes that all are equally educable, and should, as far as possible, be equally educated. He writes: 'As we strive for an equal degree of justice, an equal

---

[23] Cf. *Essay on Government*, op. cit., p. 34, where Mill refers to Representative Government as the 'grand discovery of modern times'.

degree of veracity in the poor as in the rich, so ought we to strive for an equal degree of an intelligence, if there were not a preventing cause.' The 'preventing cause' is the 'absolute necessity' of performing the labour necessary to provide the human race with the material needs and comforts of life. He continues: 'The question is (and it is a question which none can exceed in importance), what is the degree (of intellectual education) attainable by the most numerous class? ... We have no doubt it will appear that a very high degree is attainable by them ... a firm foundation may be laid for a life of mental action, a life of wisdom and reflection and ingenuity, even in those by whom the most ordinary labour will fall to be performed.'[24] He goes on to demand full-time education to the age of 15 or 16. It must be remembered that though Mill is talking here of intellectual education, he is inferring the need for it from his general view that 'the qualities which we have already named as chiefly subservient to the happiness of the individual himself, and of other men ... are desirable in all men.'[25] Intellectual education was an essential constituent in this, for a man would fail in his duty if he were unable accurately to foresee the consequences of his actions, as far as was reasonably possible. He is postulating equal moral education, as a corollary of Individualistic Utilitarianism.

There are other more fundamental results of Mill's individualism. We have seen that though Mill sometimes appears to identify 'happiness' with 'any kind of pleasure', what he really means by 'happiness' is 'what we deliberately approve'. As far as education for personal happiness is concerned, this presents no difficulty, but it raises an obvious and major problem when we come to speak of the happiness of others. For what is the position when we are doing good to others, giving them pleasures 'which we deliberately approve' and yet they do not want what we give them? Should we give strong drink to one fond of alcohol, or should we give him tea? The ideal of happiness for all, where 'happiness' means 'what we deliberately approve', implies an authoritarian benevolence, and not the democracy that Mill advocated. Only if 'happiness' means 'any

[24] *Essay on Education*, op. cit., pp. 106–7.
[25] Ibid., p. 103.

kind of pleasure' can the ideal be reconciled with Mill's individualism.

Yet the most significant thing about this problem is not the problem itself but the fact that Mill seems entirely unaware of it. There are a number of possible explanations of this, though none of them is a justification of his attitude, for there is bound to be a conflict between 'what we deliberately approve' and what people want. First of all, it might be argued that the pleasures which people ought to seek are of such a nature that, though they did not normally or naturally seek them, once they were suggested to them, they would naturally pursue them. This would mean that Mill was relying on intellectual awareness of certain pleasures, hitherto not experienced, as a motive for seeking them. While some of his writings suggest this, it is contradicted by the *Essay on Education* where we are told that not merely intellectual education, but a prolonged course of habituation is needed if we are to find personal happiness. In his own terminology, we must be accustomed from early childhood to form the right associations of ideas, and of course, we must cultivate the virtue of Temperance or self-denial.

A more tenable explanation is to be found, I think, in the England of Mill's day. Many were short of the bare necessities for existence. The immediate problem, and the problem for some time to come, was not the provision of the higher and more debatable pleasures, but the satisfactions of what Marxists call the 'basic needs' of mankind. At this level, there is no conflict between 'what we deliberately approve' and what people want. We have but to imagine the conditions of early nineteenth-century England to realize that this would be so. To an ardent political reformer—to anyone with a social conscience as strongly developed as Mill's—such social conditions would preoccupy the mind to the exclusion of the more distant future. Once again we see the dualism of Utilitarianism and Mill's failure to distinguish in his writings between the transition period which dominated his attention and the ideal state which he wanted his philosophy to portray. And the same dualism explains why Mill sometimes appears to identify happiness with pleasure when he is writing of political matters, for he is concerned with the need for meeting the basic wants of mankind.

The corollary of Mill's individualism is also important—his distrust of state or government action. As an ideal, Utilitarianism requires group or political action for its most complete and effective realization. Greatest happiness as the aim of each individual may be a laudable purpose but the individual's power of producing happiness is strictly limited to his immediate circle. Beyond this, his benevolence is perforce a benevolent neutrality, rather than active generosity. Many would argue that we have no duty to those whom we do not know, other than benevolent neutrality, and that the obligation to produce the *greatest* happiness is impossible to defend. Whether this is so or not, it is an entirely different matter when we turn to the state. Here it is much more defensible to say that the duty of the state is to promote the greatest happiness of the community. Further, it is clear that the state can do much in pursuance of this aim: it has both the power and the opportunity. Utilitarianism is primarily a communal ethic, yet Mill's individualism rules out state action, very largely, if not entirely.

In fact, Utilitarianism, if it means fostering 'what we deliberately approve' implies a state actively pursuing the greatest happiness of the community, not merely permitting its members to attain it. Some of the implications are more apparent if we consider the modern welfare state. The essence of this is not merely social justice, but surreptitious education. Where goods and services are provided free, the consumer loses his freedom of choice of how to spend his money for he is compulsorily taxed to pay for the free services. Where beer is taxed and food is subsidized, the purpose is the same: to encourage people to want what is 'deliberately approved'. All of this would have been congenial to Mill except the fact that it was done by the state. He was therefore left with the gulf between what people want, and what is 'deliberately approved'—a gulf imperceptible in his own day, but growing wider and wider as social conditions improved.

The position then is this: Utilitarianism, unqualified by individualism, implies a conception of the state which is positive in two senses—first, that the state is the active provider of the greatest happiness of the community, and second that it is the active though surreptitious educator of the community as to where true happiness lies. Individualist Utilitarianism means a democratic state, and a negative conception of its functions —it should do the minimum and leave individuals as free as possible to seek and attain their own happiness. It must therefore rely on other agencies than the state to perform both the function of educating the people to know where true happiness lies, and that of positive large scale beneficence. For Mill, private charity and individual effort was the agency of beneficence, and the example of the middle classses the instrument of education.

The second of these solutions may strike us as far-fetched, but it was more plausible in Mill's day than in our own. Professor G. M. Young has written: 'The Evangelicals gave the island a creed which was at once the basis of its morality and the justification of its wealth and power . . . By about 1830 their work was done . . . They had established a certain level of behaviour for all who wished to stand well with their fellows. In moralizing society, they had made social disapproval a force which the boldest sinner might fear.'[26] In these days 'respectability' was a very powerful incentive on personal conduct. And 'respectability' in the lower classes took the form of following the example set by the middle classes. Thus Mill's reliance on the willingness of the masses to accept the 'guidance and advice' of the middle classes is not so naïve as it appears to us today. On the contrary, it was a shrewd piece of social observation of what in fact was happening.

The general distrust of state action of any kind is more difficult to explain, however, especially when we remember two things. First, nineteenth-century Utilitarianism was originally a scheme for the reform of legislation. It was a test or criterion of the wisdom and justice of state action. It has an indisputable political parentage if not a political ancestry. Second, Mill himself believed in political action —'he cared nothing for the individual, only for the mass' lamented Francis Place when Mill declined to do him a favour. The contemporary situation does suggest some explanation of these paradoxes. The immediate problem, as it presented itself to Bentham and Mill,

[26] *Early Victorian England*, ed. G. M. Young, O.U.P., 1934, ii, p. 416.

was not to galvanize an inactive state into beneficent activity, but to inhibit an all too active state from pernicious activity. The first task was to sweep away all the anachronistic laws— legacies of the eighteenth century and earlier, of the days of planned economy, of theories of 'natural right' which to the Utilitarians had no rational basis—all those things which prevented the people from attaining happiness. And, outside the realm of law, a similar task was to reduce the privilege of the Church and aristocracy—privilege which, according to Mill, they enjoyed because the state allowed them to.[27] Thus the immediate and considerable task confronting Bentham and Mill was a negative one, rather than positive—it was to sweep away unjustified and unmerited privilege, rather than to construct a beneficent and active state. Their work would, as they saw it, leave a state much reduced in power and influence, rather than promote, as today we might expect, a welfare state. A second factor which may have influenced Mill's attitude was the very great importance of private individual effort in nineteenth-century charity. When we reflect that the foundations of a national system of primary education were laid by Lancaster and Bell, financed and organized and supported by voluntary individual effort and donation, we can see something of the dimensions of personal charity in those days. To Mill, individual effort could do far more to promote the greatest happiness of the greatest number of people than we should think either possible or advisable today.

It would be hard to say whether this last factor was a cause or a consequence of individualism. Certainly Mill's individualism was rooted in other and deeper convictions. We have already referred to Mill's lifetime of political writing, and to the fact that one constant strain through all his articles was the dangers of privilege, vested interests and the power of sectional groups. Mill saw in these vested interests a striking confirmation of Plato's wisdom in arranging that those who had power in his ideal state should have neither privilege, private interests, nor property so that they would always rule in the interests of the many. And Mill anticipates Marx in his Commonplace Book by asserting that people who are privileged invariably rule in

[27] Cf. *Essay on Education*, op. cit., pp. 118–19.

their own interests, even when they think they are serving the community, for they deceive themselves as to their true motives. The inescapable logical conclusion of all this is individualism, for on this view no-one could be trusted to seek another man's pleasure. This was of course especially true in the transition period: a benevolent aristocracy was, according to Mill's hedonism, psychologically impossible, and would in fact be a fraud upon the people. Thus, as we have seen, he regarded representative government primarily as a device for securing rule in the interests of all. He pushes the same point—the danger of vested interests and sectional groups—still further when he writes on the dangers of loyalty to small groups: 'Self-love, we know, though it moves us to many useful acts, moves us also to harmful ones. The same is true of social love in all its branches but the highest.'[28] This leads him to insist that the 'greatest number of people' means exactly what it says—all mankind, without distinction of race, class, or creed, national or other social grouping. In the end, therefore, Mill is prescribing not the duty of the state, nor the duty of the individual to the state, nor indeed to any group: he is prescribing the duty of the individual to mankind at large.

Extreme individualism in ethics usually means a subjective ethic in which each is guided by his conscience and each determines for himself where his duty lies. But Mill was scornful of such theories, and wrote of them: 'This is as much as to say that whatever a man, in the moment of action, feels himself most inclined to do, he does rightly, for his impulse is the test. In short it is impossible for him to do wrong. This is the sort of morality all must come to who make feelings their guide.'[29] To meet these objections in his own philosophy, as we have seen, he demands not merely good intentions from his agent, but intelligent anticipation of the consequences of actions, so that, but for the unforeseen, there would be an external objective situation by which one could judge whether an action was in fact good or bad. But Mill also needs to prove the objectivity of his moral ideal in terms of his general philosophy—he has to square it with his theory of knowledge, and it is in this process

---

[28] *Fragment on Mackintosh*, op. cit., p. 308.
[29] Ibid., p. 305.

that he shews himself most unmistakably to be an ethical natura-list. For if happiness is an objective thing, it must be an object of knowledge. This for Mill, means knowledge through the senses, fundamentally the same as knowledge of the material world. This leads him to reduce happiness to pleasurable sensations, and to say that the sensation and the pleasure it brings are one and the same thing. By means of Association Psychology, all moral experience is reduced to the same terms. Mill uses naturalism not to deny the existence of morals but to prove their reality in the only way he thought was valid.

It was not merely the need to fit his moral philosophy into his theory of knowledge that obliged Mill to be an ethical naturalist. A second factor, probably just as potent, lies in the political purpose of Utilitarianism. A practical criterion of immediate reform demanded something easily recognizable, something which everyone could apply to existing situations and say at once either that they conduced to general happiness or they did not, and for this to be so there must be no doubt or disagreement about what constituted a state of happiness. In this way political democracy also postulated an objective 'happiness' and it is this political purpose which leads Mill to concentrate so much on the external marks of beneficent action. And this lends support to my earlier suggestion that, had Mill elaborated his views of 'wherein happiness consists' it would have consisted of an elaboration and classification of these external marks of general happiness. In his day, this elaboration was not so necessary, for, as we have noted, the immediate basic needs of so many people were unsatisfied. But in the future, obviously it would be, and in this way Mill may be the fore-runner of the sociologist, for one explanation of later 'evolu-tionary Utilitarianism' is that its exponents found the same need for a more tangible and concrete 'happiness', which Mill foresaw, and which, as the condition of the people improved, grew more and more pressing if Utilitarianism as a political creed was to survive.

IV

Throughout this exposition of James Mill's thought on the aims of education, I have tried to keep two basic points in mind. First, I have followed his thought as far as possible in the same order he himself developed it, and I have therefore started from the assumption that he thought, rightly or wrongly, that he was explaining and analysing morals, not denying them. As we have seen, there is good evidence to support this assumption. Second, I have emphasized his constant preoccupation with contemporary politics, and have therefore indicated some of the political implications of his theories.

As a result of this approach, the many different strands which make up James Mill's Utilitarianism have, I think, been thrown into sharper relief. Five such strands can be distinguished. His moral theory is, first, a doctrine of personal conduct—a doctrine very like self-realization. Second, it is Utilitarian in its insistence on seeking the happiness of others. Third, it involves the principle of equality, fourth, it is individualistic, and finally it rests on a naturalist philosophy, and therefore reduces all moral beliefs to pleasure, simple and unqualified.

These five different strands cannot be reconciled, and it is Mill's attempt to reconcile them which makes his philosophy seem absurd to us today, and which often prevents a proper understanding of his mind. Self-realization can only include Utilitarianism and the principle of equality if at least one of our desires is other-regarding, not self-regarding—if, amongst the things we 'deliberately approve' is a desire for the welfare of others. And much of Mill's individualism would not be inconsistent with this. One thing prevents the fusion of these ideas and that is the psychological theory of Hedonism. On the other hand, Hedonism is the foundation of Mill's individualism, and with individualism goes the principle of equality. Psychological Hedonism is at once the rock on which Mill's philosophy must founder, and the basis of some of his strongest convictions.

Why was James Mill so firm a believer in psychological

5

Hedonism? The twentieth-century student is confronted with the fact that one of the most upright men of the day, with a code of personal conduct far more rigid than most, is yet the advocate of pleasure as an end, and convinced that pleasure is the only motive. The explanation of this paradox lies partly in the strong eighteenth-century philosophical tradition of English empiricism. Hedonism may have rendered parts of Mill's moral theory inconsistent with one another, but it made much more of it, to his eyes at least, consistent with English empiricism, and with the extreme environmentalist position in education congenial to the heart of the reformer. Hedonism, ethical naturalism, empiricism, and the 'bucket theory of the mind' are a logical whole, and Mill was too good a philosopher not to realize that he had to prove the objectivity of his ideal in terms of a theory of knowledge: he was too much the spokesman of his age to see that it could not be proved in terms of eighteenth-century English empiricism.

Mill's observations of the contemporary political scene also seemed to him a striking confirmation of the truth of psychological Hedonism. We have already referred to the constant reiteration in his articles of the evils of vested interests in Church and State, and to the many entries in his Commonplace Book asserting that 'judgment of good and evil almost wholly depend upon interest'. To him, the governments of his day appeared as groups of selfish people, intent on the safeguarding of their privileges, and engrossed in the pursuit of their private advantage. These are the reflections of a disillusioned man, educated for the Scottish church, and plunged into the turmoil of English politics. And Hedonism not only explained the contemporary political scene: it satisfied the aspirations of the Radical in an age when reform would necessarily be largely occupied in bettering material conditions. The crux of the matter is seen in two entries in the Commonplace Book. The first reads: 'Under a bad government there is no common interest. Every man is governed by his private interest.' To this Mill adds the comment 'a good thought'. But the second says: 'Sense of public interest—to create this sense and give it form, is the ultimate point of good education.' These two entries seem to me to summarize Mill's problem as he saw it. The association of political reform with a moral ideal need not be fatal to either, but it was the growing conviction, born of political experience, that there were no motives other than self-interest, which led Mill to infer his moral philosophy more and more from the immediate needs of the day, instead of, as he should have done, inferring the reforms needed from a contemplation of the ideal. Mill's limitations are due to his too complete immersion in his age; it must be admitted that it was an age which forced itself upon one's attention.

There is one central idea involved in Utilitarianism which was especially congenial to Mill and which explains why the theory was so influential. Any form of utilitarianism is a teleological theory of ethics, and, as such, stresses that all actions must be judged by reference to their contribution to a supreme end or purpose—a final good. With such thinking, much of life becomes not a good in itself but a means to something else, a preparation for an ultimate ideal. It may involve sacrificing the present for the future—an idea which can easily be carried to extremes. Such thinking suits the political reformer like Mill, for his whole purpose is to persuade people to change for the sake of greater happiness in the future. In another way, the same general idea operated. Ideals of personal conduct in Mill's day involved much self-denial. With the Evangelicals the justification of this was both simple and logical. Pleasure in this life was of small worth compared with the life to come: to them all life was but a preparation. Mill, brought up for the Scottish church, and as respectable a member of the middle classes as any, was profoundly, though unconsciously influenced by these ideas. Thus he gives us a Utilitarianism apparently as the eighteenth century left it: in fact, in his hands it becomes as stern a code of personal conduct as any Evangelical could wish, and as sharp a spear-point for a political crusade as the most ardent reformer could desire.

V

Theory of Knowledge

In Mill's day, Psychology and Theory of Knowledge were not distinguished as separate enquiries: they were inextricably intertwined as one and the same enquiry, perhaps best defined by the title of Mill's book, as "the analysis of the phenomena of the human mind'. Since then the distinction between Psychology and Theory of Knowledge has been recognized, and indeed insisted upon as essential to any clear or profitable thinking in either field. And the basis of the distinction may be stated very generally thus: Knowledge is a relationship between a person who knows and something which is known. While there are clearly very close connexions between the two, it is none the less true that the process of knowing on the one hand, and the object of knowledge on the other, are essentially two different enquiries. Thus one modern philosopher writes: 'Knowledge . . . must be knowledge by a mind of an object which is not that mind . . . That there is a plain, empirical difference between my knowing of an object and the object which I know, seems to me impossible to doubt.'[1] This difference was necessarily obscured by Mill's approach. The same author continues: 'Logic is not psychology; we are not in logic interested in mental processes so much as what those processes, which do not work *in vacuo*, are apprehending.'[1]

In educational theory it is essential to recognize these two different enquiries, and to examine theories from the two points of view of Theory of Knowledge and of Psychology. For, in

[1] L. A. Reid, *Knowledge and Truth*, Macmillan, 1923, pp. 182–3. Professor Reid goes on to argue that, even from the point of view of Logic, there is a subjective element in knowledge which cannot be ignored. But this is within the context which he has defined, namely, that Logic and Psychology are two different studies, and the emphasis of the first is on the object of the process called knowing, and not on the process itself.

education, psychological matters concern the nature of the pupil to be educated, and the manner in which he learns—matters which, in principle, can be resolved by observation, experiment and practical experience. But the theory of knowledge is concerned not with the processes of knowing and of learning, but with the object of knowledge, with what is learnt. Theoretically at least, it is unaffected by theories of the process of learning, or by views of the nature of the pupil. It is part of the aim in education, indeed, in intellectual education, the theory of knowledge is the analysis of the nature of the aim. The one certainly affects the other, but equally certainly, does not determine the other. We may hold with Plato that number is a concept not resolvable into particular sense experiences, and at the same time quite logically hold also the psychological view that a child learns the concept of number most successfully by starting with particular concrete examples of it. Hence although Mill did not distinguish these two studies, we must do so, if we are to understand the educational implications of his philosophy, and this means that we must consider his theory first as a contribution to the theory of knowledge, and second, as a theory of psychology.

The first written statement of Mill's views is to be found in the *Essay on Education*, 1817. Here, he starts with the question: 'How the mind, with those properties which it possesses, can, through the operation of certain means, be rendered most conducive to a certain end.' This is a question, it would seem, in psychology. But he continues that, to answer, we must know the 'whole science of human nature'—still something which, today, would be regarded as a psychological enquiry. But he then continues: 'All that passes for knowledge ... is either matter of experience, or ... matter of guess. The first is real knowledge, the properties of the object correspond to it. The latter is supposititious knowledge, and the properties of the object do or do not correspond to it, most likely not.' If we now ask what experience we have of the human mind, Mill answers that it consists of sense-experience, of experience of our own feelings, and of 'other men exhibiting signs of having similar experiences themselves'. We *infer* what other men feel because they act as we do when we have certain feelings. Mill gives this term 'feelings' a wide and general meaning: he uses it as a generic term to cover all our experience of the external world by sensation, of our own bodily sensations, and of what today we would call our feelings and emotions. On this basis, he says we have knowledge first, of the feelings themselves, and secondly of the order in which they come, and 'this is all'. Of those feelings which we should now call sensations, he distinguishes actual sensations which he calls 'impressions' from memory images —'the type or relict of the impression' which he calls 'ideas'.[2]

He then states his own position clearly: 'These two—*impressions* and their corresponding *ideas*—are simple feelings in the opinion of all philosophers. But there is one set of philosophers who think that these are the only simple feelings, and that all the rest are merely combinations of them. There is another class of philosophers who think that there are original feelings besides impressions and ideas: as those which correspond to the words *remember, believe, judge, space, time,* etc. Of the first are Hartley and his followers in England, Condillac and his followers in France; of the second description are Dr Reid and his followers in this country, and Kant and the German school of metaphysicians in general on the continent.'[3] Since he is writing for an encyclopedia, Mill does not assert his own position, but it is clear enough: he ranges himself with Hartley. Not only does our knowledge consist of 'feelings', i.e. sensations of the external world and of our own emotions, but there is no other kind of knowledge. All can be reduced to, or shewn to be originally derived from sense experience. We have no categories such as space and time which we bring to the organization of such knowledge. We have no forms of knowledge such as mathematics is supposed to be where a pure triangle conceived in the mind is made the basis of a chain of reasoning. Our categories of thought, and our concepts in mathematics can be shewn to be derived originally from sense-experience of the external world. Where Plato argued that such sense-experience was illusory and misleading—but the shadow of reality—Mill argued precisely the reverse—that it was the only real knowledge and that all else was derived from it.

[2] Mill, *Essay on Education*, op. cit., pp. 45–8.
[3] Ibid., p. 48.

He goes on to analyse sensations as we experience them into their smallest constituent parts. Most sensations which we think are simple can on analysis be shewn to be complex and the combination of several sensations. He quotes as an example the ideas or sensation of a rose which can be analysed into 'the simple feelings of sight, of touch, of taste, of smell, of which the complex idea or feeling is made up'.[4] By such analysis we may gain a 'commanding knowledge of a train of events, by observing the sequences which are formed of the simplest elements into which they can be resolved; and it thus illustrates the two grand operations, by successful perseverance in which the knowledge of the human mind is to be perfected'.[5] In other words if we define as a sensation, or in Mill's term 'impression', a single fleeting glimpse of an object such as a rose, we imagine this to be a single sensation. But if we analyse it we can find this apparently single sensation to be itself a combination of several distinguishable sensations. In like manner, we may experience a rose in a certain combination of other sensations—for instance, in a garden with lawns and other flowers, in a house, and in the company of certain people. All this Mill refers to as the 'train of events'—mental events—which make up our experience in the first place and our recollection of it afterwards. His two 'grand operations', therefore, are first, the separation of a train of events into the single events or sensations, and then the further analysis of these simple sensations into their component elements—the only genuinely simple atomic sensations.

'It is upon a knowledge of the sequences which take place in the human feelings or thought, that the structure of education must be reared . . . As the happiness, which is the end of education, depends upon the actions of the individual, and as all the actions of man are produced by his feelings or thoughts, the business of education is, to make certain feelings or thoughts take place instead of others. The business of education, then, is to work upon the mental successions.'[6] This principle operates for both moral and intellectual education. Moral education involves the association of the ideal—general happiness—with our

[4] Ibid., p. 51.
[5] Ibid., p. 51.
[6] Ibid., p. 52.

own normal appetites. Intellectual education involves the association of sense experiences with one another in the correct order—that is, in the order in which the objects giving rise to the associations are in fact associated in nature, or, in more general terms, the associations of our impressions should correspond with truth. One implication of this doctrine is that not casual but causal sequences should be experienced and thus associated.

There follows a lengthy historical account of the principle of Association, including Hobbes, Locke, Hume, Condillac, and Hartley. He then turns to the problem of motivation: 'there are two things which have a wonderful power over those sequences. They are Custom; and Pain and Pleasure. These are the grand instruments or powers, by the use of which, the purposes of education are to be attained.'[7] Mill regards them as two separate 'instruments' in that either will produce an association. Education must proceed by a repetition of beneficial sequences, and the best means of producing this repetition is to associate beneficial ideas or habits with things like eating or sleeping, which everyone has to do daily, so that daily repetition will form unbreakable habits.

The problem of motive is a problem of psychology, however, and we are at this stage concerned with his theory as a theory of knowledge. It was considerably expanded in his later work: the *Analysis of the Phenomena of the Human Mind*, which he commenced in 1822 and published in 1828, and it is to this source which we must turn for a clarification of Mill's position. The basic contention is the same: that sense-experience is the only source of knowledge, and everything else is erected upon it. But among the senses Mill included more than the five which give us knowledge of the external world—'of these unnamed, and generally unregarded, sensations, two principal classes may be distinguished: first, those which accompany the action of the several muscles of the body; and, secondly, those which have their place in the alimentary canal.'[8] The first of these we shall find important later in explaining some abstract ideas in terms of 'sensibilities'.

---

[7] Ibid., p. 58.
[8] James Mill, *Analysis of the Phenomena of the Human Mind*, Longmans, 2nd edn, 1878, ed. J. S. Mill, i, p. 3.

The term 'idea' Mill admits to being used, normally, 'with a great latitude of meaning, both in ordinary and in philosophical discourse'. But he sticks to the sense in which he used it in the *Essay on Education*: 'Another name, by which we denote this trace, this copy of the sensation, which remains after the sensation ceases, is *Idea* . . . The word *Idea*, in this sense, will express no theory whatsoever; nothing but the bare fact, which is indisputable.'[9] Thus if we describe Mill's philosophy as one reducing knowledge to experience it is important to be clear just what he meant by 'experience'. He would exclude experience of the concept of a triangle, for instance, except in terms of a particular visible and 'sensible' triangle which we are seeing, or had seen and were recalling. It would exclude many forms of imaginative experience—for example, poetic truths. On the other hand, he does not go so far as some modern educational theorists inspired by Pragmatism, and limit 'experience' to the practical and the concrete—that with which some activity can be undertaken.

The next step in the argument is the theory of the Association of Ideas. Mill defines this as follows: 'If our senses are awake, we are continually receiving sensations, of the eye, the ear, the touch, and so forth; but not sensations alone. After sensations, ideas are perpetually excited of sensations formerly received; after those ideas, other ideas; and during the whole of our lives, a series of those two states of consciousness, called sensations and ideas, is constantly going on. I see a horse: that is a sensation. Immediately I think of his master: that is an idea. The idea of his master makes me think of his office: he is a minister of state: that is another idea. The idea of a minister of state makes me think of public affairs; and I am led into a train of political ideas; when I am summoned to dinner. This is a new sensation, followed by the idea of dinner, and of the company with whom I am to partake it. The sight of the company and of the food are other sensations; these suggest ideas without end; other sensations perpetually intervene, suggesting other ideas: and so the process goes on.'[10] So far this is what we today would understand by the term 'association of ideas', but it is to be noted

[9] Ibid., i, p. 52.
[10] Ibid., i, pp. 70–1.
5*

that, in speaking of 'political ideas', Mill appears to be slipping quite illegitimately from his own definition of an idea as an image, to the more normal meaning of it, as a concept.

The problem is, according to Mill, to establish whether such 'trains of feelings' (i.e. of sensations and ideas) occur haphazardly or in some order. Sensations clearly follow 'the order established among what we call the objects of nature'—they reflect the external world. This order in nature can be classified into two—the synchronous order and the successive order. 'The synchronous order or order of simultaneous existence, is the order in space; the successive order, or the order of antecedent and consequent existence, is the order in time.'[11] Any particular group of things I see at any one time is an example of synchronous order. A match causing an explosion is an example of successive order. Neither is confined to one sense; and although Mill later subjects these notions to a minute analysis he is not concerned with the question of whether, strictly speaking, we ever receive more than one sensation simultaneously—i.e., whether what appear to be a plurality of simultaneous sensations are in fact a very rapid succession of sensations as the eye, etc., switches rapidly from one to the other. From the point of view of his theory of knowledge this question is hardly important. What is worth noticing is that this new classification into synchronous and successive order in sensation replaces the earlier distinction, in the *Essay on Education* between 'sequences' of ideas and 'trains' of ideas. The latter was by no means clear, implying as it did that all sensation was strictly successive and that there was some purpose in distinguishing between long and short associations. Such a distinction may be justified by the evidence of introspection, but it is now found to be unnecessary. The change may indicate a change of emphasis or of interest on the part of the author. The earlier doctrine is a psychological one, but he now wants to construct a theory of knowledge, and discards psychological findings unnecessary to his purpose.

He then passes to the core of his theory—the problem not of sensations but of ideas and their association. Since they are copies of sensations 'our ideas spring up, or exist, in the order

[11] Ibid., i, p. 71.

in which the sensations existed of which they are copies. This is the general law of 'Association of Ideas', by which term, let it be remembered, nothing is here meant to be expressed, but the order of occurrence.'[12] It must also be remembered that by 'order' Mill means both successive and synchronous orders.

The important thing about this law of Association of Ideas is the very wide application which Mill gave to it. First, all ordinary sensations such as the sight of a particular horse, which we should normally classify as simple, are subject to further analysis and are shewn to be a compound of sensations of the size, shape, and colour of a horse. The recollection of the horse, its image, is, like the original sensation, an example not of a single sensation, but of synchronous association. Association is here used as a weapon of analysis. But it equally explains ideas which might be recollected with the horse, for instance the field in which it stood, and the company in which we stood when we saw it. Second, we have antecedent and consequent sensations, and corresponding ideas—that is experience of one sensation invariably followed by another, so that the first sensation will recall the idea of the other, and one idea the idea of the other. As Mill's use of the term 'consequent' suggests, it is from such experiences of successive associations that we get the notion of causation.

This and other categories, however, belong to a later stage in our exposition, and the immediately next step in Mill's exposition is concerned with the strength or weakness of associations. They may be strong or weak, either between sensations and ideas, or between ideas. 'The causes of strength in association', writes Mill, 'seem all resolvable into two; the vividness of the associated feelings and the frequency of the association.'[13] The vividness in turn can be explained in three ways: sensations are always more vivid than ideas, either sensations or ideas associated with pain and pleasure are more vivid than those which are not, and the ideas of the more recent sensations are more vivid than those of the more remote.

Mill continues: 'It is to this great law of association, that we trace the formation of our ideas of what we call external

[12] Ibid., i, p. 78.
[13] Ibid., i, p. 83.

objects; that is, the ideas of a certain number of sensations, received together so frequently that they coalesce as it were ... Hence what we call the idea of a tree, the idea of a horse, the idea of a man.' We should note Mill's ambiguity here: it is not clear whether he is referring to one tree, horse, or man which we recollect, or to trees, horses, and men in general. It would appear to be the latter, when he continues: by referring to this 'high association, this blending together of many ideas' and adds that it gives us 'the power of classification and all the advantages of language'.[14]

This brings us to the second main element in Mill's thinking —his theory of language. So far his position may be summed up thus: All knowledge is originally derived from sense-experience, and from no other source. Much of this sense-experience is capable of further analysis than we suspect, by the use of the principle of association, and on the other hand, the same principle can also be a means of synthesis, and so can explain groups or trains of sensations and ideas. We have now to see how he carried this reasoning farther, with the aid of his theory of language.

He starts by saying that the process of 'Naming' is involved 'in all the more complicated cases of human consciousness'. If we are to communicate with other men we must choose 'some *sensible objects* as *signs* of our inward feelings'. The same is necessary if we are to record our feelings for future reference by ourselves. Various signs such as gesticulation, serve to communicate in rudimentary fashion. But language spoken and written came to be by far the most valuable instrument for these purposes.

He then argues that 'we cannot recall any idea or train of ideas at will. Thoughts come into the mind unbidden.'[15] He is referring here to the ideas themselves, and not to the verbal symbols marking them. Nor can sensations be recalled except in the form of ideas, which in themselves cannot be controlled. They may or may not conform to the order of the original sensations of which they are copies—that is they may be true, or they may be the wildest fantasy. It is obviously of the highest

14 Ibid., i, pp. 92–3.
15 Ibid., i, p. 130.

importance 'to be able to ensure the order of our ideas; to make, in other words, the order of a train of ideas correspond unerringly with a train of past sensations. We have not, however, a direct command over the train of our ideas. A train of ideas may have passed in our minds corresponding to events of great importance; but that train will not pass again, unvaried, except in very simple cases, without the use of *expedients*.'[16] We can control sensations, in so far as we can repeat any particular sense-experience. We cannot control ideas unless we can link them with 'sensible objects', and 'make use of them as marks for our ideas'. If we do this we can 'ensure any succession we please of the sensible objects; and, by the association between them and the ideas, a corresponding succession of the ideas'. Words are these 'sensible objects'. They may be 'evanescent signs' in speech, or 'permanent signs' in writing. The first are 'immediate marks of the ideas', and the second are 'secondary marks of the ideas' since they refer first to speech which directly refers to the ideas. Language, then, is a system of symbols referring to sense-experience and to images of it.

The main contention which Mill puts forward on the basis of this exposition of the nature of language is that every word must be tested by its reference to actual experience—i.e. to the images or sensations of which the image is a copy. If this is done, then every word will be found either (i) to have precise reference to a particular sensation or particular image, or (ii) to refer to common features of several such sensations or images, or (iii) to be, on analysis, without referent and strictly meaningless. In the first category are what we call Proper Nouns referring to particular individual persons or things and to nothing else: here the reference is precise and concrete. In the second category are common nouns referring not to John but to a man—i.e. referring to everything which falls into a certain class or group of which all the members have the same characteristics in common.

The first of these categories presents no problem. With the second, Mill takes the somewhat extreme position of asserting that economy in the use of 'names' is the only reason for classifying objects. He writes: 'Names, to be useful, cannot exceed a certain number. They could not otherwise be remembered. It

---

[16] Ibid., i, pp. 131–2.

is, therefore, of the greatest importance, that each name should accomplish as much as possible. To this end, the greater number of names stand, not for individuals only, but classes. Thus the terms red, sweet, hot, loud, are names, not of one sensation only, but of classes of sensations; that is every sensation of a particular kind. Thus also the term, rose, is not the name of one single cluster, but of every cluster coming under a certain description. As rose denotes one class, stone denotes another, iron another, ox another, and so on.'[17]

On the basis of this theory words can be more or less general —for instance, 'man' is more general than 'neighbour', and 'human being' more general than 'man'. They can also refer not only to sensations and ideas but to 'our notion of a horse'— i.e. ideas or concepts in normal usage of the word 'idea'. But essentially they consist of a composite picture of the common qualities of a number of particular sensations of particular horses. The origin of such general terms must therefore lie in sense experience, and the meaning of such words can only be resolved by reference to sense-experience.

Mill's account of the process of classification is in terms of his theory of language, and also of the association principle. 'Words become significant purely by association',[18] he writes, and quotes the example of the name St Paul's attached to the individual building. 'The word is pronounced in conjunction with the idea . . . and by degrees, the idea and the word become so associated, that the one can never occur without the other.' Now, 'suppose that our name of one individual is applied to another individual. It then calls up first one and then the other. It then is applied to an indefinite number of individuals until it has become associated with them all. What happens? It does call up an indefinite number of the ideas of individuals, as often as it occurs; and calling them up in close connexion, it forms them into a species of complex idea.

'There can be no difficulty in admitting that association does form the ideas of an indefinite number of individuals into one complex idea; because it is an acknowledged fact. Have we not the idea of an army? And is not that precisely the ideas of an

---

[17] Ibid., i, p. 137. J. S. Mill disputes this view in a footnote.
[18] Ibid., i, p. 262.

indefinite number of men formed into one idea? Have we not the idea of a wood, or a forest; and is not that the ideas of an indefinite number of trees formed into one idea? These are instances of the concretion of synchronous ideas.'[19]

A little later, Mill continues: 'It thus appears, that the word, *man*, is not a word having a very simple idea, as was the opinion of the Realists; nor a word having no idea at all, as was that of the Nominalists; but a word calling up an indefinite number of ideas, by the irresistible laws of association, and forming them into one very complex, and indistinct, but not therefore un-intelligible idea.'[20] It follows from this that the same word may, in different contexts, have different meanings—one to signify an individual example, the other to signify a class.

This is Mill's answer to the problem of universals. His asser-tion that he differs from the Nominalists is interesting, especi-ally in view of his earlier statement that 'economy in the use of names' is the sole reason for having general names at all: it is not immediately clear how he reconciles these two positions. What is quite clear is, as a later passage emphasises, that his position is the exact opposite to that of Plato. Plato spoke of 'the faculty of seeing "the One in the Many, and the Many in the One"; a phrase which . . . is really a striking example of what in classification is the matter of fact. His error lay, in misconceiving the ONE; which he took, not for the aggregate, but something pervading the aggregate.'[21]

By broadly the same technique Mill disposes of other prob-lems in the theory of knowledge. His explanation of Abstraction starts with a familiar thesis: 'We have already observed the following remarkable things in the process of *Naming*: 1. Assign-ing names to those clusters of ideas called objects; as man, fish; 2. Generalizing those names, so as to make them represent a class; 3. Framing adjectives by which minor classes are cut out of larger . . . One purpose of Abstraction, therefore, is the forma-tion of those *sub-species*, the formation of which is required for certain purposes of speech.'[22] The process is explained thus. If

[19] Ibid., i, p. 264.
[20] Ibid., i, p. 265–6.
[21] Ibid., i, p. 271.
[22] Ibid., i, p. 295.

we speak of a *black* horse, or *black* man or *black* carriage, in each case there are two associations—'horse' and 'black' and so on. Of these, the nouns—horse, man, or carriage—are 'variable clusters', but the adjective 'black' refers to a sensation constant to all clusters and is the stronger association. Mill uses his own special terminology, in inverse order to that of traditional logicians, by saying that the word 'black' *notes* a particular colour—i.e. its main association, and *connotes* the clusters (or nouns) to which it is joined. Abstraction is the dropping of the connotation—e.g. 'blackness'. Abstract terms are 'simply the concrete terms with the connotation dropped . . . It hence . . . appears that there can be no *Abstract* term without an implied *Concrete*.'[23] This explains all abstract terms such as truth, health, quantity, motion, weight, strength, and so on.

Memory is explained as an association between the idea of the thing remembered, and the idea of my having seen it. This latter contains 'two important elements; *the idea of my present self*, the remembering self; and the *idea of my past self*, the remembered or witnessing self. These two ideas stand at the two ends . . . of a series of my states of consciousness. That series consists of the successive states of my consciousness, intervening between the moment of perception, or the past moment, and the moment of memory, or the present moment. What happens at the moment of memory? The mind runs back from that moment to the moment of perception. That is to say, it runs over the intervening states of consciousness, called up by association. But "to run over a number of states of consciousness called up by association", is but another mode of saying, that "we associate them"; and in this case we associate them so rapidly and closely, that they run, as it were, into a single point of consciousness, to which the name MEMORY is assigned.'[24] Memory thus involves the concepts of Personal Identity and of Time, but both are explicable under the Association principle. Personal Identity is reduced to 'successive states of consciousness'[25] and Time is also a problem in succession. 'With every present event is associated the idea of an antecedent; with that antecedent, the

[23] Ibid., i, pp. 304–5.
[24] Ibid., i, pp. 330–1.
[25] Ibid., ii, p. 171.

idea of another antecedent; and so on without end. These are the ideas of Succession and of Infinity; forced upon us by indissoluble Association ... This is the Past; an infinity of simultaneous successions, each having antecedents, running back without end. These are successions in the concrete; successions of objects. Drop the connotation to form the abstract, as is done in other cases; you have then the successions without the objects; which is precisely the meaning of the word TIME.'[26]

Finally, there is the problem of Belief, to which Mill devotes a long chapter. First, the direct experience of a simple sensation. To have such a sensation and to believe that we have it are not two things but one, for we are 'expressing the same state of consciousness'. 'The feeling is one, the names, only, are two.'[27] The problem of Belief really arises with other cases which may be classified under three heads: 'Belief in Events, real existences; II, Belief in testimony and III, Belief in the truth of propositions.'

The first of these may be further subdivided according to whether the events in question are past, present, or future. Belief in present existences, other than by full sense experience of an object, is a case of what we should now call reduced cue perception—that is the perception of, say, a rose by sight carries with it by association all the other sensations of touch, feel, and smell which we know we should experience if we tried, but which we accept on the single perception of sight. We have also less in visual sensation than we suppose. 'Whenever we have the sensation of colour, we cannot avoid having the ideas of distance, of extension, and figure, along with it; nor can we avoid having them in such intimate union with the ocular sensation, that they appear to be that sensation itself ... Our belief that we *see* the shape, and size, and distance of the object we look at, is as perfect as belief in any instance can be. But this belief is nothing more than a case of very close association.'[28] There is, however, more to it than that, for 'along with belief in my sensations, as the *effect*, there is belief of something as the *cause*; and that to the *cause*, not to the *effect*,

[26] Ibid., ii, p. 132.
[27] Ibid., i, p. 342.
[28] Ibid., i, p. 347.

the name object is appropriated'.[29] From this Mill argues that the causes of our sensations are the separate qualities in the object, and that the object or *substratum* is the cause of the qualities, and therefore the cause of the causes of our sensations. This object or substratum 'when closely examined, is not distinguishable from Cause. It is the cause of the qualities . . . and . . . we mark it with the name substratum.'[30] Cause is rapidly reduced to 'antecedent and consequent, where the connection is constant . . . This has been established on such perfect evidence, that it is a received principle of philosophy . . . these constant conjunctions are, of all things in the world, what we are the most deeply interested in observing; for on the knowledge of them, all our power of obtaining good and avoiding evil depends. From this, it necessarily follows, that between none of our ideas is the association more intimate and intense, than between antecedent and consequent, in the order of events . . . That a cause means, and can mean nothing to the human mind, but constant antecedent, is no longer a point in dispute.'[31] So central to thought is the concept of cause that we clearly can proceed further and further back—enquiring about the cause of the substratum and so on.

Belief in the existence of objects, which I have perceived, but am not now perceiving is partly a case of belief in Memory, but also partly 'an anticipation of the future. In believing that St. Paul's exists, I believe, that whenever I am in the same situation, in which I had perception of it before, I shall have perception of it again.'[32] It is therefore part of the general problem of our belief in future events—this is dealt with later. But, in addition, my belief in the existence of St Paul's includes the belief that anyone else 'whose senses are analagous to my own' will, if he stands in St Paul's churchyard, experience a 'sensation of that edifice'. This belief in other beings having the same sensations as I do is a case of association. We see what we know to be 'marks or signs of sensations in other creatures. But the interpretation of signs is wholly a case of association, as the extra-

[29] Ibid., i, p. 349.
[30] Ibid., i, p. 350.
[31] Ibid., i, pp. 350–2.
[32] Ibid., i, p. 335.

ordinary phenomena of language abundantly testify. And whenever the association, between the sign and the thing signified, is sufficiently strong to become inseparable, it is belief.'[33] So the associations responsible for our belief in other people and their sensations are, first, our association of our own sensations with our own bodies, secondly the impossibility of thinking of anyone's body without therefore thinking of it as sensitive, and therefore capable of the same perceptions as I am.

Mill's long argument dealing with the future and our belief in it need not be stated in detail. The future, as such, he says is a nonentity—all there is to it is an 'indefinite number of tomorrows' making up the complex idea of futurity in general. Belief in future events is reduced to association—causal association, or necessary consequents, by which is meant nothing more than that a particular consequent has always followed a particular antecedent. Belief in past events is Memory, which is 'but a case of Belief'. But there is also belief in past events, or present, or future ones, on the basis of testimony. This is not fundamentally different from the problem of belief in events anyway. 'The words a man uses, are to us, sensations: belief that he uses the words is not what is meant by belief in his testimony.'[34] The problem is the relation between the words and the things they testify. And this is no problem: 'Words call up ideas by association only. There is no natural connection between them. The manner in which words are applied to events, I know most intimately by my own experience. I am constantly ... employing words in exact conformity with events.'[35] So this resolves itself into association between words and events in my mind, and corresponding events called up when other people use the words.

There remains belief in the truth of Propositions. A proposition is a name for 'a form of words which makes a predication',[36] says Mill. It must either predicate that one name is identical with another, or that one name is part of a larger class denoted

[33] Ibid., i, p. 356–7.
[34] Ibid., i, p. 383.
[35] Ibid., i, p. 384.
[36] Ibid., i, p. 388.

by another, as when we say that 'man is an animal'. Both terms of the proposition depend for their meaning on association—the association of the word with the object or with the class of objects—hence, 'the coincidence of names is all that is meant by the truth of the proposition; and my recognition of that coincidence is another name for my belief in its truth'.[37]

Before leaving Mill's theory of knowledge, it is necessary to give some account of its negative side. This consists of his treatment of words which imply the existence of something which in fact does not exist. He argues that the use of the verb 'to be', in connexion with another verb implies not only the action in question, but also that the doer of the action exists. This rests upon a somewhat crude analysis of the verb 'to be'. If I say 'I am' it means simply that 'I exist'. 'When I say "I am reading" not only reading is predicated of me but *existing* also.'[38] But, says Mill earlier, 'When we affirm of anything that it *exists*, that it *is*: what we mean is, that we may have sensations from it; nothing, without ourselves, being known to us, or capable of being known, but through the medium of our senses.'[39] Thus language may mislead us by implying existence purely because of an 'unhappy duplicity of meaning'[40] in the verb structures we habitually employ, namely the use of the verb 'to be' in conjunction with other verbs.

Mill elaborates this: 'It is the case, however, of the higher abstractions . . . that the use of the verb which conjoins the Predication of *Existence* with every other Predication, has produced the wildest confusion . . . Is it any wonder, for example, that *Chance*, and *Fate*, and *Nature*, have been personified, and have had an *existence* ascribed to them, as objects, when we have no means of predicating anything whatsoever of them, without predicating such *Existence* at the same time. If we say "Chance is nothing"; we predicate of it, by the word "is", both *existence* and *nothingness*.

'When this is the case, it is by no means to be wondered at, that philosophers should so long have enquired what those

[37] Ibid., i, p. 388.
[38] Ibid., i, p. 175.
[39] Ibid., i, p. 157.
[40] Ibid., i, p. 176.

Existences are which abstract terms were employed to express; and should have lost themselves in fruitless speculations about the nature of entity, and quiddity, substance, and quality, space, time, eternity, and so on.'[41]

This was Mill's theory of knowledge. As a preliminary, we should notice three points. First, although it is a philosophy based on sense-experience, it is not sensations as they are actually experienced which are the basis of knowledge, but sensations analysed into the smallest conceivable units—sense-experience subjected to the 'method of analysis'. Take away the analysis into the atoms of mental life—the truly simple sensations—and we should still have a theory reducing knowledge to sense-experience, but it would not be that of James Mill, with whom the Association principle is fundamental and all-pervading. This principle in turn can only be applied as widely as Mill applies it through the theory of synchronous and successive 'orders' of sensation, and these are built upon the analysis of actual sensation into its atomic elements. Secondly, although Mill, in common with other philosophers of his day, did not address himself to problems of truth, it can be noted that his theory implies a Correspondence theory of Truth. Statements are true if they refer to sense-experience, and not to fictional entities. Their truth consists, in the last analysis, in the fact that they correspond to the facts of the external world. Or, as Mill put it in the *Essay on Education*: 'all that passes with us under the name of experience is either matter of experience, or . . . matter of guess. The first is real knowledge; the properties of the object correspond to it.'[42] Finally, if his statement of the theory of knowledge is taken as inclusive of all forms of knowledge, as he evidently intends, then clearly it cannot accommodate 'moral knowledge' of the good, as anything different from sense-experience as he has defined it. No reality can be ascribed to moral sense, or intuition, if the theory of knowledge is to be maintained. His theory therefore involves a Naturalist view of Ethics.

Now, the theory itself clearly rests upon three principal elements. First, there is sense-experience—the origin of everything.

[41] Ibid., i, p. 176.
[42] *Essay on Education*, op. cit., p. 45.

Second, there is the Association principle which pervades and explains everything. Third, there is the theory of language by which all that cannot be reduced to the first two elements is shewn to be meaningless. With the first two of these, it is equally clear that the Association principle is vital as the principle in terms of which sense-experience is to be interpreted, explained, and understood.

When one considers the very wide use Mill makes of 'association' as a principle of explanation, one cannot help wondering whether it is not a blanket term which in fact does not explain very much. Let us take first the simplest case quoted by Mill—the suggestion that our sense-impression of a rose is not a simple sensation but a complex one, an example of a 'sequence of ideas' according to the language of the *Essay*, and of the 'synchronous order' in the *Analysis*.

The word 'association' signifies a 'joining together' of two or more things. It may be used more widely to refer to one man's association with another, and it may refer to many forms of such association ranging from the casual to the habitual, from the infrequent to the regular or permanent. Generally, we reserve the word 'association' for the more permanent forms of behaviour, or joining together.

If this is so, what exactly is meant when we say that the idea or sense-impression of a rose is an 'association'? Mill would say that he means that sensations of sight, touch, smell, etc., were joined together. But what is the evidence for this? Simply that an apparently simple sensation can be analysed, that is separated, into several other *conceivable* sensations. In that case, is Mill really saying anything at all when he says that the sensation of a rose is an example of synchronous association? To the ordinary man it is itself a single simple sensation. If you split it up, it must therefore be joined again, to account for sense-experience. You are really only saying that what seems to be one can be split, in theory, into two or more components, and then that the components are 'associated', i.e. joined together. Association is no explanation of anything in such a case: it is merely using different language to describe the original facts of sense-experience, subject to analysis which is outside sense-experience, and therefore to synthesis—or association—to make it into sense-experience again. The explanation is tautological in that it simply restates the fact that something which was one in experience has been split into more than one, and that we knew when we subjected it to the 'method of analysis'.

Take secondly the association in our minds of seeing a rose in a garden, or on a tree, that is in circumstances which in ordinary parlance we should describe as association. Here we have sense-experience of one object in association with one or more others. Our original sense-experience is of more than one object in association with one another. Does it *explain* this, to say that it is due to 'association'? Certainly not: it merely *describes* the data from which we start, in different language. We perceive one or more objects joined together in some way, by being part of the same scene, or occasion. It is no explanation, but merely a different word, if we say that the objects are 'associated'.

Third, let us consider the association of words with objects— an association on which Mill founds much of his argument about belief in testimony. Here again, words, such as 'rose', call up in our minds the sense-impression of a rose because we have had that experience and used that word in connexion with it. But when we use the word again we do so with the idea of a rose in our minds, that is to say, we use it associated with the same recollection. Have we explained anything by saying that this is due to 'association'? Are we not merely describing, first, our original sense-experience and how we learned words—in which case we are speaking of psychology—and second, what we mean when we now use the word?

So far, the argument suggests that association as such tells us little more than that things are joined. If they are joined it is either because we perceive them to be so, or because by analysis we claim them to be so. If this is so, the only useful explanation comes not in association as a phenomenon, since this is merely a descriptive word, but in the *causes* of association. These Mill reduces to two. He takes Hume's three principles of Association—Contiguity in time and place, Causation, and Resemblance. The first, he says, is his own synchronous order. The second is succession in time. The third he dismisses on the somewhat thin argument that we usually see like things together, and that resemblance is therefore but a case of the law of frequency.[43]

None of this, however, carries us very much farther as far as the Theory of Knowledge is concerned. For if it is valid it must be based on evidence, either of what is before our minds when we think, or of how we came to have such ideas as we have. The evidence for association by contiguity is simply that we have experienced two or more things together on a number of occasions. It is not a case of contiguity, in Mill's meaning of the term, if two things are simply before my mind here and now, for that is not a case of association—frequency of such experience being essential to the formation of an association. Hence the evidence in favour of this principle of association is necessarily in terms of past experience and this is, strictly speaking, a psychological problem, not of what knowledge consists of, but of how we come to learn. In short, the Association principle may be valuable to Mill's psychology—that we have yet to see—but it is not a necessary or useful element in his Theory of Knowledge.

The second main arm of his theory is concerned with language. The importance of this to Mill himself may be gauged by the fact that the whole approach of his *Analysis* is in terms of language and the problems it raises. He does not deal mainly with sensation and the association of ideas: rather he gives a relatively brief mention of these matters, and then devotes long sections to parts of speech, and to different terms in language that we habitually use. This all suggests that he was really concerned with problems in the Theory of Knowledge at this stage in his life. If we ask the question, which a modern philosopher has suggested is the principal question in Theory of Knowledge: 'What is before my mind when I think?'[44] then our answer must start with an analysis of language, of the words in which we are thinking, and it must then go on to decide whether these words refer to real things, or to fictions of language and so on.

Much of Mill's writing on language was traditional, and would hardly be accepted today. His analysis of the verb 'to be'

[43] *Analysis*, op. cit., i, pp. 106–11.
[44] Woozley, *Theory of Knowledge*, Hutchinson, 1949, p. 11.

for instance, as has been quoted at length earlier, is hardly adequate. For if, in using the continuous present tense of a verb, I assert existence of its subject, it seems to me to be equally asserted if I use any other form of the same verb. Thus if I say 'John is walking', I am certainly asserting that John 'is', that is that he exists. But I should equally assert this in saying 'John walks'. More interesting than the fallacy in Mill's argument is the assumption which lies behind it—that whenever, and in whatever connexion, we use the verb 'to be' we postulate 'existence'. This in turn rests on the idea that words have a fixed and invariable meaning—a particularly dangerous assumption to make with regard to the verb 'to be'.[45] It may be that Mill's admiration of the classical languages, then regarded as the perfect logical languages, blinded his judgment. But it is also true that the association doctrine, applied as rigidly and as scientifically as he applied it, would lead him to suppose that with so common a word as 'is' there was a fixed and inseparable association, that is, a meaning.

The same fallacy occurs in Mill's account of belief in historical testimony. He writes: 'The explanation is still more simple of my belief in the fire of London. The testimony in this case is of that sort which I have always experienced to be conformable to the event. Between such testimony, and the idea of the event testified, I have, therefore, an indissoluble association. The testimony uniformly calls up the idea of the reality of the event, so closely, that I cannot disjoin them. But the idea, irresistibly forced upon me, of a real event, is *Belief*.

'It is in this way that belief in History is to be explained. It is because I cannot resist the evidence; in other words, because the testimony calls up irresistibly the idea, that I believe in the battle of Marathon, in the existence of the Thirty Tyrants of Athens, in that of Socrates, Plato, and so on.'[46]

We may leave aside a number of problems raised in this as to whether historical experience is ever the same as our own, and whether it is not the special function of history to recreate for us something unlike our own experience. The relevant point

[45] Cf. I. A. Richards, *Interpretation in Teaching*, Routledge & Kegan Paul, 1949, pp. 299–337, where a number of different senses of 'is' are analysed.
[46] *Analysis*, op. cit., i, pp. 385–6.

at present is the theory of language implied. This whole account rests upon the supposition that words have, and indeed *had* a fixed meaning, in the past as well as the present. The word 'fire' to Mill calls up certain associations, in his own experience. He assumes an exact transposition of this to the experience of the writer of the testimony. With this particular example he may be right, on the whole. But it is not so in general. Words in the past had an area of reference, partially similar to, and partially different from that which they have today. We have only to think of words like 'democracy' to realize that. And indeed, words to two contemporaries may only partially coincide in their meaning, as witness the same word. Mill indeed recognized this in his own account of language in general, for he writes: 'As the combinations [of ideas] are formed arbitrarily, or, in other words, as the ideas of which they are composed are more or less numerous, according to pleasure, and each man of necessity forms his own combination to which they both give the same name. Using the same words, they have not exactly the same ideas. In the term, piety, for example, a good Catholic includes many things which are not included in it by a good protestant. In the term, good manners, an Englishman of the present day does not include the same ideas which were included in it by an Englishman two centuries ago; still less those which are included in it by foreigners of habits and usages dissimilar to our own. Prudence, in the mind of a man of rank and fortune, has a very different meaning from what it bears in the minds of the frugal and industrious poor. Under this uncertainty of language, it not only happens that men are often using the same expressions when they have different ideas; but different, when they have the same ideas.'[47]

All this is very sound sense, and modern students of language would agree with it. But although among his examples of the variable referents of words are historical examples, his account of historical testimony is inconsistent with this, and depends upon the assumption of fixed or common referents to words, in the past and in the present, to the writer of the testimony, and to its reader, centuries later. But this does not happen, and to interpret historical testimony we need first to know the referent

[47] Ibid., i, pp. 141–2.

of the words to the writer and reader of the day. In short, although the meaning of words must be in terms of their reference to experience, that experience can never be, in history, the personal and direct experience of a modern reader applied to testimony written in the past. Hence historical knowledge cannot be satisfactorily explained in terms of Mill's empiricist philosophy, and, indeed, the problem of interpreting the language of original sources in history is more complicated than Mill's account suggests.[48]

For his philosophy in general, however, the account of language we have just quoted gives a fair indication of his method, and as a result he arrives at what would now be called a Resemblance theory of universals, a theory of Causation reduced to experience of constant antecedents and consequents, a theory of Memory explained on a strict and rigid Association doctrine. All this may be termed a codification of the English empiricist tradition, with two additions. First, there is the use of the Association doctrine as a principle or law which explains everything—a principle analogous to Newton's Laws of Motion. Second, there is the approach to the problems of knowledge through the analysis of language. Although both these factors are significant in some ways, as we shall see, they do not in fact affect the Theory of Knowledge which is substantially that of Locke and Hume.

This theory has had considerable influence since Mill's day, and many modern philosophers would accept it as substantially correct. It also provoked considerable criticism, especially from Bradley and the Idealists. The debate as to its merits does not concern us, but it is worth mentioning one or two of the more crucial points in the debate in order to bring out essential features in Mill's position. And these points of criticism centre on the question of how much of our knowledge does Mill's

---

[48] Mill himself was an historian of eminence, but he was something of a 'Whig historian', that is, he tended to see the past in terms of the present, and as a story of the evolution of the present, of the march of progress and so on. He was thus concerned to stress not the unlikeness between past and present, but the more direct links, and such links tend to be conceived in anachronistic terms. In this way Mill may have felt consistent in applying his own present experience to the interpretation of historical testimony, and he may not have noticed the special problems in philosophy raised by historical knowledge as I have defined it.

account explain. Does it, as he alleges, explain everything, or does it explain part and leave some things unexplained?

It would be conceded by many that our concepts of universals are derived from the common features of particulars, and that what we mean by 'table' is the general or common characteristics of all the objects to which we give the name 'table' and all the particular occasions when we have seen such an object. But the question is, are there other concepts of the mind in addition? Is the notion of similarity, for instance, which lies behind the Resemblance theory, itself a universal which the mind brings in when it forms a universal from a number of particulars? And when Mill talks of 'synchronous association' is he not assuming a concept of Time, in asserting that any two things are 'synchronous'? Similarly with categories of Space, and Causation—when Mill defines Causation as the constant association of antecedent with consequent—is he defining its meaning, or referring to the evidence of it? Is this really all we mean by causation? Can it account for causation in History, for instance? One would have thought not. Similarly with subjects like medical science and biology, we seem to *mean* when we say that *A* is the cause of *B*, that something in *A* can be shewn to produce *B*. The evidence for this may well be a large number of instances in which *A* has occurred, followed by *B*. And in natural science the process of verification would consist essentially in isolating *A* and isolating its consequent. But this would be evidence for the conclusion, not the meaning of it.

A second line of criticism is to ask whether there are not forms of knowledge not reducible to sense-experience. We have already noted one—historical knowledge. This is however not a good example for it might be argued that, if we make the assumption that '*something* happened in the past', we can then proceed to interpret the evidence on lines not essentially different from those we use for present evidence for present events, although of course it would not be in terms of our own experience.[49] A clearer example can be found in forms of experience which are clearly not reducible to sense-experience in any shape or form. Such experience would include moral, aesthetic, and

[49] Cf. Field, *Some Problems in Philosophy of History*, British Academy, 1938.

religious experience. On all these points Mill is clear. Religion is something about which nothing can be known—he was an agnostic. There is no evidence anywhere in his writings that he regarded aesthetic experience as something which existed at all. And moral experience he reduced, by an analysis of its origins, to sense-experience and the pleasure it gives us. We have seen, and shall see in more detail later, that he was not entirely consistent in this, and that he wanted both to reduce moral experience to a naturalist basis, and to retain it as an operative motive, unchanged and in its own right. This perhaps illustrates most vividly the dilemma in which so rigid an empiricist as Mill found himself.

When we turn from the theory, to ask why Mill was so convinced he was right, we are faced with an absence of first-hand evidence. Mill came to these problems relatively late in life, after he had moved to or near London, with the result that the invaluable Place correspondence offers no help. It was past the time, too, when he made entries in his Commonplace Book. Finally, this side of his theory was unconnected with the practical political causes of his day in which he was interested, and so little connexion between his own times and his theory of knowledge can be traced. We are therefore left to conjecture.

The first point to be made is that his theory is in the tradition of his day, and that even the Scottish philosophers under whom he studied adopted enough of it to make the final step an easy one, and not a fundamental break with his upbringing, as it had been in morals. Sir Leslie Stephen sums the position up as follows: 'Until the German influence came to modify the whole controversy, the vital issue seemed to lie between the doctrine of Reid, or "intuitionism" on the one hand, and the purely "experiential" school on the other, whether, as in France, it followed Condillac, or, as in England, it looked back chiefly to Hartley.'[50]

Reid's 'intuitionism' amounted briefly to this. We believe in an external world, but that world cannot satisfactorily be accounted for by the evidence of our senses, for these give us

[50] L. Stephen, *The English Utilitarians*, Duckworth, 1912, ii, p. 268.

only 'ideas' which correspond only partly to the external world in which we in fact believe. We cannot, for instance, gain notions of space and geometry from our senses. A true consideration of our 'experience' therefore reveals elements not directly derived from sense-experience. Hence the need for 'intuition'. Dugald Stewart accepted this in essentials. But the point to notice about both Reid and Stewart is that, in accepting that some knowledge could not be reduced to sense-experience, they did not deny the empiricist and associationist doctrine *in toto*: for a very large part of the field they accepted it, and their quarrel was essentially a dispute as to whether or not it could cover the whole field. In a way, Stewart was literally an empiricist, in accepting the theory just so far, and in stopping short of creating a complete and tidy system of thought. But it was this stopping short which was a challenge to someone of James Mill's temperament and outlook. For, in accepting Associationism so far, the Scottish philosophers had to explain the rest of human experience, and this they held to be due to 'intuition'. To a hard-headed rationalist this could easily be shewn to be a circular argument, for it amounted to saying that we believe in something which could not be reduced to sense-experience, and therefore we have, in addition to the power of the senses, the faculty of intuition. But if we are asked to define 'intuition' it can only be as that faculty which enables us to perceive non-sensory experience. The concept is not in fact so circular as it sounds, because we have to start on these problems by deciding what we will or will not regard as knowledge, and from this the rest follows. Mill is in fact being equally arbitrary, and equally circular, in asserting that sense-experience is the only true knowledge, and concluding from it that the only source of our knowledge is our senses.

None the less, it is clear that Reid and Stewart, in taking this midway position, left themselves vulnerable, especially to anyone with a taste for a neat and tidy system, and for a complete solution to all problems of knowledge. Had they, like Plato before them, and Bradley later, denied the validity of sense-experience altogether, it would have required heavy guns to displace them. But in accepting some sense-experience as valid, but ruling off a portion of human experience as unexplained by this method, they left themselves open to attack to anyone who could demonstrate that this 'irrational segment' of human experience could in fact be reduced by the methods of science and reason to sense-experience. Reid and Stewart might be termed 'agnostic' in theory of knowledge, and if it could be demonstrated that the unknown could be known, the inexplicable explained, they must too easily succumb. In this way, James Mill's early philosophical training at Edinburgh laid the foundations for his later thought. In morals it did not, and as we have seen, political problems changed his mind. But in theory of knowledge the gap was not so wide or difficult to cross, and we have no such explanation in the contemporary scene to offer for his transition to full-blooded empiricism.

Halévy suggests that there was a continuous development of Mill's views on mental philosophy from a date as early as 1802, when, in the *Anti-Jacobin Review*, he reviewed Belsham's *Elements of the Philosophy of the Mind & of Moral Philosophy*—a book which expounded the association doctrine, largely following Hartley.[51] Mill's review is critical: on mental philosophy he follows Reid, and on morals he dismisses Belsham's hedonism as 'vicious and selfish'. But he does refer to Locke's *Essay* as 'an achievement in thought, the greatest perhaps on record in the treating of the human mind'.[52] This supports my suggestion that in essentials the Scottish philosophical school in which Mill had been reared favoured an advance towards the full-blooded empiricism which he adopted later.

Other evidence however does not support the view that there was a continuous development of his views. There is no other published writing on this theme until 1815, and there are no entries in the Commonplace Book, which during his early life was used regularly. It is true that John Stuart Mill says: 'At an early period of Mr. Mill's philosophical life, Hartley's work had taken a strong hold of his mind',[53] but this proves little without a definition of the term 'philosophical life'. As against this the Place correspondence shews Mill asking for a copy of Hartley in 1815, about the time when he was concerned with his *Essay*

---

[51] Halévy, *Growth of Philosophical Radicalism*, op. cit., pp. 438–9.
[52] Bain, op. cit., p. 41 n.
[53] *Analysis*, op. cit., i, Introduction by J. S. Mill, p. xvii.

on Education. [54] In August 1815 Mill published anonymously an article in the *British Review* in which he took a full associationist position. A waggish comment to Place is our only evidence that he wrote the review: 'I am glad you like the article in the *British* on Dugald Stewart. Did you observe how cunningly the author (whoever he is) makes a juggical review preach flat atheism, and proves that there is not an argument for the existence of God which will bear to be looked at for a moment? Of the author, if you continue to be a good boy, I may tell you more herafter.'[55] Mill is unusually discreet here, probably because his article attacks Stewart whom he invariably refers to privately in terms of warm personal friendship and regard.

The position then is that we can date the beginning of Mill's interest in mental philosophy about 1814: it followed his study of politics, most of his history of India, and his adoption of Utilitarianism as a political creed, and psychological hedonism as its basis. His mental philosophy, if this argument is true, had to fit his moral and political theory, and not the other way around. Actually, it seems that they marched hand in hand: not until the *Encyclopedia* articles did Mill move from articles on current political problems to the formulation of a political theory. There was only a continuous development of his thought, then, in that both the empiricists and the Scottish school had 'a common ancestry in Locke'. But for the immediate stimulus to his thought, we have to consider the year 1814—the year in which he was asked to write on the theory of education, and the year in which Bentham became interested in problems of language.[56]

[54] B.M. Add. MSS. 35152. Mill to Place, 6 September 1815. 'Hartley is a book well worth your having—though my saying so now may appear to be a little interested.' Halévy dates this letter 1818: the MS. is obscure but its position and contents in relation to other letters make 1815 the more probable date. On 16 August 1815 Place had written: 'I cannot find anyone who has Hartley—but I will persevere and you shall have both him and Beatson.' It is unlikely that three years elapsed between these two letters.

[55] B.M. Add. MSS. 35152, Mill to Place, 13 September 1815. 'Juggical' was a word used by Mill and Bentham to indicate orthodox Christianity.

[56] Further evidence to support the contention of this paragraph is contained in a letter from Mill to Place, 8 October 1816 (B.M. Add. MSS. 35152) in which he says: 'I have given a hasty reading to Hartley since I came here. Hartley's is the true scent but his book is obscurely written: and it will require no little persevering reflection to render the application of his theory perfectly familiar to

Mill had previously shewn some interest in the problems of language—he had written an article on Horne Tooke's linguistic treatise *Diversions of Purley* as early as 1806.[57] He recommends this book to Annie Place as 'the best introduction we yet have . . . to all the logical studies'.[58] It was an attempt at an historical study of language, but that was not its chief importance. 'Tooke held', remarks Stephen, 'and surely with reason, that an investigation of language, the great instrument of thought, may help to throw light upon the process of thinking.'[59] In fact, such an enquiry did more than this, for it turned the direction of philosophy from the psychology of thought to a more truly philosophical problem—what are the objects of thought. This is a natural result of approaching the problem by an analysis of the meaning of words, and this approach had its effect on Mill. His own doctrine of abstraction, for instance, echoes Tooke's comment: 'Abstract words are generally participles without a substantive and therefore in construction used as substantives.'[60] And Tooke also asserted that 'Language had the role of economy'—a thesis taken over direct by Mill.

Much more significant than Tooke's particular theories, however, was his general approach, and the fact that Bentham became exceedingly interested in problems of language, in

[57] Bain, op. cit., p. 55.
[58] B.M. Add. MSS. 35152, Mill to Place, September 1815.
[59] Stephen, op. cit., i, p. 138.
[60] Ibid., i, pp. 139–40, quoting Tooke, *Diversions of Purley*, ii, p. 18.

---

one's mind in every part of the field of thought. This I shall be going on, doing, doing—but how long it will take to the being done will depend upon many circumstances.' This probably refers to the *Essay on Education*, since a year later he writes to Place: 'If I had time to write a book I would make the human mind as plain as the road from Charing Cross to St Paul's.' There is no evidence for several years of his contemplating such a book. Next, we may observe that Locke is recommended to Annie Place as 'a sort of fundamental book' (September 1815) and to Ricardo (1817). Meantime, Mill proclaims in the *Philanthropist*: 'All men are governed by motives, and motives arise out of interests.' (Bain, p. 144.) He asserted the same view vigorously to Ricardo in two letters (August and October 1815, Sraffa, op. cit., vi, nos. 109 and 134) adding: 'you quarrel with my opinions . . . I arrived at them slowly and unwillingly myself; and so will you. They resulted spontaneously, and without my seeking them, from the studies in which I engaged.' All this supports the view that he adopted psychological hedonism for political reasons, and his mental philosophy followed, but did not precede this belief, the transition from Reid and Stewart to Hartley and Locke being a relatively small one.

6

1814, when he and Mill first came to Ford Abbey. There is little or no direct evidence that Bentham influenced Mill with his linguistic theories, but there are some significant facts. The first is the date—1814—which, as we have seen, marks the beginning of Mill's serious study of mental philosophy. Bentham's work on linguistics has been collected and edited by Mr C. K. Ogden, under the title *Bentham's Theory of Fictions*. Ogden gives 1812 as the earliest possible date for Bentham's work on language, and the first manuscript is dated 7, 8, and 9 August 1814—the time when Bentham and Mill first came to Ford Abbey, very possibly without other company.[61] Second, this is the time of the project for the Chrestomathic school on which, according to Mill, 'Bentham became hot on the subject'. The long appendix to *Chrestomathia* on the logic of Nomenclature and Classification is an essential part of Bentham's language theory and forms Part II of Ogden's edition. We know that Mill and Place assisted Bentham in this, and that, during this time, Mill acted as Bentham's amanuensis.[62] We know, too, that a regular part of life at Ford Abbey consisted of spending an hour or two each day talking with, or more probably listening to, Bentham.[63] Bain comments that, although both Mill and Bentham were working out treatises on Education, 'it is very curious to remark how few signs of action or reaction between the two minds their respective products bring to light . . .' Although Mill had 'largely meditated in the same fields . . . he could have been little more than

---

[61] Cf. Mill to Ricardo, 28 August 1814, giving an account of his arrival at Ford Abbey with Bentham. The letter suggests that no-one other than Mill's son was present, though more joined them later—'of our party', whatever that phrase might mean. (Sraffa, op. cit., vi, no. 57.) A month later Mill writes: 'The duration of my stay here does not altogether depend upon myself. I hold myself engaged to remain with Bentham, who will soon have no-body with him except myself and appendages and who would not stay a day alone as long as he finds it agreeable to remain.' (Mill to Ricardo, 30 September 1814, ibid., vi, no. 11.) Two years later we find a reference to Koe 'upon whom I counted to relieve myself here'. (Mill to Ricardo, 6 October 1816, ibid., vii, no. 180.)

[62] Mill and Place assisted in preparing *Chrestomathia* for the press. Mill edited the *Table of the Springs of Action*, 1817, and made many alterations of his own (Bain, op. cit., p. 163). The 'Instructions to Thomas Hodgskin on his Travels' is in Mill's handwriting, but the language is possibly Bentham's. (B.M. Add. MSS. 35153, undated, but apparently early, between January and May, in 1817.)

[63] Cf. Wallas, *Life of Francis Place*, pp. 75–7, quoting Place to Mrs Place, 7 August 1817.

an approving listener in all these numerous conversations.'[64] The two books were of a different type: Mill developed a philosophy of education, while Bentham produced a detailed plan. But if we look at the connexions between linguistic theory and Mill's philosophy there are some points where the influence of Bentham appears.

Bentham's basic starting point was the same as Mill's: that language must be tested by reference to experience in order to find out whether it refers to 'real entities' or to fictitious ones. But Bentham's interest was 'technological' to use C. K. Ogden's term, whilst Mill's was philosophical. And Bentham was a far more acute student of language than Mill: we cannot imagine Bentham, for instance, offering the naïve analysis of the verb 'to be' which Mill put forward: indeed, Bentham's position was that we postulated existence by using substantives 'in the same manner as names of substances are employed: hence the character in which they present themselves is that of so many names of substances. But these names of fictitious entities do not . . . raise up in the mind any correspondent images.'[65] This is surely a better explanation than Mill's of how we come to ascribe the attributes of a substance or real entity to something which does not exist, and is but a creature of the mind. It is not the verb 'to be' which misleads, it is the use of a noun, with or without this or any other verb.

Bentham and Mill give the same account of universals and of abstraction—thus Bentham writes: 'No portion of matter ever presents itself to *sense* without presenting at one and the same time a multitude of simple ideas, of all of which taken together the *concrete* one, in a state more or less complete, is composed.' Bentham is here using the word 'concrete' to refer to universals: he is distinguishing it from his fictions, which are nouns which cannot be shewn to be derived from concrete particular experiences—they are in fact adjectives turned into nouns, such as quality, quantity, length, and so on—and we cannot use any of these without referring to *something* which has quantity, quality, or length—they are, properly understood, adjectives. But in his account of universals, Bentham is in full agreement with Mill—

[64] Bain, op. cit., pp. 143–4.
[65] Ogden, *Bentham's Theory of Fictions*, Routledge & Kegan Paul, 1951, p. xxxvi.

and he adds 'the activity of detaching any one or more of the sensations from the rest is the process of abstraction'.[66] This is precisely the same as Mill's account, but Bentham carries it further when he describes the quality of 'redness', if so abstracted, as a fiction, since it can have no meaning or referent to experience apart from the noun it qualifies.

There are one or two passages in Mill's writings which are distinctly reminiscent of Bentham. In the *Analysis* he gives as examples the phrases 'thunder roars, and lightning flashes', and points out that the only sensations are the sound of roaring and the sight of the flash. 'The noise here is the only sensation; but in order to distinguish it from all other noises, I invent a name for its unknown cause, and by its means can mark the sensation with perfect precision.

'The Fictions, after this manner resorted to, for the purpose of marking; though important among the artifices of naming; have contributed largely to the misdirection of thought.

'By the unfortunate ambiguity of the Copula (verb), existence is affirmed of them in every Predication into which they enter. The idea of Existence becomes, by this means, inseparable from them; and their true nature as Creatures of the mind, and nothing more, is rarely and not without difficulty, perceived.'[67]

Here the approach is Bentham's and so is the language. But whereas Bentham would have classed the noun as a fiction, Mill ascribes the confusion to the verb 'to be'. This is certainly a linguistic approach to the problem, but not a very profound one. But it is to be noted that Mill follows Bentham in agreeing that fictions are 'important among the artifices of naming', i.e. technologically useful in communication.

The essential difference between Bentham and Mill is that Bentham was interested in language as a means of communication, and Mill was interested in the philosophical truths, if any, which lay behind the language. Bentham's test therefore was 'what was efficient in communication'. It is strictly irrelevant to this question whether what one communicates is nonsense, so long as one communicates what one means. And Bentham, at

---

[66] Ibid., pp. lv–lvi.
[67] *Analysis*, op. cit., i, p. 186.

the end of his life, marked the different road which he had trodden by an entry in his Memorandum Book (1831):

'Wherever there is a word, there is a thing; so says the common notion—the result of the association of ideas.

'Wherever there is a word, there is a thing; hence the almost universal practice of confounding *fictitious* entities with *real* ones—corresponding names of fictitious entities with *real* ones. Hence, common law, mind, soul, virtue, vice.

'Identity of nomenclature is certificate of identity of nature; diversity of diversity: how absurd, how inconsistent, to make the certificate a false one.'[68] Here the significant thing is Bentham's condemnation of association as responsible for the fallacy that words have a fixed meaning. We have seen how Mill would agree that words have a variable referent, but also how he often slips into the assumption that they have a fixed meaning. This is perhaps because he had only partly understood Bentham—thus in an article in 1815 he says: 'The only *real* truths we are acquainted with are particular truths. General truths are merely fictions of the human mind, contrived to assist us in remembering. According to Mr Stewart's chapter on abstraction, it therefore appears, that matter and mind belong to the class of fictions.'[69] The language here is the language of Bentham, but the class of fictions is extended to include universals, although the two examples given—matter and mind—are two which Bentham would have classed as fictions. Mill took as his test the ultimate experience of particulars—everything else was therefore in greater or less degree a 'creature of the mind'. But Bentham, interested in communication, was aware that none could take place in terms of particulars, and his distinction was therefore based on nouns which were genuine universals and those which were not. Mill was interested in reality, and in making language an accurate reflection of it: thus, in education, he speaks of the importance of making associations follow the order in which things really exist in nature. Thus, too, we have the impression that he sought a language which would accurately reflect reality: no doubt this explains his admiration of the classical languages. But

[68] Ogden, op. cit., p. lxvii.
[69] Halévy, op. cit., p. 450.

Bentham ridiculed them as making a 'dwelling place of a scaffolding instead of employing it in the erection of a building'.[70] Mill was undoubtedly influenced by Bentham—the linguistic form of the *Analysis* is sufficient evidence of that. Equally undoubtedly, he was too embedded in the empirical tradition to follow him more than a little of the way—he used a theory of language to support this tradition, not to found a new one. If, eventually, as we have seen, the emphasis of the *Analysis* is linguistic, then it is due to Bentham. It is also the reason why the *Analysis* subtly shifts in emphasis from psychological problems to those proper to the theory of knowledge.

A third influence on Mill explains perhaps why he did not follow Bentham more wholeheartedly, and why, therefore, he made no really new contribution to philosophy of the mind. This influence was that of natural science. J. S. Mill, to whom the talks on which the book was based were originally given, leaves us in no doubt of this factor in his editorial introduction to the *Analysis*. He writes that the object of natural science is 'to diminish as much as possible the catalogue of ultimate truths'. It proceeds by 'the resolution of phenomena which are special and complex into others more general and simple . . . Two cases . . . may be roughly distinguished . . . In one case it is the order of the phenomena which is analysed and simplified; in the other it is the phenomena themselves.' The first leads to 'a law of causation pervading all Nature', and the second to the discovery that 'the very fact which we are studying is made up of simpler facts: as when the substance water is found to be an actual compound of two other bodies, hydrogen and oxygen, substances very unlike itself, but both actually present in every one of its particles.' This process is known as 'chemical analysis' but the first kind of enquiry 'of which the Newtonian generalisation is the most perfect type, is no less analytical. The difference is, that, the one analyses the substances into simpler substances; the other, laws into simpler laws.' It was the great achievement of James Mill to apply both kinds of enquiry to the phenomena of the human mind by using the two great principles of successive and synchronous association. Mill's *Analysis* is 'an attempt to reach the simplest elements which by their combination

[70] Ogden, p. xciii.

generate the manifold complexity of our mental states, and to assign the laws of those elements, and the elementary laws of their combination, from which laws, the subordinate ones which govern the compound states are consequences and corollaries.

'The conception of the problem did not, of course, originate with the author; he merely applied to mental science the idea of scientific enquiry which had been matured by the successful pursuit, for many generations, of the knowledge of external nature.'[71]

We are so accustomed to thinking of Mill as a philosopher and political theorist, that we pay little attention to science, as a factor in his own education, and in that which he prescribed for his son. Mill himself studied Natural Philosophy at Edinburgh and also, it seems probable, attended lectures on Chemistry and Anatomy in the Medical course. Mill was also a member of a select 'Literary Society' at Edinburgh: the other five members were James Thompson, Thomas Thomson (the celebrated chemist, and a life-long friend of Mill), John Barclay (anatomist), James Carter and Dr Miller (both medical men).[72] With John Stuart Mill, we note that Chemistry was something on which his father particularly desired him to be informed—thus his arrangement for John to hear the lectures by 'really clever' Professors from Oxford and Cambridge at the 'College' at Bagshot in 1818.[73] The witnessing of chemical experiments was another part of the same course to which James Mill attached importance. John Stuart Mill's own comment on his interest in science is significant: 'One of my greatest amusements was experimental science; in the theoretical, however, not the practical sense of the word ... merely reading about them. I never remember being so wrapt up in any book, as I was in Joyce's Scientific Dialogues; and *I was rather recalcitrant to my father's criticisms of the bad reasoning respecting the first principles*

---

[71] Bain, op. cit., p. 17—Bain says he 'cannot account for John Mill's supposition that he may have studied in the Medical classes' although he agrees they drew students from all parts. But James Mill, in his own account of his education at Edinburgh, wrote: 'It is becoming more and more a practice for the general students to attend the lectures in the medical course, in particular chemistry and anatomy.' (Bentham MSS., University College London, Box 165, Folder 1.)

[72] Ibid., op. cit., p. 28.

[73] Sraffa, op. cit., vii, no. 278, 26 October 1818.

of physics, which abounds in the early part of that work. I devoured treatises on Chemistry, especially that of my father's early friend and schoolfellow, Dr. Thomson, for years before I attended a lecture or saw an experiment.'[74] [My italics.] This interest could hardly have sprung up without parental encouragement, and James Mill's ability and willingness to criticise the logic of physics is interesting.

The effect of the scientific manner of thinking on Mill's philosophy is easy to discern. Association, as a principle, is unnecessary to the empiricist philosophy, as Locke had shewn, and as modern British philosophers also demonstrate. We can hold that the only true knowledge is that which can be referred to sense-experience without all the apparatus of the association principle. Indeed, in some ways this principle, if applied as widely as Mill applies it, means that sense-experience as such is not true knowledge: it only becomes reality when viewed through the spectacles of the laws of association. But the whole idea of 'laws of thought' and the attempt to reduce them to two 'orders' of association is very typical of scientific thinking, as also is the 'method of analysis' which goes with it. Association also did violence to Mill's thinking about language: it diverted him from considering the actual referents of words, and so diverted him from the problem of meaning and the real problems in theory of knowledge to what is strictly a problem in psychology. For, if association is true, its truth is a matter of psychological enquiry and evidence, as we shall see in the next chapter. The real dichotomy is one to which Bradley pointed later: between psychology and association on the one hand, and linguistic analysis and the problem of meaning on the other, that is, between psychology and logic. Mill's account marks some hesitant steps in the right direction, when he follows Bentham on language, but he is held back first by the empirical tradition, and second by the pseudo-science of the laws of association.

We may now turn to the last problem of this chapter—what are the educational implications of this doctrine, considered as a theory of knowledge?

[74] J. S. Mill, *Autobiography,* pp. 14–15.

A theory of knowledge must cover and explain all forms of knowledge which the philosopher recognizes as knowledge. With this qualifying clause we see the major problem which faces the philosopher: what forms of knowledge is he to recognize as genuine, and what must he attempt to shew to be fictitious. Broadly speaking, philosophers have followed one of two paths. Some have been tolerant and have taken as their data any existing body of knowledge in which serious study has occurred and which has commanded the attention and respect of scholarly minds. Such philosophers have started, that is to say, on the assumption that any well-established field of study was genuine, and that it was their task to fit their philosophical theories to it, rather than to explain it away as nonsense because it did not suit some preconceived philosophical straitjacket. Those who start from such a basis are no less critical than the rest, but, naturally enough, the theory of knowledge resulting is a house of many mansions, with more than one 'way of knowing' or 'mode of experience'. Alternatively, philosophers may feel strongly that one form of knowledge only has established its right to be regarded as knowledge. They are therefore constrained either to shew that apparently different forms of knowledge are really the one true type, or to demonstrate that apparently different forms of knowledge are not really knowledge at all. Mill's theory was essentially of this second type.

The example of historical knowledge will illuminate this point. Since historical knowledge is of the past, it is not observable, and cannot therefore be reduced to sense-experience. Since it is normally confined to events beyond living memory, it cannot be explained by a theory of memory. Since it deals with particular events at particular times and places it cannot be regarded as similar to the laws of logic or mathematics. Hence it constitutes a problem for the philosopher, and philosophers have, in fact, either (a) regarded it as a separate 'mode of experience', unique in itself, unlike any other form of knowledge, as did the Idealists such as Bradley, Collingwood, and Oakeshott; or (b) argued that its preoccupation with particular events masked its real dependence on general laws, like science, as did the nineteenth-century positivists; or (c) produced a

6*

theory like Mill's, which, though he did not realize it, ruled out history as a form of knowledge altogether.[75]

The educational implications of these two types of philosophical approach to the problem of knowledge naturally differ. Philosophers who admit varied ways of knowing are naturally committed to a varied curriculum. For the curriculum, whether at school or university, is essentially an introduction to knowledge, and if there are varied fields of knowledge, the curriculum must afford varied paths of entry and progress. Such philosophers are necessarily involved in the problem of the balance of the curriculum, and in value-judgments as to the importance of different forms of knowledge. With philosophers of the second type these problems do not necessarily arise. Such philosophers may, indeed, hold that the learner should be trained in the apparently different forms of knowledge in order subsequently to appreciate that they are all one, though this is more a psychological than a philosophical application of the theory, since it deals more with the process of learning than with the object of knowledge. But such philosophers can equally hold, and with more consistency, that if all knowledge can be reduced to one type, then the best curriculum is the one which concentrates most strongly on the clearest example of true knowledge. Thus, if we held that all knowledge was scientific, there would be much to be said for a heavy concentration on whatever branch of natural science shewed most clearly to the learner the essential characteristics of scientific knowledge—the prototype of all knowledge. Such a theory would, indeed, involve some notion of transfer of training, so that the prototype could be seen to work in apparently different fields of knowledge. But, none the less, the essential conception of the curriculum would be as one basic training in thought and knowledge, common to everything, with various applications of it. No problem of 'balance' would arise.

Mill's theory was of the second type in that it reduced all knowledge to one form, and it has therefore two immediate implications. First, it would logically remove from the curriculum some forms of knowledge, or of apparent knowledge, which the theory cannot accommodate. Second, it may be expected to favour one *pro-forma* type of knowledge as the most representative form of true knowledge to which all else can be reduced. But after this problems begin, for, as we have seen, Mill's theory contains three strands, not altogether consistent with each other, and it is not quite clear which he thought was the most important. These three strands are, first, the reduction of all knowledge to sense-experience, second, the use of scientific analysis and synthesis of sense-experience, and third, the method of linguistic analysis.

A theory of knowledge which reduced all to sense-experience would imply a curriculum which gave the widest possible direct sense-experience to the learner. He would learn direct from reality, as it were, and would be spared the confusions and myths of language which inevitably result from book-learning. 'Book-learning' would be distrusted as unreal: indeed, we would expect such a curriculum to follow much the same lines as that advocated by Pragmatists today, with their emphasis on concrete experience and their view that book-learning is academic and unreal. Such a curriculum might also be expected to stress natural science both as a field of study where observation and experiment play so large a part, and as an explanation of the natural world we experience through our senses.

A theory of knowledge which placed its main stress on the *methods* of natural science would, however, differ from this. For the important thing would not be simply sense-experience as the one true form of knowledge, but sense-experience viewed in a particular way. Thus the real emphasis in such a curriculum would necessarily be on scientific methods of thinking, as a necessary preliminary to direct sense-experience. Such methods of thinking would be first those directly associated with natural science, and secondly, a more general abstraction of them, such as the technique of analysis, classification and establishing universal laws, which would be applied to other fields, such as the human mind. The stress in such a curriculum would not be on knowledge but on a technique of thinking: it would inevitably involve, in psychology, a theory of transfer of training. But it would not favour direct sense-experience except as a means to an end, and then only after the necessary theoretical training had been given. It would not therefore despise 'book-learning' or abstractions at an early stage; indeed, it would need them.

A curriculum which regarded an understanding of the nature of language and Logic as the main element in intellectual education would also have little use for direct sense-experience, save perhaps in the very early stages. But it would necessarily involve much 'book-learning', and, almost inevitably, considerable stress on the learning of a foreign language, either ancient or modern, since it is difficult to reflect about the nature of language if one never gets out of one's native tongue. It would also involve a varied curriculum of other subjects, since, like the second type of curriculum, an important part of its educational value would be the *application* of the principles of Logic to other fields of thought. Since it would involve a varied curriculum, there is the possibility of the problem of balance arising, though in a different form. Where the faculty psychologists of the later nineteenth century wanted balance in order to train different faculties in due proportion, where others might want different 'ways of knowing' cultivated in due proportion, a curriculum based on either scientific method or Logic might want balance in demonstrating the application of the principle as effectively as possible. And someone like Mill might be expected to hold that, for moral reasons, some fields of thought—the political and social sciences, for instance—were more important than others, and that it was particularly important to demonstrate the application of Logic in those fields. But Logic would be the queen of the sciences and would dominate the curriculum as the key to all else. All other subjects would have to be taught with this end in view: hence, in this sense, there would be no question of balance in such a curriculum. Finally, a curriculum in which Logic was the centre-point would necessarily be a lengthy one, and would postulate either a much longer school life, and later age of leaving than was customary in Mill's day, or a much earlier start than most people would think possible.

We may now turn to Mill's practice in the matter of the curriculum and discover how far he was consistent with either of these views, and perhaps gain some indication as to which one he actually favoured. We have three main pieces of evidence: the curriculum prescribed for his own children, which was entirely of his own devising; that advised for Annie Place; and finally the outline of the course of lectures which he wrote for the students of the new university college in London.

John Stuart Mill's education commenced very early, with the study of Greek, and subsequently Latin; throughout the early stage there was a heavy bias on the classical languages. In the later stages there was science, but the bias was towards philosophy, culminating in Logic. The later stages included some economics and history. All Mill's children had to study 'the hated Latin', James Bentham Mill took in addition Greek, and later, at University College, Science, Logic and Philosophy. Annie Place was not advised to do Latin, possibly because she had not commenced it sufficiently early, but she was recommended to study Horne Tooke on Language. In the outline of courses in Logic, Moral Philosophy and History for University College, Mill remarks that education has two main branches— the one natural science, and the other the study of the human mind. This latter is divided into two parts: Logic—or the study of the problem of knowledge, and moral philosophy—the study of conduct. Both are 'the highest parts of a complete and finished education', and they come 'last in order among the subjects of tuition; and the pupils who enter the university for a complete course of education, will have attended two or three years before they reach the time at which the study of Logic and Moral Philosophy commences'. The same is true of History: it is 'a branch of study which also comes at rather a late period in a course of education; and for which in the University of London pupils during the first two years will mostly be in a course of preparation'. This subject will 'teach the mode of prosecuting the study of history, and of deriving from it the lessons it affords'. Much stress should be laid on 'the mode of drawing sound inferences' from historical facts.[76]

The salient points from all three sources are the inclusion of science, and the emphasis in one form or another on Logic. The first of these needs no elaboration, but the second has some

[76] James Mill, *Outline of a Course of Lectures*, bound with other lectures by Grote, etc., Goldsmiths Library, University of London, Senate House.

connexion with the emphasis on classical languages. Mill, we
know, valued Greek as an entry to Greek philosophy. But Latin
rested on another justification. It was thought, at the time, to
be the logically perfect language in that its forms, structure,
and grammar presented a truer picture of reality than did
other languages. Thus, for instance, it avoided the continuous
present tense, with the use of the verb 'to be' which Mill
thought so misleading. And, of course, it avoided the ambiguity
in the English 'should' and 'would'. In these various ways,
Latin was held not only to be a necessary preliminary to the
study and understanding of the English language, but also
likely to make people think more logically. Bentham certainly
did not accept this, but, as we have seen, some of Mill's thought
seems to be seeking an ideal language, rather than an efficient
means of communication. In this search, although we have no
direct evidence of it, it is probable that Latin was thought to
be, if not the solution, a study which would lead to it, and this
explains the emphasis on this subject in Mill's ideas of the
curriculum. It is to be seen as a preliminary step to the study
of Logic.

　　It is clear then that the sense-experience on which all is
based, and from which all originates, does not in fact bulk
large in Mill's theory of the curriculum. The crux of his theory
is Logic, the method of analysis and scientific method. He followed Bentham in regarding language as important: he parted
from him in thinking that a perfect language was possible, from
the point of view of the logician. But in so far as he followed
this path at all, he was accepting universals as an object of
knowledge, and following his own distinction between himself
and the Nominalists.[77] In this he marks an advance on the
empiricist tradition towards the later view which held that the
distinction between the object of thought—universals, and
psychic experience—particular impressions or images, was
vital. His views on history are clearly part of his political
philosophy and will require further examination: he makes it
in fact a social science from which the past may be interpreted
and the future foretold. And his moral philosophy would
naturally lead him to regard political and social science as

[77] See above, p. 135.

among the most important subjects of study and constituents of knowledge.

His curriculum in education rules out all subjects which he cannot fit into his theory of knowledge. English literature, art, music, and religion, have no place in it. This is consistent enough, as we have seen. But since the highest point is Logic and philosophy, Mill is committed to a lengthy curriculum, and one which would bring little value unless it was completed. If we have been right in our conjectures, Latin, to Mill, would be of little value, unless it culminated in a study of Logic. Most, if not all subjects in the curriculum were regarded as a preparation for this highest point in a full education. Thus, as we know, Mill was intent on starting academic education much earlier than most would think possible, and he regarded nineteen as the age at which it should terminate in the University of London. On the whole Mill's practice is consistent with his theory: for the importance of sense-experience, association, and the influence of environment on character, we have to look at his theory from a second point of view—that of the psychologist.

VI

Psychology

If Mill's theory is to claim to be the psychological basis of a theory of education then it must deal with two main problems, or at any rate suggest lines on which they should be approached. First, how do we learn in the intellectual sphere, and secondly, how do we learn in the moral sphere, that is how do we change our characters towards ideals of right conduct and becoming good people? Involved in these two main problems are two further ones: first, how is learning motivated, in either the intellectual or the moral sphere, and second, with what native endowment of intellectual ability, or traits of character does the child start?

We may start by considering the psychology of intellectual education. Mill's explanation is this. Learning consists in the first instance of sense-experience, and subsequently of forming the correct associations between different sense-experiences. We may associate old experiences with new, two or more similar experiences, or experiences regularly succeeding one another. In either case the process is fundamentally the same, and is one of association. All learning therefore depends upon first, what we experience through the senses, and second, upon the order of our experiences.

Prima facie, this theory has the following implications. First, no learning can take place without sense-experience, and all learning must be based on it. Second, the learning of abstractions, whether of number or of universals in language must proceed by learning first the concrete instances of the abstraction, for the concept comes only as a result of successive perceptions of particular examples of it. Third, the attention and interest which the learner displays are relatively unimportant: what counts is the experience itself. And perception is unselective

—whatever is exposed to view, so to speak, is indiscriminately absorbed by the percipient. In this sense, learning is a mechanical response to environment. Fourth, it must follow from this that learning, and, indeed, intelligence are the product of environment, for, if they were not, then we should have to explain the mind's contribution to the process of perception, and this would involve some doctrine of selective perception. But the theory says differently: if, for instance, 'intelligence' is defined as the power of conceptual thinking, or of seeing relations between ideas and sensations, then Mill's theory asserts that any concepts can only come from successive experiences of the concrete, and that relations such as causation are to be explained in the same way, as passive reception of sensations in antecedent and consequent order. Finally, it follows from all this that, for effective learning, the whole environment must be controlled since any part of it will affect the learner equally, and it is quite wrong to assume that he will give special attention to one part of it, for example, school.

So far the theory is a theory of a passive mind absorbing without discrimination the environment about it. It is, in short, a mechanistic theory. But Mill adds to this a doctrine of motive which makes an important change in that, once the idea of motive is introduced, so is the idea that the individual may pay more attention to some things than to others, may select from the environment certain things and ignore others, and so on. We cannot, that is to say, retain the mechanical form of the association theory, or the conception of the mind as the purely passive receptacle of environmental influences, once we introduce notions of motive. If, for instance, people liked all red articles, then they would tend to seek them, and certainly to notice them, more than things which were not red. The explanation of their behaviour would be in terms of a motive—they liked red things. But the effect of such a theory is selective perception of and influence by the environment, and a major modification in the mechanistic form of the associationist theory.

Mill's doctrine of motive is a simple one: two things determine what we attend to—Custom, and Pain and Pleasure. The first means that, in a fully controlled environment, we could see that the child experienced frequently and 'customarily' what we wanted him to experience. Custom, in fact, is not really a doctrine of motivation at all, for it is merely repetition of experience, on the assumption that every experience will 'count for one and none for more than one', and that the attention brought to each will be equal. The second is another matter. Other things being equal, says Mill, we pay attention to and seek those experiences and associations which bring us pleasure, and avoid those which bring pain. To Mill, 'pain' and 'pleasure' are generic terms which cover all kinds of pleasure and pain. He regarded them both as equally effective motives, that is, he held that no greater effort would be made by the pupil from the prospect of pleasure than would come from the prospect of avoiding an equivalent amount of pain.

The Association theory as such, without the addition of a doctrine of motive, seems more readily applicable to some forms of learning than to others. Habitual skills such as riding a bicycle seem to be formed by associating one movement with another until the whole operation appears to be mechanical and 'instinctive'. Learning by rote is another example. In memorizing dates and events in history we normally use associationist techniques: as a consequence we can recall the dates much more readily if we are prompted by the name of the event than if we are not. It is an example of recognition rather than recall, and it might be said that association as a psychological doctrine is a generally accepted explanation of recognition.

On the other hand, some of the higher branches of learning— 'meaningful' learning—do not seem to fit the theory so readily, for, if it can be shewn that the pupil learns more readily and more efficiently if he first perceives the meaning of what he has to learn, then an element is introduced into the learning process which the associationist theory explicitly leaves out—namely, the organizing and comprehending powers of the learner. Thus, if, in memorizing a poem, it can be shewn, as some tests have shewn, that more effective learning results when the pupil first reads and understands the *whole* poem, than when he learns it blindly line by line, then we have something more than association taking place. And if we consider various kinds of problem-solving, such as riders in geometry, the accent upon the pupil's powers of understanding the problem before attempting its solution is still more marked.

This involves a more general problem: do we, in perception, see the whole before the parts, or do we see various components and add them together to make a whole. In one sense of the term Mill would say that we do see the whole before the parts: our sensation of a rose appears to be a single simple sensation, and it is only after analysis that it is found to be complex and made up of distinguishable parts. But do we perceive a garden by perceiving one flower, one shrub, and so on after another, and adding them up in our minds to make a garden? Mill would say yes, for the validity of his analysis of apparently simple sensations into their component parts depends upon the thesis that is actually what happens—that we actually experience separate sensations, although we are only aware of it on reflection. The crucial point here is what is *real* sense-experience. If it is the whole sensation as common sense would have us believe, then analysis into component parts or atoms is the introduction of an extra-sensory technique to produce something which is not in fact experienced, but which may be called a series of concepts of what makes up experience. But if the atomic parts are the only true experience then the analysis reveals the psychic fact of which we are not aware: although we think we perceive the whole before the parts, in fact it is the other way about, and it is the whole which is a concept drawn from sense-experience of its component parts.

In another way, too, Mill is compelled to insist that the whole is made up of separate perceptions of the parts. If he took the opposite view, then he must explain why, and the only explanation is that the mind brings to its perception some organizing ability, and is not, as Mill's theory appears to imply, the mere passive recipient of anything that is going on before it. If the mind directs and organizes perception in some way, then, and then only, can we talk of any form of selective perception from total available sense-data. And seeing the whole before the parts is essentially selective perception. The same principle is involved in learning. Do we group material in order to learn it? Is learning more effective this way? If so, we must bring selective and organizing powers to our learning. Mill cannot, so it would appear, admit this and to him learning must therefore consist of a painstaking mastery of each step with an understanding of the whole following, not preceding, knowledge of the parts.

This is the essence of all later criticisms from psychologists of Mill's position. They may be summed up as challenging the doctrine that we ever perceive all there is to be seen, as it is to be seen. Hence, the critics assert that we bring from our own minds something to our perceptions, and that what we actually see is not sense-data as it was later called, but a fusion between the perceiving mind and the sense-data, and the latter, as a constituent of actual perception, was always less than the total sense-data available to our senses. The critics took a parallel view with regard to learning: we bring 'insight' to our learning, especially to our learning how to solve problems. And in any case, our success in learning depends very much on factors of attention and interest, so that the same experience may not have the same effect on the same pupils at the same time. In both spheres, the assumption is that we perceive the whole before the parts, for the grasp of the meaning of sense-data, or of a problem, precedes the perception of the first and the solution of the second. We see a garden and subsequently the flowers which make it up. But we only see the garden by grouping in our minds the sense-data presented to us. We select, and we organize, and we see what is familiar, and what has meaning. With problem-solving, we proceed not by regular progress as if our response was mechanical, but, after many false starts by sudden success, and this success dates from the point at which we have insight into the problem. All this is backed by a good deal of experimental evidence, and the crux of the argument is the assertion that perception is selective, that learning proceeds by insight, and therefore that the mind brings something to experience. The same critics dealing with Memory, naturally stressed the point that the remembered image never precisely coincided with the original sensation: memory, like perception, was a fusion between the remembering mind and the thing remembered.

These criticisms have been made over a long period, ranging from Mill's original doctrine to modern debates on the subject, and some of the criticisms refer more to the modern debate than to Mill's doctrine. During this period, psychology has become separated from philosophy as a distinct field of study, with its own problems and techniques of study, particularly experimental techniques. Some of the problems studied by Mill are no longer considered relevant to psychology.

On the other hand, it is perhaps worth noting that some modern associationists have shewn, by a series of experiments, that their theory can accommodate selective perception in terms of the influence of earlier associations upon later. And in the same way they could claim to explain 'meaningful' learning, namely, that when a pupil sees the meaning of new material he is associating it with his previous experience.[1] All this would appear to substantiate their hypothesis that the powers of the mind, on which the Gestalt theorists lay so much stress, are themselves the result of previous learning, and can be explained by the associationist hypothesis.[1] It is through these existing associations, the result of previous experience or learning, that new sense-experience is selectively perceived, and it is through similar associations that we learn new material.

But there is no evidence that Mill thought this. On the contrary, an example he gives in his *Analysis* shews him as the apostle of mechanical step-by-step learning, and therefore typical of what is normally held to be the associationism of his day. Speaking of the process of memorizing the Lord's Prayer, he writes: 'In learning the passage, we repeat it; that is, we pronounce the words, in successive order, from the beginning to the end. The order of the sensations is successive. When we proceed to repeat the passage, the ideas of the words also rise in succession, the preceding always suggesting the succeeding, and no other. *Our* suggests *Father*, *Father* suggests *which*, *which* suggests *art*; and so on, to the end. How remarkably this is the case, anyone may convince himself, by trying to repeat backwards, even a passage with which he is as familiar as the Lord's Prayer. The case is the same with numbers. A man can go on with numbers in the progressive order, one, two, three, etc., scarcely thinking of his act; and though it is possible for him to repeat them backward, because he is accustomed to the

[1] D. O. Hebb, *The Organization of Behaviour*, Chapman & Hall, 1955. Cf. especially chapter 6.

subtraction of numbers, he cannot do so without an effort.'[2] The most noteworthy thing about this passage is the complete absence of any importance ascribed to meaning. We can say the Lord's Prayer forwards purely because we experienced it that way on many occasions, and not because, said forwards it has meaning, and said backwards it has none. With numbers the case is different: either backwards or forwards they may have meaning, and our facility in reciting them may be, as Mill says, purely a matter of habit, or frequency of experiencing the order of association. But what is true of the Lord's Prayer is presumably true of the memorizing of a poem, and it is certainly an astonishing thing to say that the fact that we can say it forwards and not backwards has nothing to do with the meaning of the words. Mill may indeed have regarded memorizing as a purely mechanical operation: if so, he would be challenged in this by all modern psychologists, whether associationist or not.

Does this mean that Mill regarded all learning as mechanical, or can his theory accommodate 'meaningful' learning? If so, it is necessary for him to ascribe some importance to early learning and its influence upon later. In one passage he appears to do so: 'To this [early family upbringing] the groundwork of the character of most individuals is almost wholly to be traced. The original features are fabricated here; not indeed, in such a manner as to be unsusceptible of alteration, but in such a manner, decidedly, as to present a good or bad subject for all future means of cultivation . . . It seems to be a law of human nature, that the first sensations experienced produce the greatest effects; more especially that the earliest repetitions of one sensation after another produce the deepest habit; the strongest propensity to pass immediately from the one to the idea of the other. Common language confirms this law, when it speaks of the susceptibility of the tender mind. On this depends the power of those associations which form some of the most interesting phenomena of the tender mind. From what other cause does it arise, that the hearing of a musical air, which, after a life of absence, recalls the parental mansion, produces as it were a revolution in the whole being? That the sympathies between brothers and sisters are what they are? On what other

2 *Analysis*, i, pp. 80-1.

cause originally is the love of the country founded?—that passionate attachment to the soil, the people, the manners, the words, the rivers, the hills, with which our infant eyes were familiar, which fed our youthful imaginations, and with the presence of which the pleasures of our early years were habitually conjoined!

'It is, then, a fact, that the early sequences to which we are accustomed form the primary habits; and that the primary habits are the fundamental character of the man. The consequence is most important; for it follows, that, as soon as the infant, or rather the embryo, begins to feel, the character begins to be formed; and that the habits, which are then contracted, are the most pervading and operative of all. Education, then, or the care of forming the habits, ought to commence, as much as possible, with the period of sensation itself; and, at no period, is its utmost vigilance of greater importance, than the first.'[3]

This passage from the *Essay* is a piece of observation rather than a constituent part of a psychological theory. It is a family man's comments on the facts as he sees them. As it stands it is concerned more with character training than with intellectual education: if the general association hypothesis be accepted, however, it would obviously apply to intellectual education. But there is no attempt to follow up these observations with their theoretical implications, and there is little or nothing in the *Analysis* which suggests that these observed facts were regarded as ones which had to be accommodated in Mill's general psychology. If they were to be so accommodated then some doctrine of the influence of earlier learning upon later would be required. This in turn implies the acceptance of the fact of selective perception, and also an explanation of the origins of this selectivity. For, if we say that selective perception is due to notions which the mind brings to perception, and then say that those notions are themselves due to earlier learning or perception, we are implying that those notions are sufficiently firmly fixed to dominate future perception, and this requires an explanation of their origins.

Now, in two ways, Mill's psychology *could* accommodate something of the theory required, although there is no evidence

[3] *Essay of Education*, op. cit., pp. 91–3.

that he ever perceived these implications of it, and it is therefore stretching the truth to ascribe to him anything like a conscious realization of the influence of earlier learning upon later, save in the terms of his casual educational observations. But, first, his doctrine of abstraction, classification and 'universals' is relevant to this problem, and, second, his frequent re-iteration that he was explaining the 'origins of mental phenomena' is significant.

As we have seen, Mill describes classification as the abstraction of the common features of particulars, and this is accounted for because the common features have, by association, a stronger attraction on our minds than the less frequently experienced uncommon ones. Now it could be argued that such a doctrine implied selective perception, that we do not see all there is to be seen, that we notice the familiar because of previous associations, and ignore the unfamiliar, that we distinguish figures from background and so on. But, although this is a possible argument, it is not Mill's brand of associationism. We must distinguish the actual process of perception from that of forming or strengthening associations. Mill's version of perception is a crude one: we see all there is to be seen, every part of the scene makes an equal impact on our senses. But the familiar objects strengthen the association. In short, familiarity, or frequency of experience, influences the association but not the perception. On the other hand it is certainly possible to argue, on a general basis of associationism that the associations influence subsequent perception, as well as the other way around. Hence selective perception, if accepted as a fact of experience as it is, is not fatal to associationism in general, but it is not part of Mill's particular form of associationism. Despite his comments on the importance of early upbringing, with the apparent implication that it will dominate future perception, his fully developed psychological theory makes no attempt to accommodate these points, and we cannot therefore credit him with acknowledging either the fact of selective perception, or an explanation of it in terms of the influence of earlier learning upon later.

In considering Mill's theory, it is worth noting first, what is involved in any explanation in terms of origins. It may be defined as an explanation which excludes contemporary or present factors. This is a wide definition, and it may exclude either the remote past only, or everything which is not present, in the strict sense of the term. If we speak of the origins of a tree, we may mean the seed from which it grew—this would be our normal meaning. If we speak of the origins of a house, we are referring to factors prior to the completed building of the house, and these factors may be yesterday, with a new house or a hundred years ago. But the essential point is that, if we exclude contemporary factors, as an explanation of something now before us, we do imply that it will not change, that is, that it is no longer subject to formative influences. If we do not mean this then an explanation in terms of origins is an incomplete explanation: in some respects it is incomplete with regard to a tree, for instance, in so far as it goes on growing, and is subject to influences of weather and climate and so on. Now, it is clear, that we are rarely as rigid in our thinking as this, when we speak of explaining something in terms of its origins, for we rarely completely exclude contemporary modifying factors. What we do imply, however, inevitably, when we speak of origins, is a formative period, to be distinguished from a subsequent period when formative influences have relatively little effect. During the formative period the object or phenomena we are explaining was being moulded or changed by various factors, and during the subsequent period, nonformative, it either ceases to change, or changes very little. How long the formative period is depends on how loosely we use the word 'origins', but, however it is used, the word necessarily postulates a subsequent non-formative period when little or no further change occurs. Thus, if we explain an adult's character in terms of the influences of early childhood, and maintain that that is a complete explanation, we are postulating a formative period, and also, what is so often overlooked, a subsequent non-formative period, when the character in question does not change.

Such an explanation therefore insists that past factors alone are determinate, that after a certain point present or future influences have no effect; if it did not, no account of past factors, however full, could be a complete explanation of present phenomena. When applied to human character, ability or personality, such an explanation implies that, after a certain point, environment ceases to influence man. It follows that education, and in the broadest sense, learning, ceases at this point. All this is a corollary of explaining something in terms of origins, if such an explanation is strictly adhered to. And if it is not, it still carries the implication that relatively little change occurs after the formative period, and therefore, that education and environment in general are relatively ineffective.

Now, Mill's use of the association principle is in part as an explanation of origins and derivations, and in part a doctrine of continuous change or learning—he makes the same principle serve both purposes. When he asserts that 'Custom' has great power over the associations, he is stating a doctrine not of origins but of continuous change, or at any rate potential continuous change. For, if custom is a determining factor then it follows that the more frequently two things are associated, the stronger will the association be, and, conversely, that if the custom is interrupted or broken, the association will be correspondingly weakened, and might be dissolved altogether. But Mill also speaks of 'firm assocations', meaning, apparently, indissoluble ones, and this implies that after a certain point such associations are permanently established for life, unaffected by future custom, and so on. Such associations could properly be explained in terms of origins.

The clearest example of such firm association is Mill's doctrine of the complex sensation and idea. The sensation and idea of a rose is analysed into its constituent parts of smell, shape, feel, colour, and so on, and it is therefore regarded as a complex idea and an example of association. Here, it might be argued, he is using the association principle backwards. As a matter of common experience we invariably have these experiences together, and it is only when we subject them to analysis that we become aware of the fact that they are not one single sensation but a complex of several sensations. But it might also be argued that we never experience these particular sensations except in association, and hence that experience is constantly renewing the strength of the association—custom unites, and custom preserves. But this is not so, for in fact each successive perception of a rose is an example of reduced cue perception. We see the shape and perhaps the colour, and *by association*, recall the other sensations. We do not constantly renew the whole complex of associations: we recall them by experience of one or two, and by associating the rest. Hence the association is a firm one: once formed it survives experience and is uninfluenced by it.

The same is true of Mill's explanation of certain abstract ideas such as extension and weight. They may be due in origin to sense-experience, but the essence of his thesis is that once formed they persist: what he has done is demonstrate the origins of something which is a permanent part of our mental experience. As I have pointed out, one cannot logically offer an explanation of anything in terms of its origins without assuming that it will no longer change. Hence in so far as Mill's explanation in terms of origins, of ideas such as extension and weight, is sound, he must assume that such ideas are not modified by future experience. He certainly shews no indication of accepting any such implication, but it is none the less a corollary of his thesis. And it may be argued that the explanation of universals in general involves the same assumptions. Is my general idea of a tree renewed by each experience of a new particular tree? Strictly speaking it is not, for what is renewed is the general idea, and not a series of particular experiences— that is to say, what is renewed is an abstraction from a particular experience, the result of selective perception, and that in turn rests upon the thesis of a previously formed firm association of trees in general. In short, as Bradley remarked, 'association marries only universals'.

So far we have examined the general theory of Association of Ideas as set forth by Mill, on the basis that it is, as its language suggests, and as many experts have alleged, a mechanical theory. Or to put the matter as Mill does, we have examined what the theory is if custom were the only source of the Associations. From this we have concluded that although the fact of selective perception can be accommodated by association theories, there is no evidence that Mill saw this problem. Further, a major point is whether there is a formative period when firm and life-long associations are formed which might govern what we perceive and learn subsequently. Mill's remarks on the importance of early family education and his explanation of various mental phenomena in terms of their origins both suggest that he believed in a formative period. But the mechanical form of the theory cannot accommodate this. If custom favours the association then custom is needed to renew it: without such constant renewal new associations would displace old ones: on the basis of custom, no early associations can dominate later ones.

The crux of the matter is that the term 'association' is a very wide and flexible one: it means a 'joining together' of two or more things, be they ideas, sensations, or entities in general. The term therefore signifies not only the joining, but the existence of the entities joined, that is, that they can be separated, identified and seen to exist by themselves. In this sense, any associationist theory is an atomic one, though different theories naturally differ as to what the entities are thus joined. This being so, an association theory can be used, as James Mill did use it, as a weapon of analysis, to show the atomic elements of which our apparently simple sensations are composed. To be a psychology of education it should also demonstrate how synthesis can occur and so far Mill has told us little. But the essential reason for this is that the term 'association' is, in itself, not an explanation but a description—namely of the fact that two or more things are joined. Until we know why they are joined, we have not explained the association. We have explored the first reason given by Mill for Association, namely Custom: it remains to turn to his second, Pain and Pleasure, and to examine what effect the addition of psychological hedonism has on the theory.

II

The problem of motive affects intellectual education as an incentive to learning, and it affects character training in the same way. It also involves stating Mill's view of human nature as it is, and as it has to be modified in order to comply with an ideal.

A motive may be defined as a reason for doing something—
e.g. we give from motives of charity to the poor, our motive is
pity, and it may be classified as unselfish. A motive may be the
one a person gives for doing something, or we may and often
do speak of his 'real motive', meaning usually something different—'ulterior' motives, for instance. The notion of motive is
thus related on the one hand to that of desire, and on the other
to that of purpose. Whereas we may often have desires which
don't lead to action, the term 'motive' is always used in connexion with action, generally retrospectively, in discussing past
actions. It is thus more akin to purpose than to desire.[4]

Now, Association Psychology has little affinity with either of
these notions. In its traditional form, explaining association in
terms of Recency, Frequency, and Contiguity, it had no place
for motive of any kind. When it has gone further, in modern
times, it has tended to think in terms of peripheral response to
stimulus, owing to its inherently atomic nature. It is impossible
to draw a rigid line in these matters, since modern associationists
have to account for more complicated behaviour than simple
responses,[5] but it is fair to say that the more one tends to explain
behaviour in terms of motive and purpose, the more is one
moving away from the natural structure of associationism,
towards explanations in terms of goal-seeking—explanations of
the type developed by the Gestalt theorists and their successors.
It is in the light of these preliminary observations that we must
examine Mill's thesis.

Mill's view on this subject is stated at length. In the *Essay* he
writes: 'The grand object of human desire is command over the
wills of other men. This may be attained, either by qualities and

[4] It should perhaps be noted that Mill distinguished motive from intention: the
latter embraced all the expected consequences of an action, whereas motive was the
desire for pleasure or relief from pain which prompted the action.

[5] Cf., for instance, more elaborate modern forms of stimulus response theory
in which the formula is S–O–R, i.e. stimulus–organism–response which can
accommodate some account of the organism and its particular state, as well as
the peripheral response. The main point is that the theoretical model imposed
on the facts by different psychological theories, affects the emphasis. Owing to its
atomic nature, associationism more readily explains simple actions than complicated ones, but that does not mean that it cannot accommodate the latter.
The essential point is that explanation in terms of motive and purpose more
naturally belongs to the field theorists. (Cf. Hilgard, *Theories of Learning*, especially
chapter I.)

acts which excite their love and admiration, or by those which excite their terror. When the education is so wisely conducted as to make the train run habitually from the conception of the good end to the conception of the good means; and as often, too, as the good means are conceived, viz. the useful and beneficial qualities, to make the train run on to the conception of the great reward, the command over the wills of men; an association is formed which impels the man through life to pursue the great object of desire, by fitting himself to be, and by actually becoming, the instrument of the greatest possible benefit to his fellow men.'[6] There is hardly a word in this description at which any field-theorist would cavil, except possibly the word 'association' to which he might be allergic. But the process described is a process of purpose, of associating means with ends, of goal-directed behaviour, where each action is seen as part of a larger whole, directed to a general purpose.

Further evidence of the way Mill looked at these problems is contained in the *Analysis*. He distinguishes between pleasurable and painful sensations in themselves and the causes of such sensations. By association, these causes 'are apt to become greater objects of concern to us, to rank higher in importance, than the sensations themselves. It is a vulgar observation, with respect to money, for example, that, though useful only for the purpose of obtaining pleasure, or saving from pain, it is often employed for neither purpose, but hugged as a good in itself.'[7] This passage is significant in two ways. As an analysis of human behaviour it focusses attention on remote objectives—Mill even talks of 'causes of causes of pleasurable sensations': this inevitably moves from the stimulus response framework to the goal-directed theory. Second, it emphasises the need to regard means as means only, and to assess them in relation to the purpose which they serve.

Later he writes: 'One important observation is to be made; that the remote causes of our Pains and Pleasures are apt to be objects, far more interesting, than those which are immediate. This at first sight appears paradoxical. It is the necessary result, however, of the general law of our nature.

[6] *Essay on Education*, op. cit., p. 100.
[7] *Analysis*, op. cit., ii, p. 188.

'The immediate causes of our pleasurable and painful sensations have never any very extensive operation. The idea of any
one is rarely associated with more than a limited number of
pains or pleasures. Food, for example, the cause of the pleasures
of eating; pleasures, perhaps, from the frequency with which
they are repeated, and the portion of life over which they are
spread, more valuable as a class, than any other which we
enjoy; has never appeared as object of sufficient interest, to
make the affection with which it is regarded be thought worthy
of a name. The idea of Food, though associated with pleasures
which constitute so important a class, is associated with the
pleasures of but one class; some of the remote causes are
associated with the pleasures of almost every class. Money, for
example, instrumental in procuring the causes of almost all our
pleasures, and removing the causes of a large proportion of our
pains, is associated with the ideas of most of the pleasurable
states of our nature. The idea of an object associated with
a hundred times as many pleasures as another, is of course a
hundred times more interesting.'[8] This passage is to be contrasted with the modern associationists' theory of motive.
Where the latter talks of stimulus and response in terms of an
individual action, Mill says that such limited pleasures are 'not
interesting' and by this he means 'not operative as motives to
action'. The modern associationist experiments with rats in a
maze: not food in general, but a particular piece of food at a
particular time is his motive, and the basis of his theory. Mill,
by contrast, insists that the really operative motives are much
more general, even though they are but the means to a thousand
particular pleasures.

A little further in the *Analysis,* he writes: 'As among the
remote causes of our pleasures and pains may be reckoned
everything which in any way contributes to them, it follows
that the number of such causes is exceedingly great. Of course
it is only the principal causes which have been attended to, and
classed under titles. They are mostly comprehended under the
following: Wealth, Power, Dignity, as regards the pleasurable
sensations; Poverty, Impotence, Contemptibility, as regards the
painful sensations.' 'The three, above named, grand causes of

8 Ibid., ii, pp. 206–7.

our pleasures . . . are the means of procuring for us the Services of our fellow-creatures, and themselves contribute to our pleasures in hardly any other way. It is obvious from this remark that the grand cause of all our pleasures are the service of our fellow-creatures.' Thus Mill returns to his assertion in the *Essay*, that the grand object of human desire is command over the wills of other men.

We can see from this how far removed Mill is from the modern associationist standpoint. Of any simple action, he would say that the operative motive to perform it was the desire which lay behind it, and that that desire would be for the cause of the pleasure, or for the cause of the cause of the pleasure. It would be in most cases focussed on general but remote objects—upon a distant goal or purpose towards which the particular action contributed as a means. These, according to Mill, are the motives which in fact move men to action. Thus although associationism has usually been taken to imply that each action should be viewed in isolation, and its motive explained in atomic terms, to Mill it means precisely the opposite. *Because* of association, no action is ever, in fact, isolated, it is always linked with long trains of ideas and sensations and it can only be explained, not in terms of itself, but in terms of the whole train with which it is linked. Mill's psychology, like his Ethics, is purposive and teleological, despite a terminology which suggests the opposite. To him, all behaviour, good or bad, was purposive. It may seek the grand objects of desire by beneficent means such as by earning the respect and good-will of other people. But it may seek the same object by the methods of the tyrant: his behaviour, too, is only to be explained in the light of its ultimate object. Threats, bribery and blackmail are his means, and if we ask why he adopts them, the explanation lies in terms of his purpose. All this underlines the point that, in his explanation of actual human behaviour, Mill never departed from the cynical psychological hedonism to which he was led, in part, by his observation of contemporary politics. It also suggests that here, as elsewhere in his psychology, it is important to distinguish in Mill's analysis between actual human behaviour and its origins.

It is clear that if moral education consists in forming new

associations with Wealth, Power, and Dignity, Mill is assuming a firm and fixed association between Wealth, Power and Dignity, and the particular pleasures on particular occasions which these general factors can bring. It follows that to explain them as operative motives in terms of previous associations is an explanation in terms of origins, and it further follows, and is indeed assumed by Mill, that, as motives, these general objects of desire will not be changed by subsequent environment or education. This is clearly demonstrated in his account of the moral sentiments, and it is worth quoting him fully on this. In answering Sir James Mackintosh he says: 'Sir James must mean, if he means anything, that to trace up the motive affections of human nature to pain and pleasure, is to make personal advantage the only motive. This is to affirm, that he who analyses any of the complicated phenomena of human nature, and points out the circumstances of their formation, puts an end to them.'[9] Certainly this contention of Mill's is true but it rests on the assumption that the 'phenomena' once formed, persist unchanged and uninfluenced by society and the way of life of the individual. He who 'points out the circumstances of their formation' is formulating an explanation in terms of origins, with all the implications of this form of explanation.

Mill continues: 'Gratitude remains gratitude, resentment remains resentment, generosity, generosity, in the mind of him who feels them, after analysis the same as before. The man who can trace them to their elements does not cease to feel them as much as the man who never thought about the matter. And whatever effects they produce, as motives, in the mind of the man who never thought about the matter, they produce equally, in the minds of those who have analysed them the most minutely.

'They are constituent parts of human nature. How we are actuated, when we feel them, is matter of experience, which everyone knows within himself. Their action is what it is, whether they are simple or compound. Does a complex motive cease to be a motive whenever it is discovered to be complex? The analysis of active principles leaves the nature of them unchanged. To be able to assert, that a philosopher who finds

[9] *Fragment of Mackintosh*, op. cit., p. 51.

7

some of the active principles of human nature to be compound, and traces them to their origin, does on that account exclude them from human nature, and deny their efficiency as constituent parts of that nature, discovers a total incapacity of thinking upon these subjects. When Newton discovered that a white ray of light is not simple but compound, did he for that reason exclude it from the denomination of light, and deny that it produces its effects, with respect to our perception, as if it were of the same nature as the elementary rays of which it is composed?'[10] It is hardly necessary to comment on the significance of Mill's use of the term 'constituent parts of human nature' as indicating that they were part of the permanent furniture in our minds. Nor need we comment on the analogy with Newton, which shews how much the methods of science influenced him. The vital point is that, whatever is true of the constituent elements of a ray of light, Mill's analysis of the constituent elements of human nature is necessarily an analysis in terms of past associations, and therefore an explanation in terms of origins.

He continues to criticize the same doctrine as applied to personal pleasure: 'The compound pleasures of human nature; curiosity, the being an object of esteem and affection, the feeling of esteem and affection, the sense of merit, and others too numerous to mention; are among the most valuable pleasures of human nature. We know them, by our inward experience of them, to be so. Are they less pleasures because they are compound? Does he who shews them to be compound do anything to lessen their value? or to prevent their being, as Sir James expresses it, "a most important part of that interest which reasonable beings pursue"? Is there a single syllable in Hobbes which implies that he did not set the same value on them, as all other men? To infer from his treating them, not as ultimate facts, but capable of being traced to a common source, that he did not allow them to be objects of rational esteem, is to the last degree contemptible.'[11]

This passage shews clearly the difficulty of Mill's position which we noted in an earlier chapter, in discussing his aims,

10 Ibid., pp. 51–2.
11 Ibid., pp. 52–3.

and this difficulty is fundamentally the one which we have been elaborating now—namely, that he assumed, as he states quite clearly here, that his analysis of the origin of human motives did not change them. Hence, if we want to know Mill's view of the actual psychology of human behaviour, his theory of the motives which in fact animate man, we shall not find it in terms of association for this explains only the origins of the motives and does not describe their nature now.[12] It has often been pointed out that to say that man was basically and irretrievably selfish and to postulate an altruistic moral ideal is inconsistent. We can now see that there is a further and more subtle inconsistency involved. Man's moral ideal is conceived in teleological terms: he must strive always for the general happiness, and his actions are right in so far as they contribute to this end. But his nature is explained in the atomic and mechanistic terms of association psychology, and this is a form of explanation which does not readily suit purposive explanation. Mill is not only talking of a selfish being acting unselfishly; he is talking two different languages. The gap is bridged by saying that, by original association, man rapidly comes to seek not the objects which actually bring him pleasure, but more general purposes such as possession of money which he associates with many pleasures. Thus man's selfishness is also conceived in teleological terms, and, the transition having been made, the psychology of moral behaviour is more readily accommodated. As an explanation of the origins of human motives, Mill's theory is atomic and mechanistic. As a statement of the psychology of human behaviour, and how man may improve it, the theory is neither atomic nor mechanistic it is purposive, and moral education requires the substitution of one purpose for the other.

This point is underlined if we turn for a moment to Mill's moral theory. Association psychology in principle seems to us today to involve a notion of character-training which is mainly a matter of acquiring habits. This at least fits most readily its

12 Strictly speaking the term 'association' by itself does not explain anything: it only describes, and the explanation is to be found in what causes association. In this case Mill is describing a process in early childhood, and not describing its result—adult human nature.

doctrine of learning in this sphere. As far as habit was concerned, Mill would certainly have agreed that it was a matter of
association. But this was not his main theme. He was concerned
to connect by custom and frequent recurrence certain trains of
thought with sensations regularly experienced, rather than
habitual or unconscious action. He did not think of courtesy at
the table as habitual action. He argued that since eating was
one of those things we most regularly did, it was a very useful
sensation with which to connect beneficent trains of ideas, since
the association would be strengthened and renewed by constant recurrence. But it should not produce habitual courtesy
and consideration for others—that is, unconscious, or as it is
loosely described, 'instinctive' good manners. On the contrary,
it should produce a careful consideration of our actions in the
light of the general happiness, or in Mill's language, eating
should be associated 'with the trains which lead most surely to
the happiness, first of the individual himself, and next of his
fellow-creatures'. Habitual action is in fact a bad thing in
general to Mill, for it is action without calculation, and that, to
his eyes, is immoral.

   In fact, habitual action, or any stress on the development of
good habits as part of moral education, is quite alien to his
moral theory. For, if moral education is mainly a matter of
habit, it must be a moral training in terms of principles rather
than of ideals, of obedience to moral rules rather than of fidelity
to moral ends. Habitual conduct consists in identifying successive situations as identical in certain respects and of acting
accordingly. For instance, we may identify in the action of
lying to a patient suffering from an incurable disease, simply
the point that it is deceit, notwithstanding all the beneficial
consequences which may follow from the action. Once we thus
identify it, we act habitually, automatically, by association with
the rule with which the action is identified. And it is a corollary
of any moral theory based on principles or moral rules that we
should so act and, in particular, that to us the consequences of
particular moral actions are irrelevant. It may be maintained
that promises should be kept, though the heavens fall. This has
been defended by many philosophers, and there is much more
to be said for it than is said here. But such a doctrine is entirely

alien to the doctrine of James Mill. To him, no action was right unless it led to the greatest general happiness. This implies that all actions are theoretically subject to review, that all actions should be based on calculation. Lying may generally lead to bad consequences, and a habit of not lying may be generally good. But, to a utilitarian, to identify an action as lying is not the end but the beginning of the problem of resolving its moral nature. The evil consequences of the deceit have to be balanced against all the other consequences of the action which may be, on balance, good. All action, in a perfect world, would be an individual calculation—'to act without calculation is the property of an irrational nature'[13] and is immoral, according to Mill. Moral rules are only rough guides to right conduct: when calculation of good or bad results requires it, such rules must be disregarded. That being so habitual action can only be a makeshift, a rule of thumb generally valid but never the core of moral behaviour, or the centre of moral education. Any such habits formed by association must not be too strongly ingrained for they might well hinder rather than aid moral conduct. The vital thing is the general habit of associating the general happiness with our own personal pleasure. But this is not the formation of a habit of action, it is the formation of a habit of thought, by which every action becomes the subject of intelligent foresight and careful calculation. It is the use of association terminology, but not a genuine associationist principle of explanation, to suit a teleological theory of ethics.

The essential point is that, with Mill, associationism is irrelevant to his Ethics, or to his strongest convictions about human nature. It is used purely to explain the origins of our feelings, desires, and motives, and, just as we saw in the preceding section, this is psychologically beside the point. From a philosophical standpoint, to reduce moral sentiments to hedonism, by tracing their origins to childhood training, is a method of accommodating his moral theory to the naturalism necessary to his general empirical position. But it tells us little or nothing about character training. The problem here is to reconcile, not associationism, but psychological hedonism with Utilitarianism, an ethic with which it appears to be fundamentally inconsistent.

13 *Fragment on Mackintosh*, op. cit., p. 163.

To try to resolve this by speaking of our learning to associate our own pleasure with other people's is quite inadequate. Either it means that we seek other people's pleasure because we want their good opinion, that is for selfish reasons, or that we seek it because we like to see other people happy. The latter could just as well be the result of early upbringing, and still be a genuine sentiment. In this case, the association terminology is merely a misleading form of words to describe the fostering of 'other-regarding' tendencies in human nature. It explains nothing. The crux of the matter is do we like other people's happiness? Mill would say that we do, especially after a good education. Reference to the origins of this sentiment is irrelevant.

It is worth noting that Mill speaks with two voices on the subject: 'Pains from the moral source', he writes, 'are the pains derived from the unfavourable sentiments of mankind ... These pains are capable of rising to a height with which hardly any other pains incident to our nature can be compared. There is a certain degree of unfavourableness in the sentiments of his fellow-creatures, under which hardly any man, not below the standard of humanity, can endure to live ... To know how to direct the unfavourable sentiments of mankind, it is necessary to know in as complete a way ... as possible, what it is which gives them birth. Without entering into the metaphysics of the question, it is a sufficient practical answer ... to say that the unfavourable sentiments of men are exerted by everything which hurts them. They love that which gives them pleasure; hate that which gives them pain. Those acts of other men which give them pleasure or save them from pain, acts of beneficence, acts of veracity and so on, they love. Acts, on the other hand, which give them pain, mendacity and so on, they hate. These sentiments, when the state of mind is contemplated out of which the acts are supposed to come, are transformed into approbation and disapprobation, in all their stages and degrees.'[14] Here there is no question of unselfishness, or even of association,

---

[14] *Essays on Government, Jurisprudence, Liberty of the Press and Law of Nations*, 1824 edn, 'Essay on Jurisprudence', pp. 21–2. Macaulay used this passage to refute Mill's political theory that no man could seek another's interest. Cf. Macaulay's *Essays*, 1860, i, p. 292, 'Mill on Government', reprinted from *Edinburgh Review*, March 1829.

for we promote other people's pleasure because of our own powerful desire for their approbation. On the other hand, in the *Essay on Education*, he writes: 'In reality, the happiness of the individual is bound up with that of his species, that which affects the happiness of the one must also, in general, affect the happiness of the other.'[15] This might be taken to mean something quite different—that man can only be fully happy if others are happy too, simply because their happiness is something he desires in and for itself. It is perhaps unwise, and possibly unfair, to try to force Mill into a strait-jacket, as it were, of precise terms and definite theories, when faced with such apparent inconsistencies, especially if our purpose is to understand what he really thought.

The truth appears to be that Mill gave two different meanings, or at least, emphases, to psychological hedonism. When he is speaking of existing corrupt society he means, by hedonistic man, selfish man pursuing his own pleasure, regardless of that of others. When he is talking of ideal society he regards the pleasure of the individual as 'bound up with that of his species' —a form of thinking which has close affinities to that of Plato. It is the use of the language of hedonism—speaking in terms of pleasure, simple and unqualified—which reduces this to naturalism, and means that, even then, we desire other people's pleasure for some other reason than for itself alone. And the language of hedonism has another unfortunate effect. By talking in terms of pleasure, Mill conveys the notion of something objective, and also the idea that different situations have pleasure-giving properties. This conveys the suggestion that what gives men pleasure is more fixed than Mill really thought it was. But if, as we noted in an earlier chapter we substitute 'satisfactions' of desires for 'pleasure', and talk in terms of desire, then the matter is different, for the emphasis is not on external factors to the person, but on his own attitude to them. This, it seems clear, Mill thought could be changed by appropriate education, and the right kind of society. It is to be noticed, too, that this means that, when he says that other people's pleasure give us pleasure, he is really only saying that we desire other people's pleasure—in short, he is hovering uneasily

[15] *Essay on Education*, op. cit., p. 98.

between ethical naturalism, and saying that we ought to cultivate other-regarding tendencies. His language makes him
appear much more of a hedonist than perhaps he is.

We may now draw together our conclusions about Pleasure
as a motive. We originally asked what effect it had on Association Psychology and whether it constituted an *explanation* of a
process which Association as such describes. Whatever modern
developments may show, the evidence seems overwhelming
that, in Mill's hands, Association Psychology was not the
mechanical theory it is usually thought to be: it is essentially
teleological, with many more affinities with goal-directed
theories than at first sight appears. Equally, although Mill lays
great stress on Association as a method of analysis and on the
atomic structure thus revealed, from a psychological standpoint
his theory is not atomic, for the whole stress is on large and
general associations. He says little in psychological explanation
of such associations, but concentrates on their psychological
effects once they are formed. In this, he assumes that early
associations once formed will persist. Finally, pervading everything, is Mill's psychological hedonism: in so far as he makes
explicit the psychological assumptions of his philosophy, it is
hedonism rather than association which is important. For this
is what 'pleasure', as a dominant factor in associationism,
comes to: the doctrine that men will invariably pursue their
own pleasure. In Mill's philosophical writings this is obscured
by the pseudo-scientific language of Association Psychology,
and by his own expressed purpose of writing a science of the
human mind. In this enterprise, which in the event was far
more a philosophical than a psychological enquiry, we have the
language of a science, but not its characteristic logic nor its
appropriate mode of explanation. From a psychological standpoint, particularly in the field of conation, it is a teleological
theory based on purpose as the explanation of human behaviour.

III

It is not easy to draw together these conclusions about Association Psychology and to discuss their implications for education, for we have really two rather different theories—the theory of cognitive learning, which in part seems to be traditional associationism, and the addition of hedonism, especially in the sphere of character-training, which fundamentally changes the theory. It is implied, though not worked out in any detail, that hedonism as a motive would operate in the sphere of intellectual education. It may be useful to focus our discussion on three points which we noted earlier. First, according to the theory, no learning could take place without sense-experience, second, that abstractions can only be learned from concrete instances and finally, a very general point, that the environment is all-powerful.

With the first two of these, it is clear that logically some such doctrine as that of the modern pragmatists would be implied for education. But it is equally clear that this was neither Mill's practice nor the twist which he gave to his theory. In practice, his son remarks that it was a defect of his father's teaching that it was 'too much in the abstract'. In theory, he held that universals and abstractions once formed were the spectacles through which we saw the rest of experience, the basis of all study through language, and that the most important thing was to learn to use language correctly as a means of learning, and this meant understanding the pitfalls of language. Mill was not in this sense an apostle of learning through the senses. They are the origin, but after the earliest stages, learning takes place through language, and that means through abstractions.

Of incentives to learning, and of motivation in general, Mill tells us little. Pain and pleasure are the sovereign masters, but these are generic terms. Presumably they imply rewards to hard-working children, and punishment for the idle. But we must note that Mill also held that intellectual study was pleasurable in itself—'he never varied', wrote his son, 'in rating intellectual enjoyments above all others, even in value

7*

as pleasures, independently of their ulterior benefits.'[16] This would suggest that until this stage was reached, Mill believed in an authoritarian education, guiding the young on to paths at the time uninteresting, and providing incentives by pains and pleasures extraneous to the work itself. Certainly if we contemplate the curriculum he devised for his son, at the ages for which it was designed, there were no concessions at all to childish interests, or to providing work of the type which would suit different ages of development. But such a curriculum and educational practice again involves certain assumptions about association. If a child tackles work which it does not like under the incentive of extraneous rewards or punishments, one would expect to be formed in its mind an association between reward and good work, and punishment and bad. This association, if it lasted, would inhibit the love of learning for its own sake, and thus hinder the achievement of part of Mill's general aim in education—the cultivation of the most rewarding personal pleasures. If this is not to occur, there must be some transfer of motive, some doctrine that an activity may be started by one motive, and continued for quite another. This it might be said is sound, and many modern psychologists and indeed common experience would suggest that it took place.

So far these are rather negative conclusions. But there are two other points of interest, both of which underline the point that Mill's theory of the mind was not a psychology. Firstly, we should note that, if it were, it would contain at least some affinities with modern association psychology, which is a theory of learning, based on experimental evidence, and with a highly technical analysis of its subject. With Mill, we are told only in the most general terms about the learning process, and even this is not applied by him when he comes to the practice of education. Nor are his theories based on psychological evidence: the most he could argue would be that they were based on the evidence of introspection. But even here it is not really the evidence of introspection which is offered, but introspection seen through the spectacles of a theoretical science of the mind. It is not sensation as it is experienced which is adduced as evidence, but sensation subject to atomic analysis. Mill in fact

[16] *Autobiography*, op. cit., p. 41.

is never really clear whether he is analysing *how* we learn or *what* we learn and the latter is a philosophical question.

Perhaps more interesting and significant is to consider the relationship of another feature of associationism—its atomic nature—with the monitorial system of teaching, which was recommended by Bentham and practised by Mill. It is odd that its possible affinity with association psychology was never noticed or argued. For the monitorial system rests essentially on the assumption that as soon as a monitor had acquired a particle of knowledge, so to speak, he could pass it on to his pupils. For this to be so each portion of knowledge had to be intelligible by itself and it could be passed on as a separate and intelligible unit. All this would be challenged from more than one quarter nowadays, but it was the ineluctable basis of the monitorial system, and it fitted in well with the atomic nature of Mill's associationism, where it is also implied, as we have noticed, that knowledge consists of a series of individual truths each of which could be comprehended in isolation, and that when subsequently they were welded together by association, such a union was but the sum of the individual parts. In practical terms in education, the monitorial system could only work if this assumption held: it is possible to defend it at the primary stage, and for the more mechanical parts of learning involved there at the time. But with Bentham and Mill it was thought good at the *secondary* stage: Mill educated his entire family by this system, and the curriculum studied was a formidable one. It would be wrong to make too much of an omission, but the fact that Mill never saw this connexion between his theory of education, and a practice which he favoured, does suggest that he never really saw the association principle in psychological terms.

It remains to consider Mill as an environmentalist. He is clearly an environmentalist in that he ascribes nothing to inheritance, and with Helvétius asserts that 'L'éducation peut tout'. But that does not take us far. When he ascribes special importance to early childhood, he is ascribing special importance to early environment, and correspondingly less to the later. He does this as we have seen in respect of the formation of universals, of abstraction and of long trains of associations of pleasures with their causes. All these are formed early in life and persist. In addition to his direct comments on the importance of early upbringing, we have the fact that, as we have shown, association was used by Mill to explain the *origins* of present phenomena, and this in itself implies a formative period and also, a subsequent period, when environment exercises much less influence, at any rate, through the principle of association. This point is relevant to Mill's very wide definition of education as 'everything which operates, from the first germ of existence to the final extinction of life'. It is also relevant to his doctrine of Social and Political education or the educative influence of society and the state respectively. Such concepts of education could be justified on the basis of a mechanical form of Association psychology, where custom alone governed the strength and durability of an association. But it is not readily apparent how Mill's form of associationism, and especially the notions of a formative period, can form the basis of his theories of Social and Political education. It seems that hedonism rather than association psychology may be found to be the psychological basis of these social theories.

Such a conclusion, however, should not be pushed too far. A major point to remember is that 'association', as we have noted, is in itself not an explanatory term, it is descriptive. It is more than this: it is a very general term and potentially both vague and ambiguous in its operation. It is when we ask the more precise questions of modern psychology that we realize how vague, and therefore how flexible, Mill's theory was. It is empirically based, yet accommodates learning in the abstract; mechanical in form, yet made the explanation of meaningful learning; implies individual motivation of each step in learning, yet turned by Mill into goal-seeking and purposeful behaviour of the most broad and general kind. It may in fact explain little: to him it explained matters of fundamental importance, namely, the power of the environment to change and improve people, the possibility through education of producing a community of literate and rational people who could discern the merits of the 'middling ranks', perceive the truth of the utilitarian ideal, and who would eventually bring about a reformed state and society. Environmentalism in some form is central to Mill's faith in reform at every point: associationism is central because it is the explanation of the extreme environmentalist position which was the basis of everything Mill stood for. It perhaps underlines what we have noted in our study of Mill's life and thought, namely that he became a political utilitarian first, and a philosopher of utilitarianism later. The latter had to fit the former.

This may explain why Mill set such store on association psychology, but it does nothing to mitigate or answer the criticisms we have made which may be summed up as saying that when it is considered as a psychology, it tells us little, and what Mill does say on psychology cannot be ascribed to the association principle. Behind this lies the larger problem of the failure to distinguish philosophical questions from psychological ones, with the result that Mill was in the main expounding not a psychology but a theory of knowledge. Later in the century, Bradley was to criticize the union of philosophy with psychology as obscuring the real questions in philosophy. But it was equally damaging to psychology. It may be that the basic question asked: 'What are the phenomena of the human mind?' is essentially a psychological question and that, to explain the origins of such phenomena is, strictly, an essay in educational psychology. But with Mill it never is, because he departs from psychic facts and from the actual manner in which we learn, in his zeal for the atomic analysis borrowed from natural science and the laws of association which he thought to be the fundamental principles of explanation. Neither is permitted to affect his political theory, nor his theory of education in either the moral or the intellectual sphere, and neither is worked out as a theory of psychology.

VII

Political and Social Education

We have now to examine Mill's theory of Social and Political Education, which follows from his definition of Education which is much wider than the normal usage. It will also be necessary to examine briefly his Political Theory as such, as set out in his *Essay on Government*, in order to see whether this has implications for education, and whether it throws further light on his educational theories.

Mill's definition of education is as follows: 'Education, then, in the sense in which we are now using the term, may be defined, the best employment of all the means which can be made use of, by man, for rendering the human mind to the greatest possible degree the cause of human happiness. Every thing, therefore, which operates, from the first germ of existence, to the final extinction of life, in such a manner as to affect those qualities of mind on which happiness in any degree depends, comes within the scope of the present enquiry.'[1] This, Mill admits, is a wide definition, and it follows the example of Helvétius who regarded education as all-powerful as a determinant of character, and who defined it in the same wide terms. Mill writes: 'One of the causes, why people have been so much startled, by the extent to which Helvétius has carried the dominion of education, seems to us to be their not including in it nearly as much as he does. They include little more than what is expressed by the term "schooling"; commencing about six or seven years of age, and ending at least with the arrival of manhood. If this alone is meant by education, it is no doubt true that education is very far indeed from being all-powerful. But if in education is included everything, which acts upon the being as it comes from the hand of nature, in such a manner as

[1] *Essay on Education*, op. cit., pp. 41–2.

to modify the mind, to render the train of feelings different from what it would otherwise have been; the question is worthy of the most profound consideration.'[2] Mill does not commit himself to Helvétius' famous assertion: 'L'éducation peut tout', but he does say, on empirical grounds: 'This much, at any rate, is ascertained, that all the difference which exists, or can be made to exist, between one *class* of men, and another, is wholly owing to education.'[3]

This definition enabled Mill to include under the term 'education' the influence of the family, both before and during school-days: this he entitled Domestic Education. More important from the point of view of this chapter is that he also extended the term education to apply after school-days, and throughout life and therefore arrived at concepts of Social and Political Education, or the influence of Society and of the State upon our characters and abilities.

'Social Education', says Mill, 'is that in which Society is the Institutor. That the Society in which an individual moves produces great effects upon his mode of thinking and acting, everybody knows by indubitable experience. The object is, to ascertain the extent of this influence, the mode in which it is brought about, and hence the means of making it operate in a good, rather than an evil direction.

'The force of this influence springs from two sources: the principle of imitation; and the power of the society over our happiness and misery.'[4]

The first of these is due to association and the frequency with which we are in the society of our personal group or groups. 'It is very evident, that those trains which are most habitually passing in the minds of all those individuals by whom we are surrounded, must be made to pass with extraordinary frequency through our own minds, and must, unless where extraordinary means are used to prevent them from producing their natural effect, engross to a proportional degree the dominion of our minds.'[5]

[2] Ibid., pp. 69–70.
[3] Ibid., p. 71.
[4] Ibid., p. 114.
[5] Ibid., p. 115.

The second is more complicated. Mill first draws attention to the 'intense desire which we feel for the favourable regards of mankind. Few men could bear to live under an exclusion from the breast of every human being. It is astonishing how great a portion of all the actions of men are directed to these favourable regards, and to no other object . . . Whatever, then, are the trains of thought, whatever is the course of action which most strongly recommends us to the favourable regards of those among whom we live, these we feel the strongest motive to cultivate and display; whatever trains of thought and course of action expose us to their unfavourable regards, these we feel the strongest motives to avoid. These inducements, operating upon us continually, have an irresistable influence in creating habits, and in moulding, that is, educating us, into a character conformable to the society in which we move.'[6] So far, this too refers to personal groups and direct associations. But Mill then applies the argument more generally. After arguing that good early education might protect an individual from a corrupt society, to some extent, he continues: 'but still the actual rewards or punishments which Society has to bestow, upon those who please, and those who displease it; the good and evil which it gives, or witholds, are so great that to adopt the opinions which it approves, to perform the acts which it admires, to acquire the character, in short, which it "delighteth to honour" can seldom fail to be the leading object of those by whom it is composed.'[7] He continues: 'And as this potent influence operates upon those who conduct both the domestic education and the technical, it is next to impossible that the trains which are generated, even during the time of their operation, should not fall in with, instead of counteracting, the trains which the social education produces; it is next to impossible, therefore, that the whole man should not take the shape which that influence is calculated to impress upon him.'[8]

Finally, we have Political Education, which 'is like the keystone of the arch; the strength of the whole depends upon it. We have seen that the strength of the Domestic and the

[6] *Essay*, op. cit., pp. 115–16.
[7] Ibid., p. 116.
[8] Ibid., p. 116.

Technical Education depends almost entirely upon the Social. Now it is certain, that the nature of the Social depends almost entirely upon the Political; and the most important part of the Physical (that which operates which greatest force upon the greatest number, the state of aliment and labour of the lower classes), is, in the long-run, determined by the action of the political machine. The play, therefore, of the political machine acts immediately upon the mind, and with extraordinary power; but this is not all; it also acts upon almost every thing else by which the character of the mind is apt to be formed.

'It is a common observation, that such as is the direction given to the desires and passions of men, such is the character of the men. The direction is given to the desires and passions of men by one thing, and one alone; the means by which the grand objects of desire may be attained. Now this is certain, that the means by which the grand objects of desire may be attained, depend almost wholly upon the political machine.'[9]

It should be noticed from this that in speaking of Social and Political Education, Mill is concerned with two things—the direct and the indirect effect on character of these influences. Directly, Society moulds our characters in the way he suggests: indirectly, it affects the family and the teacher, and therefore the education which they in turn give. Political education is similar—but here Mill stresses the indirect effect more strongly —'the nature of the Social [education] depends almost entirely upon the Political'. This indirect effect which is mentioned first as a *secondary* effect of Social education, becomes progressively more important as he develops his argument, until, in his summing up, he seems concerned mainly with a chain of indirect influences, the government determining society, and society in turn determining family and school education. Involved in this is a political theory which is typical of Mill's day—that the state is the 'keystone of the arch' and determines the form which society shall take.

It is not so easy to summarize the second main problem we mentioned—the educational implications of Mill's political theory, for they were never explicitly stated and we must infer

[9] Ibid., pp. 118–19.

them, as best we can, from the *Essay on Government*. It is clear, from what we have so far quoted from the *Essay on Education*, that Mill would have regarded the search for the educational implications of a system of government as a perfectly proper enquiry. Since he did not develop this question, we must perforce state briefly his political theory and then see what it implied for education.

In the *Essay on Government* Mill describes the end of government as the greatest happiness of the greatest number, and then proceeds to analyse this. Happiness consists in a balance of pleasure over pain, and a man's pleasure comes from two sources—either his fellow-men, or from other causes. Government is concerned with the first of these. He then continues: 'Of the laws of nature, on which the condition of man depends, that which is attended with the greatest number of consequences, is the necessity of labour for obtaining the means of subsistence, as well as the means of the greatest part of our pleasures. This is, no doubt, the primary cause of Government; for, if nature has produced spontaneously all the objects which we desire, and in sufficient abundance for the desires of all, there would have been no source of dispute or of injury among men; nor would any men have possessed the means of ever acquiring authority over another.

'The results are exceedingly different, when nature produces the objects of desire not in sufficient abundance for all. The source of dispute is then exhaustless; for every man has the means of acquiring authority over others, in proportion to the quantity of those objects which he is able to possess.

'In this case, the end to be obtained, through Government as the means is, to make that distribution of the scanty materials of happiness, which would ensure the greatest sum of it in the members of the community, taken together, preventing every individual, or combination of individuals, from interfering with that distribution, or making any man have less than his share.'[10]

Most of these objects of desire are the product of labour, and therefore labour must be ensured, either by slavery, which denies

[10] James Mill, *Essay on Government*, ed. E. Barker, C.U.P., 1937, pp. 3–4.

the greatest happiness principle, or by reward. If reward to any man goes beyond the product of his labour, then it can only be at the expense of others: hence 'the greatest possible happiness of society is . . . attained by insuring to every man the greatest possible quantity of the produce of his labour'. Since each man has an inducement to maximize his own satisfaction, if need be at the expense of others, this ideal 'can best be attained when a great number of men combine, and delegate to a small number the power necessary for protecting them all. This is Government'.[11]

Mill continues that this raises two questions—how much power should the government have, and what use should they make of it. The problem is that the government are like any other group of men and 'lie . . . under the same temptations to take the objects of desire from the members of the community, if they are not prevented from doing so'.[12] Since their powers of coercion are well known, Mill concentrates on this second problem—precisely the one to which Plato gave so much thought, how to ensure that the powers of government are used not for the rulers but for the good of the community.

His answer is 'the grand discovery of modern times, the system of representation'.[13] If all are represented then the interests of none can be disregarded, and government in the interests of all is ensured. But this rests in turn on the assumption that the people are 'capable of acting agreeably to their interest'.[14] This point Mill examines at some length. He concedes that the people may make mistakes but 'the evils which arise from mistake are not incurable; for, if the parties who act contrary to their interest had a proper knowledge of that interest, they would act well. What is necessary, then, is knowledge. Knowledge . . . would be an adequate remedy. But knowledge is a thing which is capable of being increased: and the more it is increased the more the evils on this side of the case would be reduced . . . It is no longer deniable that a high degree of knowledge is capable of being conveyed to such a portion of the

11 Ibid., p. 5.
12 Ibid., p. 6.
13 Ibid., p. 34.
14 Ibid., p. 63.

community, as would have interests the same with those of the community'. It is therefore necessary to work to the utmost to increase 'the quantity of knowledge in the body of the community'.[15]

None the less, in all ranks, some will mistake their own interest. On this, Mill says, first, that 'prudence is a more general characteristic of the people who are without the advantages of fortune, than of the people who have been thoroughly subject to their corruptive operation', and, secondly, that, as a general truth, it may be accepted that 'the wise and good in any class of men do, to all general purposes, govern the rest'.[16] From this he moves to praise the virtues of the 'middle rank'—'the most wise and most virtuous part of the community'. They are, in Britain, numerous, 'and form a large proportion of the whole body of the people'. The people below this middle rank, in the opinion of all observers, have their 'opinion formed and their minds . . . directed by that intelligent and virtuous rank who come most immediately in contact with them . . . There can be no doubt that the middle rank, which gives to science, to art, and to legislation itself, their most distinguished ornaments, the chief source of all that has exalted and refined human nature, is that portion of the community of which, if the basis of Representation were ever so far extended, the opinion would ultimately decide. Of the people beneath them, a vast majority would be sure to be guided by their advice and example.'[17]

Mill's theory of government then, rests upon the representation of interests, and this in turn rests upon the view that people will know their own interests. This is to be attained by widespread education, and by depending on the example of the middle rank—an example which will always be wise, and which is likely to be followed owing to the intimate connexions which the lower ranks have with the middle. The implications of this for education are, then, that all should be educated, as far as possible, to know their own interests. The pursuit of the general happiness comes, not because men seek it directly, but because the system of representation ensures it as the result of each

[15] Ibid., pp. 65–6.
[16] Ibid., p. 70.
[17] Ibid., p. 72.

pursuing his own interest. Just as, in economics, there can be
an identity of interests, so, in the state, there can be a similar
identity, through the system of representation.

II

As summarized in the previous section, the theory of Political
and Social Education depends upon three main points. It is a
theory about the influence of Society upon its members: it
therefore requires some elucidation of what is meant by
'Society'—a term which is decidedly ambiguous. It requires,
secondly, an examination of the reasons given by Mill for this
powerful influence of Society—the means by which, according
to him, Society affects the individuals of which it is composed.
These means are the tendency of people to imitate one another,
and the doctrine of psychological hedonism, that everyone,
inevitably, pursues his own interest. If either of these doctrines
are found, on examination, to be untrue, we cannot accept
Mill's particular theory of Social Education, for it depends
explicitly upon these two pillars. Finally, the concept of Political
Education has two parts to it—the direct influence of the State
on the citizens, and the indirect power which it has over
Society in general. This last point obviously involves an examination of Mill's assertion that the State was supreme—'the
keystone of the arch'.

The first question to ask, then, is what is meant by the word
'society'. We can, first, describe our personal circle of friends
and acquaintances as the 'society' in which we move. If this
has influence, it is by personal and direct contact with ourselves.
We sometimes meet, however, a second and more general
meaning, as when we talk of a whole community as a society—
in Graham Wallas's term, the 'Great Society'. Here, we obviously cannot speak of influence by means of direct and personal
contact, and if we wish to talk of the 'influence of society' in
this sense of the word, we must assume some kind of chain
relationship, by which a small personal group so influences the
whole of society that it makes sense to talk of the influence of
society as a whole. Thus we might think of a court which was a

personal group but where each member had social relation-
ships of some kind stretching through society, so that the small
personal group at the top effectively influenced the whole
society. The church, at different periods in history, has had an
influence of this kind. Or we may hold a theory such as the
Marxist one which holds that one factor is the dominant social
influence in any society large or small. In order to see which
applies to Mill, we must consider the means by which he
considered society exerted its influence.

For the most part Mill seems clearly to be referring to a personal group. Thus his explanation of the principle of imitation
is entirely in these terms. So also are his comments on our desire
for the social approval of people with whom we mix. But in the
latter part of his comments, as when he speaks of 'a vicious and
ignorant society' he is ambiguous and seems to be thinking, at
least in part, of the wider meaning of the word 'society'. We
may gain some understanding of his thoughts by looking at the
society of his day.

The England of Mill's day was not sharply divided into two
or three broad classes in the manner later portrayed by Marx:
it is significant that Mill himself writes not of the 'middle class',
for instance, but of the 'middling ranks'. For England had, in
those days, a multitude of groups and minute social gradations,
each merging into the other. A modern historian has written of
these gradations and particularly of the 'middling ranks' as
follows:

'Many factors were at work to neutralize any tendency
towards the formation of a caste system, or even towards the
development of acute class-consciousness. The greatest of these
factors at that time . . . is the plurality, one might almost say
the ubiquity, of what is generally known as the "Middle Class".
Rarely, if ever, synonymous with a "Bourgeoisie" of the con-
tinental type; shaded with a multitude of gradations within its
hazy outlines; easy of access from below, and no less easy of
exit from the top: it has served as an enormous shock-absorbing
feather-bed or cushion between the "Classes" and the "Masses".
Common men are always springing into it, and uncommon
men (and more especially women) are always springing out of
it. Almost anyone might belong to it, at almost any time, from

the younger son of a Peer who has gone into trade, to the successful son of an artisan who has set up as shop-keeper. A bridge, a buffer, a vestibule, an escalator: it has been all these things at different times, and often all of them at once. Its top level is always within sight of aristocracy; its lower levels are never far removed from the life of the labouring poor. In Regency England, Lord Eldon, the son of a Newcastle coal-merchant, presided over the House of Lords.'[18]

We may set beside this modern comment, Mill's own comment on the society of his day: 'In England we have never had this arrangement [of exclusive classes, as in France]. The great wealth of the mercantile classes, and the privilege which every man possesses of aspiring to every situation, has always prevented any such separation of the high and the low-born even in ordinary society, and made all large assemblages of people to a certain degree promiscuous. Great wealth, or great talents, being sufficient to raise a man to power and eminence, are necessarily received as a sufficient passport into private company, and fill it, on the large scale, with such motley and discordant characters, as visibly to endanger either its ease or its tranquillity ... With us, therefore, society, when it passes beyond select clubs and associations, is apt to be either distracted with little jealousies and divisions, or finally to settle into constraint, insipidity and reserve.' He continues, 'It is obviously to our free government, and to nothing else, that we owe that mixture of ranks and of characters, which certainly renders our large society less amiable, and less unconstrained than that of the old French nobility. Men possessed of wealth and political power, must be associated with by all with whom they choose to associate, and to whom their friendship and support is material. A trader, who has bought his borough but yesterday, will not give his influence to any set of noblemen or ministers, who will not receive him and his family into their society, and agree to treat them as their equals. The same principle extends downwards by imperceptible gradations; and the whole community is mingled in private life it must be owned with some little discomfort, by the ultimate action of the same principles which combine them, to their incalculable benefit, in public.'[19] This was written in 1809, and at first sight may seem to shew more satisfaction with the existing state of things than Mill felt —certainly later in his life, though 1809 was after his meeting with Bentham, and his conversion to political Utilitarianism. It is at an early date in Mill's radicalism, but none the less, a careful reading will shew that it is not inconsistent with his later views. He is praising English society in comparison with that of France; he says nothing of the defects of the English system of government. But what he does say, and insist upon, is important, namely, that English society was not stratified into watertight classes, that one mingled with another, and that, through wealth, a man could always rise from one to another.

These extracts gives us the explanation of social influence in Mill's day. Just because the 'middling ranks' stretched so far, both up and down, and just because there was no precise demarcation between the middling ranks and the aristocracy, and between them and the labouring classes, the 'middle class' was not only a 'feather-bed' but a transmitter of influence. This, no doubt, was why Mill placed such reliance on it as an instrument of educating the poor as to where their true happiness lay. If it had been a class, sharply cut off from other classes, one would expect to find little influence outside its own ranks. But because it was not a class, its influence permeated everywhere.

Was England, however, a society about which one could generalize? In a predominantly rural and agricultural land, as yet little touched by the Industrial Revolution, and with a sparse, and apart from London, largely scattered population, one might expect local differences to be considerable. But to set against this we have the predominant position of the landowning groups who controlled both Parliament and their own localities, and of the Church, attached by unholy alliance to the landowning aristocracy, and carrying its influence into every village. The great landowners, as we saw in the opening chapter, dominated Parliament, and also in large measure

[19] *Edinburgh Review*, January 1810, Art. xiii, 'Correspondence inédite de Mme du Deffand avec D'Alembert, etc.', Paris, 1809.

controlled appointments in the Church of England, from bishops down to direct control in many cases of the choice of local rector or vicar. Mill would argue that this meant that those qualities had to be cultivated which pleased the land-owning class, and that this would be so throughout the land, affecting aspiring bishops, aspiring vicars, aspiring curates, those who sought to enter Parliament, and in most cases and most localities, people in all positions high and low. Social education, by means of the reward of certain qualities, becomes translated as the influence of a dominant group of landowners throughout the community—in short, all strive to gratify the interest of this all-powerful and all-pervading group. It is obvious that the 'principle of imitation' worked in much the same way, on the basis that 'imitation is the sincerest form of flattery'.

It is true that there were very different conditions in the Lancashire cotton towns. But these, as we noted earlier, figure very little in Mill's private writing—he seems ignorant of their existence. And in the *Essay on Government* he dismisses them as an aberration from the normal order of things. After speaking of the virtues and influence of the middling ranks, he goes on: 'The incidents which have been urged as exceptions to this general rule, and even as reasons for rejecting it, may be considered as contributing to its proof. What signify the irregularities of a mob, more than half composed, in the greater number of instances, of boys and women, and disturbing, for a few hours or days, a particular town? What signifies the occasional turbulence of a manufacturing district, peculiarly unhappy from a very great deficiency of a middle rank, as there the population almost wholly consists of rich manufacturers and poor workmen; with whose minds no pains are taken by anybody; with whose afflictions there is no virtuous family of the middle rank to sympathise; whose children have no good example of such a family to see and to admire; and who are placed in the highly unfavourable situation of fluctuating between very high wages in one year, and very low wages in another? It is altogether futile with regard to the foundation of good government to say that this or the other portion of the people, may at this, or the other time, depart from the wisdom of the middle rank. It is enough that the great majority of the people never cease to be guided by that rank; and we may, with some confidence, challenge the adversaries of the people to produce a single instance to the contrary in the history of the world.'[20]

This passage bears out the interpretation we have suggested —that Mill was writing not of an England divided into classes, but of an England in which each class or group was attached to another, influenced by it, and in touch with it—an England which was socially an organic whole. Anything else he seems to regard as a departure from the course of history. And it is clear, too, from this passage, what he meant by the principle of imitation—when he speaks of having some good family 'to see and to admire'. In this, perhaps he was thinking of his own youth, where he gained so much help from wealthy people in the district. And this reminds us to be careful not to impute too much to him. Most of what he says, under the heading of Social Education, seems to have reference to the influence of personal groups. Even his comments about 'vicious and ignorant society' could apply to that. But it seems to have a wider application, certainly when he goes on to speak of *indirect* social education, that is, the influence of society on teachers and parents. And it is understandable that he may have thought in terms of national society in commenting upon the corrupt society of his time. We shall gain further enlightenment by examining in detail the second means by which this influence was exercised—the reward of qualities by 'society', and finally by analysing what the connexion was between Social and Political Education as Mill saw it.

III

According to Mill, Society influenced its members owing to their tendency to imitate one another, and because of the power of Society over the happiness and misery of its members. It is now necessary to examine these two arguments, and especially the latter, more closely.

The principle of imitation seems fairly straightforward. We can concede as a matter of common experience that people in

[20] *Essay on Government*, op. cit., p. 73.

fact do tend to conform to those about them; whether we have done much more than restate this fact by calling it 'the principle of imitation' is doubtful. But, granted the fact, it would tend to produce a standard pattern of behaviour, if different social groups observed the same conventions, so that the pressure to conform was always towards the same pattern and set of habits. And Mill does more than state the principle of imitation: he explains it in associationist terms. 'It is very evident', he writes, 'that those trains which are most habitually passing in the minds of all those individuals by whom we are surrounded, must be made to pass with an extraordinary frequency through our own minds, and must, unless where extraordinary means are used to prevent them from producing their natural effect, engross to a proportional degree the dominion of our minds.'[21] But he could also, quite logically, associate the tendency to imitate and conform with his second principle—the power of society over our happiness and misery, and our desire to 'obtain the favourable regards of those among whom we live', which, he says, 'is one of our most intense desires'.

This second point is the really crucial one in the argument. Society has power over our happiness and misery because, first, of our strong desire for the favourable regard of other people, and, second, of its power to reward those qualities which suit it, and punish those which don't. The ambiguities in the term 'society' have already been discussed: there remain the questions of the reward of qualities, our desire for the favourable regard of those about us, and the assertion that 'Society' has the 'power' to reward qualities, and control our happiness and misery. Of these questions the last one is a political one, and belongs to the next section. I propose here to discuss the implications of the assertion that those who can reward qualities can produce a certain type of character, and that all men have a desire for 'other people's approbation'. The first of these is the more fundamental since, if reward of certain qualities or certain behaviour is to succeed in producing a certain kind of character, it must be an efficient incentive, and reward is an incentive so long as men are assumed to be essentially selfish. The point is not stressed in the *Essay on Education*, but in view of the frequent

[21] *Essay on Education*, op. cit., p. 115.

and re-iterated belief in Mill's other writings, that men always pursue their own interests, it is this which we should examine first. The desire for other people's regard must be viewed in this context of psychological hedonism. And although in common sense and ordinary experience we might concede that a situation in which material rewards worked one way, and the path of duty another, was inherently unsound, the whole argument has heavy overtones and a special significance in view of Mill's strong belief in psychological hedonism. Our first task, then, is to ask what is meant by 'pursuing one's own interests'.

To say that 'everyone pursues his own interest' is apparently to assert that everyone is irretrievably selfish: this would be the normal meaning of the term. In this sense, a man is pursuing his interest when he feeds himself, clothes himself or houses himself. We can speak similarly when a man pursues a personal ambition. But the phrase is potentially much vaguer and wider than this. What if a man seeks wealth for the sake of his family? Here he is serving other people, but since he is interested in doing so, it is still correct to say, in a sense, that he is pursuing his own interest. And the assertion can, in this sense, be made of any object of desire, providing it is desired. This point brings out the justice of Macaulay's comment that, as Mill used it, the phrase was 'an identical proposition'. And if it be thought that we are extending the meaning too far from its normal usage, we have to remember Mill's assertion that one of our strongest interests was the favourable regard of other people.

If 'our interests' are defined as 'what in fact we desire to do' as expressed by what we choose to do, then the phrase is tautologous, in that the desire is inferred from the action, and not independently established, and it is assumed, without argument, that what we choose to do is what we most want to do, merely on the evidence that we choose to do it. Whatever we in fact do, can under this argument be called 'pursuing our interests', but only by begging the question and assuming that whatever in fact we do must be what we selfishly want to do. Apart from this there is an inherent ambiguity in the phrase 'pursuing our interests' in that it may describe the object of desire—e.g. a miser's hoard—or it may describe the motive from which anything is pursued—e.g. wealth for the sake of one's family. It is this ambiguity which Mill exploits when he speaks, first, of rulers 'pursuing their own interests' by policies designed to enrich themselves and preserve their own privileges, and, second, of our strong interest in 'the favourable regard of other people', a desire which can only be gratified by serving the interests of other people. In this second sense Mill is using 'interests' to refer to a motive, and not to describe the object of desire.

When Mill is speaking of politics and society in his own day, he means by 'pursuit of interests', man's essential selfishness: 'it is obvious that every man, who has not all the objects of his desire, has inducement to take them from any other man who is weaker than himself . . .' In speaking of government, he writes: 'Not a man is there, I fear, in that house who would not compromise the good of his country in many, and these far from trifling particulars, to gain the favour of a ministry, of a party, or if despising the favour of ministries and parties, to push some other personal end . . . it is an easy thing to contract opinions which favour one's corrupt inclinations . . . It is curious to trace, even in those who seem to be the farthest removed from the hope of directly sharing in the plunder, by what secret links the opinions which favour misgovernment are really and in fact connected with the feelings of the plunderers; even by vain imitation; an idea that it gives them an aristocratical air, where there is not a stronger bond of connexion—but in truth I have very seldom, indeed, found in real life, any man a friend to bad principles of government, who did not in some way or another foster the idea of deriving advantage from them.'[22]

So far as this passage is concerned, and it is typical of Mill's view of the society in which he lived, the assertion is that whatever the proclaimed motives of those in positions of power, or those who hope for advancement, the motive is really selfish, even though it may be unconscious. A bad society will corrupt: those at the top will consciously seek to preserve their power, riches, and privilege, those beneath will seek their favour for the same reason, and others will be unconsciously corrupted by the general influence of these all-powerful forces. Hence such a

[22] Sraffa, *Ricardo's Correspondence*, vi, no. 109, Mill to Ricardo, 23 August 1815.

society will exercise 'social education', no matter what the preceding education may have been, but it will be an adverse influence. Clearly this kind of social education can only occur in a community where only the few have power, and that power is virtually absolute. In short, if Mill's doctrine stopped there, it would be little more than a commentary—some would call it a diatribe—on the conditions of his day. That it was true, there is little doubt, but that does not suffice to make it the basis of a general theory of education.

Let us turn to the desire for 'other people's approbation', which is essentially different. Whereas the first extract concerned selfish motives in the objective sense—it asserted that men actually pursued an object of desire which was their own interest, despite proclaimed motives to the opposite, here we have an altruistic object of desire, pursued, so Mill asserts, from selfish motives. He stresses this latter point: 'Nothing is more remarkable in human nature, than the intense desire which we feel of the favourable regards of mankind. Few men could bear to live under an exclusion from the breast of every human being.' This applies to the great despots of history, who, if asked the motives for their wars and conquests, would reply with Frederic of Prussia 'pour faire parler de soi'—'to occupy a large space in the admiration of mankind'. And 'it is the easy command ... over the favourable regards of society ... which renders the desire for wealth unbounded'.[23] The same attitude pervades the subjects of any state, and they therefore cultivate the qualities which please their superiors and which are rewarded. In this way a bad society can do much harm.

Mill stresses the same point in his *Essay on Jurisprudence*, where he writes: 'Pains ... from the unfavourable sentiments of mankind ... are capable of rising to a height, with which hardly any other pains, incident to our nature can be compared.'[24] This passage prompted Macaulay to make an important criticism: why, if this is so, does it not cause rulers to rule in the interests of their subjects, in order to gain their favourable

[23] *Essay on Education*, op. cit., pp. 115–16.
[24] *Essay on Jurisprudence*, quoted in *Mill's Essay on Government*, by Macaulay, *Lord Macaulay's Miscellaneous Writings*, Longmans, 1860, i, pp. 292ff.

regard? The immediate answer to this would be that, in this article, Mill is referring to the limited context of criminal prosecution, and stressing the punitive effects of publicity, the censure of the Judge, and the opprobium of one's fellow men. But in view of his wider insistence on the same subject, this by no means suffices to meet Macaulay's point.

Macaulay's point rests on the assumption that other people will only give their approbation if the rulers look after their interest in a genuine sense. But Mill would say that this does not necessarily follow. Approbation might be sought and given for material reward which, in turn, might be given not for qualities which are good, or to people because they were human beings and deserved respect and justice but for qualities which suited the rulers, and preserved their power. They would thus reward subservience and acquiescence rather than good qualities. They would be seeking other people's approbation up to a point, by limited material reward, but not by doing them good. And, Mill would also argue, that the rulers would depend upon the poorer classes not knowing their interests, and therefore extending their acquiescence, if not their approbation, blindly. Having said this, however, Mill's bald statement that it is characteristic of all human nature to seek other people's approbation, coupled with citing the example of a dictator, seems to mean two different things. In the case of a ruler it can mean acquiescence and possibly respect, but between equals it means respect owing to mutual consideration of each other's interests. For 'other people's approbation' to mean a morally good state of things there is therefore an assumption either that there are no rulers, so that no-one can command another's approbation for other than genuine altruism, or that the rulers are enlightened and good and reward only the right qualities.

Mill's allusion to Frederick of Prussia suggests that he does not rule out the possibility of a genuine 'enlightened despot'. And his article on *Aristocracy* written at the end of his life, shews what he would have regarded as an ideal situation in a socially unequal society: 'When a society exists, well constituted for the pursuit of intellectual attainments and of the elegancies of life, a style of social intercourse is cultivated, which whets the understanding and improves at once the morals and the

taste. Men of independent, but few enormous incomes, sufficiently numerous to form a class and a public, are obliged to sell
distinction among themselves by qualities which recommend
them to the respect and affection of their fellows. These are,
the high qualities of the intellect, the practice of virtue, the
endearing affections, and the elegance of deportment in life. In
the social intercourse of persons so circumstanced, the principal
ambition must be to make manifest the possession of such
qualities. It needs but little stretch of the imagination to see the
consequences. Think what a society must be, in which all that
is respectable in intellect and correct in conduct is the object
of display; what effusions of knowledge, what ingenuity of discussion, what patience with the ignorant, what gentleness in
the contest of differing opinions, what tasteful disquisitions on
the slighter ornaments of life, and what grace in the enjoyment
and display of them. Social intercourse of this kind is a school
of all that is grand and lovely in human nature. And where
such is the style of that intercourse in the leading class—a class
not separated from, but intimately mixed up with, the rest of
the community, the imitation of it is inevitable. The community
becomes intellectual and refined.'[25] He goes on to argue that
in his own day 'distinction arises from wealth . . . high mental
qualifications, not being the cause of distinction to such men,
are not possessed by them'.

This extract has several points of interest, not least its assumption that the aristocracy would not be cut off from, but intimately bound up with, the rest of the community. For our
immediate purpose the point is that Mill does not here think
that the possession of wealth is necessarily a corrupting factor.
In short, it supports the view that rulers can be enlightened and
good despite their power. But other passages in Mill's writings
speak in a different vein, and speak repeatedly of the evil of
'interest allied with power' and say that 'such evils are altogether incurable'. He writes: 'And Plato seeing thus clearly the
necessity of identifying the interests of the guardians . . . with
those of the people, bent the whole force of his penetrating
mind to discover the means of affecting such identification; but
being ignorant, as all the ancients were, of the divine principle

[25] James Mill, *Aristocracy*, Art. i, *London Review*, ii, July–January 1835–6.

of representation, found himself obliged to have recourse to extraordinary methods.'[26] In Mill's day the trouble was the system—'the constitution of the honourable houses ... by placing men's interests and their duties not in concord, whence alone the performance of duties can be expected: but in direct opposition, whence violation of duties is ensured.'[27] Later in his life he wrote more temperately, in replying to Macaulay: 'Interest in its rough and ready acceptation, denotes the leading objects of human desire; Wealth, Power, Dignity, Ease ... I suppose that nobody, at least nobody now alive, will dispute that, taking men generally, the bulk of their actions is determined by consideration of these objects. As little, I suppose, will it be disputed that in deliberating the best means for the government of men in society, it is the business of philosophers and legislators ... to look to the more general laws of their nature, rather than the exception.'[28] This is Mill's essential line of thought. There may be saints, and there may be altruists—that he does not deny—but it is highly imprudent to found a system of government on this basis for, like Acton later, Mill would say that government means power, and 'power corrupts'.

The root of the apparent inconsistency between Mill's article on Aristocracy and the above extracts lies in a further ambiguity—namely, what is involved in 'seeking other people's approbation'. Everything depends upon what prompts this approbation, upon what kind of conduct and what qualities of character call forth praise and approval from our fellow-men, whether they are our equals, our superiors, or our inferiors. Macaulay assumed, perhaps understandably, but none the less erroneously, that this approval would only be forthcoming if we catered for the selfish interest, in the literal sense, of other people. But this is not necessarily so, nor is it a true interpretation of Mill, when we put his educational theory alongside his political theory. First, as a general proposition, men may accord praise and blame for a variety of actions and qualities of character. Some may praise those who serve them, and those

[26] *Fragment on Mackintosh*, op. cit., p. 289.
[27] Sraffa, *Ricardo's Correspondence*, op. cit., vi, no. 134, Mill to Ricardo, 19 October 1815.
[28] *Fragment on Mackintosh*, op. cit., pp. 278–9.

8

who flatter: others may praise independence of character, morally worthy actions, actions shewing 'a sense of public interest' as Mill commented in his Commonplace Book, and so on. 'Desire for other people's approbation' in itself does not mean very much, beyond the essential assertion of self-interest in other people's opinion, until we know for what that approbation is accorded.

Broadly speaking Mill means two different things when he talks of 'seeking other people's approbation'. A corrupt government and leaders of a vicious society will award its approbation to its own kind, to those who flatter it, are subservient to it, who do not menace its privileges and power. But in an ideal state, with an aristocracy of the kind he portrayed in his article, things would be very different. Approbation would only be accorded for morally praiseworthy behaviour: right action and upright behaviour would be the path to social approval and, indeed, to material and perhaps political advancement. And all this could be attained by education.

There is clear evidence to support this interpretation in the *Essay on Education*. Mill's essential doctrine is stated in associationist terms. He writes:

'The grand object of human desire is a command over the wills of other men. This may be attained, either by qualities and acts which excite their love and admiration, or by those which excite their terror. When the education is so wisely conducted as to make the train run habitually from the conception of the good end to the conception of the good means; and as often, too, as the good means are conceived, viz. the useful and beneficial qualities, to make the train run on to the conception of the great reward, the command over the wills of men; an association is formed which impels the man through life to pursue the great object of desire, fitting himself to be, and by actually becoming, the instrument of the greatest possible benefit to his fellow men.

'But, unhappily, a command over the wills of men may be obtained by other means than by doing them good; and these, when a man can command them, are the shortest, the easiest, and the most effectual. These other means are all summed up in a command over the pains of other men. When a command over the wills of other men is pursued by the instrumentality of pain, it leads to all the several degrees of vexation, injustice, cruelty, oppression, and tyranny. It is, in truth, the grand source of all wickedness, of all the evil which man brings upon man. When the education is so deplorably bad as to allow an association to be formed in the mind of the child between the grand object of desire, the command over the wills of other men, as the means; the foundation is laid of the bad character —the bad son, the bad brother, the bad husband, the bad father, the bad neighbour, the bad magistrate, the bad citizen— to sum up all in one word, the bad man.'[29]

The point here is really the one which emerged repeatedly in our discussion of Mill's aims in education—the dual purpose he wanted his theories to serve. They are at once a comment on the society of his day and a programme of the ideal society which might be created by the right education. But since the right education was itself the product of a good society which in turn depended on a good government, we are apparently at an impasse. We have noted, in chapter IV, one part of Mill's solution: the device of representation to ensure that the selfish interests of none were disregarded. This requires no reform of character but would reform the government, by force as it were. It would ensure a government, even of selfish and corrupt men, paying some regard to the general happiness. But it would not by itself do more than this. Before arriving at final conclusions on this matter we should examine Mill's theory of Political Education.

IV

In his introductory section in the *Essay on Education* Mill does not distinguish Political from Social education; he groups both under the heading 'social' which he defines as 'the mode in which the mind of the individual is acted upon by the nature of the political institutions under which he lives'.[30] This, in our language, suggests that 'social' is subsumed under 'political'

[29] *Essay on Education*, op. cit., pp. 100–1.
[30] Ibid., p. 44.

rather than the other way about. But we must remember that Mill used the phrases 'political' and 'political institution' very broadly and in a sense which we would equate with 'social'. The important thing is that, in explaining how the political machine affects us, he speaks in the same terms as he uses for social education: the political machine moulds character by rewarding certain qualities and so on. It must always be remembered that Mill's theory of the state rested essentially on an economic basis: we need government to assure each person a reasonable reward for his own labour and without good government he would never get this, as he did not get it in Mill's day. Thus far the concept of Political Education raises no new problems, beyond those we have already discussed in connexion with Social Education. Where Political Education does raise new problems is in Mill's theory of its indirect influence: his assertion that the political machine 'acts upon almost everything else by which the character of the mind is apt to be formed', and his comment that politics was 'like the keystone of the arch: the strength of the whole depends upon it'.[31]

This is the view, typical of Mill's time, that the state really was supreme, as in legal theory it is supposed to be. This would be challenged in more than one quarter nowadays, if it were put forward as a general theory of society and the state. In particular, a Marxist would argue that the state, far from being supreme, was in fact always the reflection of the economic organization of society, and that powerful capitalist forces were always in fact supreme, whatever the legal forms suggested. We have, therefore, two main problems to discuss: first, was the state supreme in Mill's day, and secondly, would this be so in an ideal society—in other words, can we accept the doctrine, not only as a comment on his times, but as a valid political theory true of all organized societies. But both problems depend upon a clear understanding of what is meant by saying that the state was 'supreme', or in other words, that it had the 'real power'. The preliminary question is, what does the word 'power' mean, in the context of politics?

'Power' is a word which is used in many contexts other than political ones, for instance, when we speak of 'mechanical

[31] Ibid., p. 117.

power'. With these we are not concerned. In political contexts, 'power' may be taken to mean 'ability to secure obedience'. It thus raises problems similar to those raised by the more technical term 'sovereignty'. If we take this definition as a starting-point, we can say that those with power give orders, and the rest of the population obey. In so far as the orders of those with power are in fact disregarded, their power is apparent, but not real. The Marxist thesis, according to this, means either that, although the government apparently gives the orders and commands obedience, those with economic power can resist, and in fact decide whether obedience is forthcoming, that is, whether the government's power is real, or that the economic forces themselves determine what orders the government gives.

Now, it seems clear that the terms 'power' and 'obedience' express two sides of a relationship—the same relationship— between one person, or group of persons, and others. The one commands and the other obeys, but for this to happen there must be a certain relationship, and this relationship is what is described by the words 'power' and 'obedience'. It might be argued that 'power' was the ability to force someone to do one's will. When we turn this into a practical situation, however, it means that a person causes another to obey him by threat of unpleasant consequences if obedience is refused. It is not literally forcing obedience, but rather securing acquiescence by having the power to impose punishment or sanctions if obedience is refused.

If this is so, then it is clearly possible to speak of someone having the 'power' to secure the obedience of others by other means than physical coercion, or threat of punishment. It could be said that a person has power if he controls the media of education and propaganda in a community, or, if religious faith is strongly held, the leaders of the church will have power. In each case the person is in a position to secure obedience. Conversely, a person may nominally hold power, and yet in practice be inhibited from exercising it. Macaulay quotes examples of this in illustrating his point that although the government and the magistrates have the power to order cruel punishment for breach of the game laws, if they exercised it to the legal limits, public opinion would be affronted, and their

action would not in fact secure obedience. In these circumstances, the 'power' of the landlords, magistrates, and government, is what they can in fact do, not what legal theory or
formal institutions state they can do. The point is that power is
not, as language seems to suggest, something possessed by someone, or by some institution. It is the expression of one side of a
relationship—the other being obedience. And since obedience
can be obtained by many and varied means, by propaganda,
by threat, by direct coercion, by bribe—economic or social—
and, indeed, by free consent and respect, the proper starting
point is to enquire into the fact of obedience or acquiescence in
any particular situation, and to find out why it is accorded.
'Power' is strictly a derivative concept from this.

How does the Marxist contention appear, in the light of this
argument? If it is argued that business and capitalist interests
have the real power, it must mean, so I have argued, that other
people accord their obedience to such interests, either because
they fear the consequences of not doing so, or for other reasons.
It could be an indirect power, in the sense that the people
obeyed the government and the government, in turn, but more
discreetly, obeyed the capitalist interests. Thus far, the Marxist
thesis would survive unchanged. But once we put the argument
in terms of obedience and acquiescence, it becomes difficult
to assert that obedience and acquiescence is always, in capitalist
communities, given to the same group, for the same reasons.

For obedience is an attitude of mind, and it is influenced to
a considerable extent not only by the *fact* that some individuals
have powers of punishment and coercion, but also by what the
people in general think—whether they *think* the individuals in
question have the power. Thus, in country districts, long after
the ballot was secret, the vote was not strictly free, because
people thought that landlords would evict Liberal sympathizers,
and this meant that they thought that landlords had powers of
eviction, legally, which was true, and much more vital, that
they would in fact exercise them for this purpose and succeed.
We have only to contrast this with the present day to see the
point. With tied cottages in the country legal powers are, I
believe, the same as they were. The economic power of the
landlord has not changed, nor has the economic dependence

of the peasant: what has changed is the attitude of both. It would be unthinkable today for eviction or threat of eviction to be used to secure votes in a particular direction: what has changed is an attitude of mind, and in changing, it has removed this particular power from the landlord.

In this sense, public opinion creates power. If the public believe that certain individuals have power over them, then, *because of that belief*, the power is there. In this sense, a doctrine like Marxism helps to create the situation it purports to describe. In this sense it is impossible to generalize about different periods of history as to who had the power, since it depends in each case upon the public opinion of the day, and to whom the public accorded their obedience and acquiescence. Hence, in examining the circumstances of Mill's day, we must ask 'To whom did the people accord their obedience?' and secondly 'To whom, if anyone, did the government accord its obedience?'

In Mill's day, what would now be called 'vested interests' undoubtedly had the power, but they did not operate behind the government, or even through the government, for they *were* the government. Power was not hidden or discreet, it was openly in the hands of the landowners, and overt in that they, in person, or through direct nominees, sat in Parliament, and controlled appointments in the Church. The theory of Virtual Representation is, indeed, a defence not a denial of this situation. The crux of the problem of reform in any direction was to reform the government since it was in fact, not merely in form, the source of the power of the landlords, of the Church, of the magistrate. Resistance to it was not by appeal to law, but in defiance of the lawful authority of the country. Mill may not have seen the heart of the problem in saying that reform of government was the vital thing, but he certainly saw the start of the problem. It may be that when government was reformed, vested interests would still exercise the real power, behind the scenes, but this situation had not arisen, and until government itself was reformed, any such thesis could not be tested. We may find Mill out of date with his assertion that 'Politics is the keystone of the arch', but in his day this was true: questions of the power of government to coerce large economic interests had not arisen because the government openly and avowedly represented those interests.

If we regard 'power', as we have suggested, as something founded on public acquiescence, and as the expression of one side of this relationship, then the government was supreme in Mill's day because all people thought it was supreme—not surprisingly, in view of its composition which openly reflected the alliance of Church, landed interest, and State. It would follow from our argument that the Reform movement, whether in its intellectual leaders, such as Mill, or in its mob following, helped to create the power of government by their own conviction that reform of government was the key to all else. We find echoes of this in the later Chartist movement. And when we remember that the government, in these days, was a government with an active economic policy, it is not surprising that it was regarded as 'the keystone of the arch'. It was not the laissez-faire of the mid-nineteenth century, it was rather the planned economy of the eighteenth. It was the government which enacted the Corn Laws, which maintained the Navigation Laws, import duties and controls, and which shewed itself strangely reluctant to enact an effective factory act, while maintaining old rules regarding apprenticeship. It was not capitalism exploiting the people because the government refused to intervene, it was landed interest exploiting by the medium of government intervention.

V

We may now draw together our various conclusions about Mill's theory of Social and Political Education. The key to understanding it is to realize that it performed two functions: it described the corruption and evils of his own society and it tried to portray what an ideal one might be like. This dual purpose is apparent in the final paragraph of the *Essay on Education* where Mill writes: 'When the political machine is such, that the grand objects of desire are seen to be the natural prizes of great and virtuous conduct—of high services to mankind, and of the generous and amiable sentiments from which

great endeavours in the service of mankind naturally proceed—
it is natural to see diffused among mankind a generous ardour
in the acquisition of all those admirable qualities which prepare
a man for admirable actions; great intelligence, perfect self-
command, and over-ruling benevolence. When the political
machine is such that the grand objects of desire are seen to be
the reward, not of virtue, not of talent, but of subservience to
the will, and command over the affections of the ruling few;
interest with the *man above* to be the only sure means to the
next step in wealth, or power or consideration, and so on; the
means of pleasing the man above become, in that case, the
great object of pursuit. And as the favours of the man above are
necessarily limited—as some, therefore, of the candidates for
his favour can only obtain the objects of that desire by dis-
appointing others—the arts of supplanting rise into importance;
and the whole of that tribe of faculties denoted by the words
intrigue, flattery, back-biting, treachery, etc., are the fruitful
offspring of that political education which government, where
the interests of the subject many are but a secondary object,
cannot fail to produce.'[32]

The psychological basis of both theories was association
psychology but not in the commonly accepted mechanical
meaning of that term. For the whole basis of Mill's Political and
Social Education, in either a bad society or a good one, was the
concept of long trains of ideas as means associated with the end
of Wealth, Dignity, and Power. In a bad society these were
attained by and associated with causing pain to others: in a
good, there were comparable and much more beneficial associations with giving pleasure to others. Either way it is a means-end
analysis, a goal-directed psychological explanation, and
although couched in associationist terms, is the reverse of what
would now be regarded, and has traditionally been regarded
as the associationist model of explanation. It was, like any form
of associationism, an environmentalist theory, but it was one
which ascribed power to a formative period, and especially to
hedonism as a motive.

To this psychological basis Mill adds a second factor—that
all education is determined by society and by the political

[32] *Essay on Education*, op. cit., pp. 118–19.
8*

machine. The latter controls the former and both control the rewards. Hence both parents and teachers were the product of society and a corrupt society had no hope, and it may be added, no intention, of producing or allowing teachers uncongenial to it. There is no doubt at all that Mill attached considerable importance to this indirect influence of the State and society on education. Late in his life he wrote: 'Among the objects which require the attention of reformers Education stands in one of the highest places; though it is never to be forgotten that it is the operation of the political machine which has the greatest effect in forming the minds of men. We are not able to go into that subject here, because it is closely connected with the means adopted for the teaching of religion . . . we confess we despair wholly of seeing any beneficent plan of state education carried into effect so long as we have a clergy on its present footing. There might be a clergy so happily circumstanced as to have an interest in good education, and then we should obtain inestimable advantage. The clergy of the Church of England are so unhappily circumstanced as to have a decided interest against it, and till their position is altered, a good state education is hopeless.'[33] And we have, from quite early days, his violent attacks on the Church in his pamphlet *Schools for All*, 1812, and other articles. Although as we noted in chapter III there were other and very practical reasons for these attacks, it is important to note that it was the position of the Established Church—where it was put by the State—and of its connexion with privilege, which was to Mill the real evil.

We should remember the close association of existing organs of formal education with particular social institutions such as the Church. The idea that educational institutions should be independent of particular social pressures was a new one, embraced by reformers, but not illustrated by the practice of the times. The Church of England quite overtly proclaimed its desire to control education, and, to Mill, this was a clear admission that it sought to control the minds of youth, rather than to bring forth people able to think critically for themselves. Hence Mill's doctrine of indirect education, describing as an

[33] Extract from *London Review*, no. 1, 1835, *The State of the Nation*, pp. 23–4. J. Mill.

agent of education not only the schools and teachers but the social institutions behind them whose interests they were designed to serve.

Mill was therefore faced with a reform of the state and of society before there could be a reform of education. We have already noted that he thought that the essential first step was to make the government fully representative of all the people: if the selfish interests of all were represented then none could be disregarded and even a corrupt government would have to aim at the general pleasure, if not happiness. But there is one further point which is a matter of conjecture, for there is no direct evidence to support it. It would follow from Mill's theory that monitorial teaching was much less corrupted by social influences than the teaching of adults, providing the supervising schoolmasters were, as was intended, specially trained for the work. It may be that this was one of the reasons for Mill's support for this system, and indeed for his opposition to the Church of England monitorial schools, who would, in his eyes, suborn it to their own purposes. There is no evidence to support this conjecture, but Mill's own practice is significant. He controlled the whole environment and the whole of the education of his nine children by means of the monitorial system. He did this till the end of his life and in the early days amid circumstances of the greatest difficulty and indeed penury. Even when John Mill's education had reached an advanced stage, he refused tempting offers to send him to Cambridge. It is hard to resist the conclusion that a major purpose in all this was to insulate his children from the influence of a corrupt society, and that in general he might have regarded monitorial education as the logical means of reforming education in a corrupt society.

VIII

Conclusion

James Mill's theory of education rests on three basic elements. These are his moral philosophy, his theory of knowledge and associated psychology, and his political and social philosophy. Owing to the existence of full-scale analyses of his moral philosophy and of his theory of knowledge and psychology, we have been able to explore in some depth the full basis of his educational theory, and to examine the relationship between his general philosophical position and his educational theory. But in political and social philosophy he wrote little: most of what we know, apart from the *Essay on Government*, is derived from his various articles on contemporary political events, and from his private correspondence. Yet a study of his life would suggest that, with the possible exception of education in theory and practice, politics and political philosophy were his dominating interests.

As such, his philosophy of education is a model of what a theory of education should be, whether or not we agree with Mill's conclusions. For any such theory should make explicit three main problems. First, it should state an aim or purpose: this is ultimately a matter of moral philosophy, and of indicating the kind of adult which a suitable education might hope to produce. No educational theory could be complete without a statement of purpose, for all education involves some change in the pupil, and such change will achieve some aim or purpose, whether it is explicitly acknowledged and stated, or not. Hence a theory of education needs to be explicit about the aim of education. Second, such a theory should concern itself with psychology, with examining the nature of the pupil, his abilities and aptitudes, his stages of development, in order to ascertain how best he will learn, both in the intellectual sphere and in the area of character-training. Thirdly, any theory of education needs to contemplate that department of philosophy called Theory of Knowledge: all intellectual education is the introduction and training of the pupil in various forms of knowledge, and one determinant of educational practice is the kind of knowledge to which it is desired to introduce the pupil. It may be, as common sense would suggest, that there are several different forms of knowledge. Or it may be, as James Mill implied, rather than argued, that there is only one true form of knowledge and that all other subjects in the curriculum are examples of the application of this one true form. Either way, the content and method of education will be affected by our decision on these points. But Mill added a fourth area of enquiry: by his very wide definition of 'education', as covering all environmental influence from 'the first germ of existence . . . to the final extinction of life', he was able to develop, or at any rate outline, concepts of social and political education, or the influence of society and of the state respectively on its members.

The aim of Mill's education was the utilitarian ethic and this is generally understood to mean that children should be trained to further the greatest happiness of the greatest number of people. Certainly it did mean this, but our examination of Mill's educational theory and of his moral philosophy has shewn that it meant much more besides. We distinguished five strands of thought in Mill's statement of the ideal: education for personal happiness, the search for the happiness of others, the adoption of the principle of equality in distributing it, the individualism which left each person the final judge of where his or her own happiness lay and finally, psychological hedonism—the doctrine that man must, in fact, invariably seek his own pleasure. It was this last factor which seems to stop the theory being acceptable, for it is essentially inconsistent with the altruism demanded by Utilitarianism: it was the same factor, which, in Mill's eyes, rendered his moral philosophy consistent with his general philosophical position which was basically that of the English empirical tradition and involved a reduction of moral experience to ethical naturalism, i.e. that the desire for the Good is not different from any other desires, or, in Mill's terminology, that the Good is pleasure, simple and unqualified.

Without the insistence on psychological hedonism, however, the theory has much more to be said for it, particularly since it is clear that education for one's personal happiness formed a major part in it, both as part of the ideal itself and as guiding us as to what to seek for other people. It is here that we encounter the pitfalls of language. To most people, the term 'hedonism' conveys a life dedicated to the search for pleasure and to those with a high sense of duty, of whatever kind, such a philosophy is repugnant. But to Mill, the pursuit of personal happiness meant almost precisely the reverse of what we would call a life of pleasure, or, indeed, if we recall the 'pleasures' of both rich and poor in his day, outlined in the opening chapter, of what they would have called 'pleasure'. To Mill the attainment of personal happiness meant stern self-control, the temperance or moderation which his son tells us was 'the central point of moral precept' with him, an understanding that 'most pleasures were overvalued' and the untiring search for 'what we deliberately approve'. A glance at his personal life confirms this interpretation: the routine at Ford Abbey was puritanical rather than hedonistic in the ordinary meaning of the term. Yet such a doctrine, if not carried to the extremes that James Mill carried it in his personal life and in the education of his children, has much to be said for it. For it is a very tenable proposition to maintain that the ultimate Good is a state or attitude of mind in ourselves, towards both ourselves and other people: a state of mind which wished to cultivate the highest part of our natures because only then would we find ultimate satisfaction, which desired the same for others, which treated men with equal respect and which finally was sufficiently tolerant to leave to them the judgment of where their own happiness lay. Pre-occupation with Mill's psychological hedonism, understandable because of his frequent re-iteration of his belief in it, should not obscure our minds from realizing the many important truths which his moral philosophy contained.

When we turn from the Aims of Education to the psychological basis we find ourselves in the difficulty that in those days there was no psychology in the modern meaning of the term. The question to which Mill addresses himself, 'What is the nature of the human mind?' can just as well be a question in philosophical theory of knowledge—a question of *what* the mind knows—, as a question in psychology, or of how the mind perceives and learns. To do him justice, he does not claim to be writing a psychology, rather he uses the term 'philosophy of the human mind'. But since he also says that the essential question is 'How the mind, with those properties which it possesses, can, through the operation of certain means, be rendered most conducive to a certain end', it is proper to ask what kind of psychological basis to education is implied, if not directly stated in his theory.

When we came to do this we found that Mill's theory was of relatively little value as an explanation of how we learned. All knowledge derived from sensations and from the order or association in which we encounter sensations. This might be thought to tell us how children learn and to prescribe an educational method of using as much practical experience as possible. But this was not Mill's practice: his own tuition, says his son, suffered from the disadvantage that it was 'too much in the abstract'. From the standpoint of a theory of education we are left with the conclusion that to say that sense-experience was the original source of all knowledge, was, to Mill, a statement of the nature of knowledge rather than a prescription of how it was to be acquired, or transmitted.

The association principle, however, served another purpose in Mill's philosophy. Under the guidance and stimulus of the desire to obtain Pleasure and to avoid Pain, we can associate beneficent means of attaining these ends, and become morally good people, or we can find such ends associated with causing pain to others, with corruption and so forth, and be morally bad. This use of the principle depended upon the statement of a goal or purpose of all human behaviour, namely that of pleasure to oneself, and the association with it of long trains of ideas or 'means' of attaining the goal. The result was the assumption of firm associations, of a rather lengthy kind, which dominate character and behaviour: such associations were formed early in life and tended to last, though the fact that they worked, or produced results, in a corrupt society was an important factor in securing their permanence. Here Mill seems to be speaking more as a psychologist, for this does contain clear implications for the educator: it is his business so to train the young that they associate the general happiness with their own, and with only beneficent means of attaining such happiness, i.e. means which bring pleasure rather than pain to others.

When Mill thus speaks as a psychologist, however, he ceases to be an Associationist in any recognizable psychological meaning of the term. Association psychology has a long history and one of its features is its adaptability, in modern times, to several different psychological theories, each of which, it could be argued, was founded on the associationist model. The most obvious example is the theory of the conditioned reflex. But a glance at modern associationist theories will shew what, in psychology, the term means. It has generally concentrated on peripheral response to a stimulus—that is, a response by part of the mind to a particular stimulus, it asserts that what we learn are, in the general use of the term, 'habits' and not cognitive structures, and thus that intellectual learning is basically the same as learning a skill and finally that learning is a process of trial and error rather than insight.[1] As such it stands in the opposite camp to that of the Gestalt theorists whose theories have stressed a purposive explanation of action and a goal-directed theory of learning. It is true that some modern associationists such as Hebb have met Gestalt criticisms by shewing an associationist explanation in terms of the influence of earlier associations on later, but this does not alter the general nature of the associationist model of explanation. It is, as it has been traditionally described, necessarily an atomic theory, and, stripped of any doctrine of motive, a mechanistic one.[2] When motives have been introduced, the associationist model most comfortably accommodates the stimulus–response theories.

Mill, in his theories of character-training, is completely at variance with this. He uses the language of association, but not its appropriate explanatory model or its logic. Although he claimed to have founded a science of the human mind, with one single explanatory principle, that of association, he in fact did nothing of the kind. Where he is scientific in his arguments

[1] E. R. Hilgard, *Theories of Learning*, Appleton-Century-Crofts Inc., N. York, 1965, pp. 9–11.
[2] Cf. G. Humphrey, *Thinking*, N. York, 1963, p. 12.

and explanation he ceases to be a psychologist: thus, when he insists upon analysing sensations into their atomic elements, he is departing from the actual evidence of introspection and offering instead a scientific, theoretical, and hypothetical analysis. Conversely, when he does speak as a psychologist, both in analysing what people are, and in portraying what they might become, he does so not in the scientific terms of a mechanistic theory, but in the language of means and ends, of purposive behaviour and of a teleological form of explanation. The addition of the Pleasure-Pain principle to his associationism makes a fundamental change in it.

When the theory is looked at, not as a Psychology, but as a Theory of Knowledge, it is at least clear, explicit and consistent. It is, in fact, a very competent codification of the English empirical tradition and many modern philosophers would argue that, in essentials, it was on the right lines. In educational theory, its ultimate implication was, as Mill himself conceived it, a curriculum in which the central point was logic, and that logic was the logic of natural science. This, the art of thinking rationally and logically, was to him the highest point of intellectual education. But it meant that there was only one true form of knowledge, that which could be 'verified in experience' and only one kind of logical thinking, that of science. Mill's views on curriculum were consistent with his philosophy, though he himself never demonstrated the connexion. And if his theory of knowledge and his proposals for the curriculum are looked at together, they raise problems of some importance, namely whether the traditional way of looking at a curriculum, as demonstrating varied ways of knowing, each requiring to be in 'balance' with the rest, is in fact soundly based in philosophy. Mill would have said not, as we have seen, and here as in other places his views give those who differ from him a case to answer. In our own day it is rather odd that students of curriculum theory have not noticed that Logical Positivism poses a similar challenge.

His doctrines of Political and Social education were not original for, in essence, they were formulated by Helvétius: they arise essentially, and quite logically, from Mill's wide definition of 'education' as synonymous with all environmental influence, and from his position as an extreme environmentalist, holding that changes in the environment in which they lived could make all men both good and intelligent. They also arise from his observations of the contemporary scene and whatever their value in general, the doctrines of social and political education were a true comment on his times, providing, that is, that one overlooks the somewhat eccentric use of the word 'education' to describe such influences.

The basis of these doctrines in practice might be the society and political machine of his day, but the theoretical and academic justification lay in Mill's association psychology, although the connexion between the two is not as systematically demonstrated as one could wish. Association psychology *could* be the basis of a theory of social and political education, on the obvious grounds that the mechanical form of the theory would mean that whatever constituted the environment of the individual for most of his life would automatically have most influence,[3] and it would follow that society would certainly be more influential than a relatively brief period of formal schooling in the context of a man's whole life. But such a theory would ascribe no special importance or influence to the environment during a formative period in one's younger years: Mill did think them important, and, as we have seen, he was not in fact a mechanical associationist. To him, Society and the State exercized their influence because of their powers of social approval and disapproval, and finally and crucially mainly because the political machine could reward the qualities which suited it, and man, being a hedonistic animal, would therefore cultivate those qualities. Most of the theory as stated is a comment on the corrupt society and government of Mill's day: in so far as it is made a theory of general application, it is on the basis of education forging different and more benevolent associations of means. with the end of the ultimate objects of desire which men will in any case seek. In this sense, and it is a special sense, the theory of social and political education *does* rest on association psychology.

To many, these doctrines of social and political education

[3] And Mill does sometimes talk in these terms, as when discussing 'imitation' as a means of social influence.

will be Mill's most significant contribution to educational theory. Unfortunately not only were these doctrines only sketched in Mill's *Essay on Education,* but our knowledge of his political philosophy is also all too limited and virtually our only source is the article on *Government* in the *Encyclopedia Britannica.* This, despite its considerable prestige at the time, is in fact far from a complete statement of a political philosophy, and in particular, it fails to work out what the ideal state might be like. It rests the case for government squarely on an economic basis—the need to secure to each man an adequate reward for his labour, and from this sees the case for representative government purely in terms of unreformed man whose selfish interest, if represented, could not be disregarded by any government, however evil the proclivities of the ruling class might be.

All this is a recipe for the day rather than a statement of the ideal. To have immediate application as a practical reform was, as we have noted, characteristic of much of Mill's thinking, and the key to understanding him is to realize his dual purpose of wanting to promote immediate reform and to portray an ideal. But with his political theory, it is nearly all rooted in the problems of the day, and we are told little or nothing of what an ideal utilitarian state might be like. Two examples will suffice to underline this point. In an ideal utilitarian state would the government have no other function than to secure to each member an adequate wage? Perhaps Mill's individualism would move him to say 'yes', but if so, it reduces the doctrine of political education to a very minor role, and certainly one could envisage a good government playing a much more active part in educating the character of its citizens. The second point is this: Mill speaks of the 'reward of qualities' approved of by the political machine and makes clear enough the evil effects of the corrupt government of his day. But would the same situation hold in a fully democratic state? Would there be the same social structure, in which there were people in a position to reward qualities? Would not an ideal society postulate a more equal relationship between its members, where social approval and disapproval might still be a potent influence, but where material rewards counted for far less, and where fewer people were in a position to control them? These are largely matters

of conjecture, but only because we are told so little of the positive role of the State and of social and political education in a
reformed England. The indications are, however, that Mill
never carried his thinking as far as this. There is evidence that,
on the whole, he thought in an eighteenth-century context—we
have already noted his comment that factory disorders were an
aberration from the natural order of things. His article on the
Aristocracy also bears this out. And though it may seem that
Mill's psychological hedonism has in it the seeds of Marxism,
Mill was in no sense a socialist, and condemned with vigour
those who attacked the rights of property, as the following
extracts from a letter to Brougham make clear: 'The nonsense
to which your Lordship alludes about the rights of the labourer
to the whole produce of the country, wages, profits and rent, all
included, is the mad nonsense of our friend Hodgskin . . . These
opinions, if they were to spread, would be the subversion of
civilised society . . . This makes me astonished at the madness
of people of another description who recommend the invasion
of one species of property, so thoroughly knavish and unprin-
cipled, that it can never be executed, without extinguishing
respect for the rights of property in the whole body of the
nation.'[4] A cynic might comment that Mill was not the first
radical reformer, nor indeed the last, to grow more conservative
in his views as he grew older, and, incidentally, wealthier. But
it is fair to say that, with Ricardo, he had never sympathized
with extreme views on economic matters.

The failure to develop the positive side of his doctrines of
social and political education really stems from his failure to
develop his political philosophy as a whole. Unlike the rest of
his thinking, his political theory, such as it is, is inferred from
the needs of the day, instead of the other way about, that is,
that the practical reforms needed might have been inferred
from a contemplation of the ideal. In the field of law reform in
particular, this was how the Utilitarians proceeded and it was,
of course, the essence of the argument of Plato's *Republic*. On
the other hand, Mill's influence on practical political reform
was greater than historians have given him credit for and Bain
comments of 1832 that 'Had Mill not appeared on the stage at

[4] Mill to Brougham, 3 September 1832, quoted in Bain, op. cit., p. 364.

the opportune moment, the whole cast of political thinking at the time of the Reform settlement must have been very inferior in point of sobriety and ballast to what it was. His place could not have been taken by any other man that we can fix upon'.[5]

Before leaving the subject of social and political education, there are two general points to be made. Mill mentions not only the direct but the indirect effect of society and the state upon education, and by this he means that they influence the teachers and the parents directly responsible for education. This influence, he felt, was all the more perverse, if it were embalmed in an institution, such as the established church, with its position guaranteed by the State, with many privileges and much wealth, and with every incentive to preserve these, and to give an education which would produce people to whom the established church was acceptable. Many and bitter were Mill's complaints about the church, and especially about the fact that it was a state church. As we have quoted, he wrote that he despaired of seeing any advance in education 'while the church is on its present basis'. The general point to emerge from this is a plea for the independence of educational institutions or, as he puts it in the *Essay on Education*: 'An institution for *education* which is hostile to progression, is, therefore, the most preposterous, and vicious thing, which the mind of man can conceive'.[6] And for this open-mindedness to progressive ideas, educational institutions must be independent of the state and of other powerful institutions in society who would have an interest in something other than reform.

The other general point is associated with this. Despite the fact that the theory of social and political education was never elaborated, it seems to me to raise points which all educational theorists should consider. For we do not need to be extreme environmentalists to appreciate the essential logic of Mill's position that, in so far as we ascribe powers to deliberate educational measures, we are implying that the environment in general has power to modify the character and intelligence of individuals. If this is so the influence of first, the family, and secondly of at least the personal society in which individuals

---

[5] Bain, op. cit., p. 447.
[6] *Essay on Education*, op. cit., p. 112.

live, cannot be ignored. The inference is that the power of formal education to effect social change is limited: schools are more likely to reflect social change and social attitudes than to cause them. There have been two developments which might be regarded as illustrations of this point since Mill's day. The first is the long sectarian controversy over education throughout the nineteenth century and for part of the twentieth. According to the Mill doctrine, the controversy reflected the importance which society attached to religion and while this was so, all attempts like his own, however rationally based, were doomed to have only marginal success, as he discovered. But when, in the twentieth century, social attitudes to religion changed, so did the educational controversy die down. It was, however, replaced by one over comprehensive schools, and this too seems rooted in problems of society and what we think it should be, and whether what is called 'divisive' schooling is properly reflecting society as it now is, or perhaps, as some would wish it to be. What Mill would have denied, however, was that you could change society by changing the schooling: to him society and the state inevitably were the dominant factors. It is when the state and society are at variance with the ideals of educationists that conflict inevitably occurs.

When we draw together the various strands of Mill's educational theory and of his philosophy, we have first to notice that it is a logical whole. The ethic determines the shape society and the state should take and it is the aim of education. Education can do all that Mill wanted, and for everyone and not only the privileged, because of his environmentalist psychology. Environmentalism in psychology was explained and supported by the association principle which both explained a bad society and pointed the way to a good one. It did so, essentially, by fusing, or attempting to fuse, Mill's most central conviction—of the truth of psychological hedonism, with his altruistic ethic. By this means, his moral philosophy became naturalistic and was thus consistent with his general philosophy of sensation. The crux of all this was the association principle.

Mill would probably have regarded his *Analysis of the Human Mind* as his greatest work, with the possible exception of his *History of India*. For many years after his death the association principle as he developed it was the basis of philosophical discussion. In the analysis offered here, we have not found it to be a major contribution, principally because the term, and indeed the theory of Association of Ideas is potentially a very vague and flexible one and Mill took full advantage of its flexibility.[7] Just for this reason it does not explain very much—it is too general a theory—and for precisely the same reason, because it appeared to explain everything, it cannot be doubted that Mill himself saw it as central and crucial to his philosophical thinking. Most of all perhaps, it provided a theoretical basis to his environmentalism and this in turn was the basis of his theory of education.

One of the most interesting things about Mill as a philosopher and as a political reformer was the importance which he attached to education in his scheme of things. Thus he saw associationism as vital because, to him, education, in the wide sense in which he defined it, was the key to everything. But in fact his educational theory does not necessarily depend upon association psychology although it certainly requires some kind of environmentalist psychology. For this reason it is impossible to agree with Professor Cavanagh, that he 'definitely grounds educational theory on psychology',[8] for when we examined his theory from the psychological point of view, we found that it told us little. In fact, the importance of the educational theory lies elsewhere, first in his moral philosophy, and second in the width of his conception of what the term 'education' covered.

The moral aims in education seem to me important in two ways. First, if it is accepted, as I have argued, that despite the language of Pain and Pleasure and associated mechanistic terms, Mill was in fact following the general line of Greek philosophy, then it seems to me he is stating some points which all moral philosophers would accept as important. The central plea is that we should cultivate the highest desires in our nature and, if we do, we shall find that this gives us the greatest satisfaction. Although in practice this moral training requires much

[7] Thus although in the main he accounts for social and political education in hedonistic and teleological terms, when he talks of Imitation as a source of social influence, he speaks as a mechanical associationist.

[8] Quoted in *James Mill on Education*, op. cit., p. 40.

self-control, and many occasions of resisting immediate pleasures or 'passions' as Mill termed it, the ultimate ideal was not
a conflict between duty and pleasure, but a position in which
man did good because that is what he most wanted to do. Those
who differ from this explanation have to explain why anyone
should ever want to do the right thing and also, of course, why
it should not be morally better if they did desire the Good, or
as Mill put it 'actions are still more moral, if good to others is
intended'. Arising from this is a second point, which is a direct
corollary of Mill's grounding his educational theory not on
psychology but on a moral ideal. It was, and it had to be, a
democratic theory of education or else to deny to some the
possibility of becoming morally praiseworthy individuals. Mill
was, I think, the first educational theorist to face this problem
squarely. For democracy rests on the assumption that each
citizen, however humble, should have a voice in public decisions
and the ultimate basis of this is that such decisions are in the
end moral ones. But with Mill the matter went further than
what we ordinarily understand by the term 'moral education'.
To him all moral behaviour required calculation of the consequences of one's actions and this required a certain standard
of intellectual education for all.

Moral education conceived as Mill conceived it seems to me
to have important elements of truth. During the nineteenth
century the English public school, as we understand the term,
was at the height of its popularity; many existing schools were
founded then and other foundations were transformed. At their
best, perhaps because, like Mill, they controlled the whole
environment of the pupil, they turned out adults with a high
sense of duty, and many in later life lived up to this early
training. But a sense of duty is only part of what moral education should consist of, for by itself it does not produce a critical
attitude towards what one's duty really is, whether the code or
principle one is following is in fact the path to the ideal. Mill's
conception of moral education stressed this latter point: all
action involved calculation and intelligent forethought, and
all action involved constant critical reflection as to what would in
fact promote the general happiness. I feel that this is an essential,
and frequently neglected, part of moral education.

The second main contribution of Mill lies in his wide definition of education, and the associated doctrines of social and
political education. As we have noted, the questions posed by
these doctrines are important, even if the answers given by
Mill are either erroneous or inadequate. What is more doubtful
is whether it is right to use the term 'education' for such political and social influences. In our normal use of the term we
regard 'education' as a deliberate, purposive activity—a
deliberate manipulation of the environment to effect certain
changes, thought desirable, in the pupil. And it is deliberate
and purposive by both teacher and pupil. Does this apply to
concepts of society and the state as educators?

One answer to this would be to note that we sometimes use
the word 'education' for less deliberate activity, as when we
speak of foreign travel as educational. Here we refer to an
activity undertaken for pleasure, but which has, as one of its
effects, an improvement in some way in the intellectual or moral
character of the traveller. What we seem to mean here is that
education can be an aspect of an activity undertaken for other
reasons. This may be what Mill's doctrine would come to in an
ideal state, but all his comments, both public and private,
would suggest that he meant something stronger than this
when he refers to society and the state as educators. Incidentally, there is no reason to suppose that he disagreed with Bentham in the letter sent to Thomas Hodgskin on how to use his
travels: this was certainly a very deliberately planned programme to ensure that travel was educational. The point of
using the term 'education' is perhaps not of major importance,
and it is not one which can be clearly resolved. What we can
say is that by using the term 'education' to describe the influence
of society and the state upon its members, Mill achieves a
striking effect and he also calls attention to a point which most
political philosophers would accept as important, namely that
the form of the state will affect the character of its members
and that, for example, the ultimate justification of a democratic
state lies in the claim that the active democratic citizen is morally a better person than the citizen produced or fostered by a
non-democratic state. What needs to be worked out is the
relationship between such educative purposes, and other

purposes of the state and Mill's failure to do this stems from his failure to develop in any detail a political philosophy, and to concentrate instead upon immediate remedies for the political problems of his time.

A point of more substance is to consider the logical corollary of ascribing to society and the state as much power and influence as Mill did. Does it not lead inevitably to a doctrine of the social determination of morals, and indeed, of ideas? Such a doctrine is in the end circular, for it cannot logically explain the existence of Mill or other critics of society. But just as Mill stopped short in his hedonism of what some would regard as the logical conclusion of Marxism, so in his social and political theory did he avoid the determinist position which he sometimes seems to be hinting at. For Mill's ultimate faith, and a very powerful conviction, was in the rationality of man.

This faith in human reason is a distinguishing characteristic of utilitarianism, and it seems to me to take two forms. Utilitarianism is rationalist in holding that you could state an ideal, which reason and argument could shew to be good, and which men could work out the best means of attaining. But it was also rationalist in its faith that, if the ideal were good, and logic could demonstrate this, *all* men would realize this and work towards it. In this it stood in sharp contrast to any form of determinism, whose circular argument must eventually lead to a denial of the possibility of rational thought. It is also in contrast with more moderate theories such as those of Graham Wallas in *Human Nature in Politics* which emphasize the irrational motivation of various kinds which in fact brings about political change.

So far as James Mill himself was concerned, the development of powers of human reasoning and the belief that reason would prevail were almost a central article of faith. He once wrote to William Allen: 'I am afraid I have expressed myself in favour of my opinion, with an appearance of warmth, which may induce you to yield more to my *will* than to my *reason*. I beg you will let it have no such effect.'[9] And the same man who wrote this placed Logic, or the power of correct reasoning, at the head of every educational curriculum with which he was

[9] Mill to Allen, 17 January 1811, Brougham MSS. 10775, U.C.L.

concerned, whether for his son, Francis Place's daughter, or the students of University College. Even more significant was his, albeit reluctant, belief in a state-controlled system of education, despite all the dangers which both his theory and his observation implied, that such education would be corrupt and twisted by the government to produce a docile population. Mill thought a literate and educated populace would prevail, despite the dangers, for he wrote: 'And with regard to the danger of training the people generally to habits of servility and toleration of arbitrary power, if their education be entrusted to Government, or persons patronised by the Government—we can only say, that although we are far from considering the danger either as small or chimerical, it is still so very great and good to have the whole facility of reading and writing diffused through the whole body of the people, that we should be willing to run considerable risks for its acquirement, or even greatly to accelerate that acquirement. There is something in the possession of those keys of knowledge and of thought, so truly admirable, that, when joined to another inestimable blessing, it is scarcely possible for any government to convert them into instruments of evil. That security is—the Liberty of the Press. Let the people only be taught to read, though by instruments ever so little friendly to their general interests, and the very intelligence of the age will provide them with books which will prove an antidote to the poison of their pedagogues ... But grant ... a reading people and a free press—and the prejudices on which misrule supports itself will gradually and silently disappear. The impressions, indeed, which it is possible to make at the early age at which reading and writing are taught, and during the very short time that teaching lasts, are so very slight and transitory, that they must be easily effaced whenever there is anything to counteract them.'[10]

In this study of James Mill and the relations between his philosophy and his educational theory two essential points have guided me. The first has been to study him as an individual thinker, not as Bentham's disciple, nor as a member, or even a founder-member of a movement. The second has been to see him and his thinking in the historical context of the time in

[10] *Edinburgh Review*, February 1813, pp. 211–12.

which he lived and the social and political problems of the day which were ever before his mind. I should maintain that both these guiding principles were essential to the study of any past thinker, for unless such people are studied as individuals we cannot really penetrate their minds and reconstruct their thoughts, and unless we study them in their historical context we cannot really ascertain what those thoughts were, for we are tacitly assuming that their society had no influence on them and this is as absurd as the determinist view that thinkers are merely the product of their society. However true these two principles are as a generalization, they are especially true of the English Utilitarians. Here we have a movement, which can be argued to be a climax of a development of thought for several centuries, which was a dominant way of thinking in England for the whole of the nineteenth century, and in many ways, the twentieth. It is all too easy to slip into facile generalizations about the movement, to talk of the Utilitarians, rather than to study individual thinkers, forgetting the fact that, in so far as Utilitarianism has permanent value, it is the individual thinkers who made it what it is. But here also we have a movement which, much more than most philosophies, was rooted in the problems of the day, whose advocates were deeply concerned to reform their own society and who, far from living in an ivory tower, were men of action as well as of thought.

As a result of such a study of James Mill I differ from those such as Plamenatz and Halévy who regard Utilitarianism as the climax of a tradition. It is true that there was a continuous development of thought which could generally be described as Utilitarian. But with James Mill all the evidence suggests that he came to the movement by a different path and was in the main, influenced both in his early days and throughout his life, by the Greek philosophers. Guided by this proposition I have suggested an interpretation of his moral philosophy which might otherwise have been overlooked, and which certainly suggests that there is more to be said for it than is commonly supposed. Yet, when we consider his early unpublished writings, containing a decisive refutation of Utilitarianism, it cannot be doubted that, with all the other references to the Greeks in his Commonplace Book, and with his son's testimony, Mill thought he was developing their philosophy, and was in no sense the mere spokesman of an eighteenth century tradition. Even in his doctrines of social and political education, apparently taken over from Helvétius, we find an early entry in the Commonplace Book, quoting Plato to the same effect.

Not only did Mill arrive at his Utilitarianism by a different path from that of the eighteenth century tradition, and markedly different from that of Bentham, he also gave it a new emphasis, for his philosophy was the reverse of 'pleasure-loving' in the ordinary meaning of the term. It is when we study him against the background of his day that this is most apparent. And it is this historical context which prompts another essential principle in interpreting his philosophy, namely to recognize its dual purpose—to be at once a criterion for immediate reform and a portrayal of the ideal. It is only when we apply this principle, I should maintain, that we can resolve the apparent inconsistencies in his thought. It is always much easier to point out the errors in philosophers of the past than to answer the much more interesting question: Why did they think they were right? With Mill, the answer to this lies generally in the society in which he lived.

When we have examined Mill in his historical context we have found that important parts of his theory, for instance, of political and social education, are largely a comment on his times. This does not mean that his theories have only an historical interest. For here, in his moral theory and in his theory of knowledge and related views of the curriculum, he presents a case to answer and it is difficult to resist the conclusion that James Mill deserves much more attention than he has received, from philosophers, from historians, and most of all, from educationists. Not all philosophers who have written on education have done so in a philosophical manner: with Locke, for example, his educational writings are largely common sense, and almost entirely unrelated to his philosophy. But with Mill, as with Plato, it is difficult to understand his educational theory without studying his philosophy and for that reason alone he merits attention and, like Plato, it is the questions which he asks, rather than the particular answers which he gives, which will be found to be the most important and to have the widest application to societies and states unlike his own.

It is this close relationship between Mill's philosophy and his educational theories which may explain another feature in which Mill is distinctive among educational writers. We noted in the opening chapter that this period in English history was a time when 'change was in the air' and when there was much debate about education. Yet Mill is curiously isolated and even insulated from the discussion. If we think, for example, of Rousseau and his ideas of 'education according to nature'—such notions are almost ignored by Mill. And when we recall that he was writing for an encyclopedia, this is the more surprising. Previous writers are discussed, certainly, but, apart from Helvétius, what are discussed are the writings of philosophers—Hobbes, Locke and Hume, and so on. And with the discussion of Locke, it is his philosophy which Mill is concerned with: there is no mention of *Thoughts on Education* or of *Conduct of the Understanding*.

It is the same when we look at the contemporary demand for a 'relevant' education which would include science and technology. Despite the fact that Bentham, Mill's close friend and collaborator, was the most distinguished protagonist of such curricula, despite Mill's active support for the Chrestomathic school, he significantly declines to follow Bentham in this matter of school curricula. Instead, the education of John Mill, and of the rest of the family was based on other criteria, notably philosophy and, where possible, the classics, or, as his daughter put it, the 'hated Latin'. This classical curriculum was conceived in an enlightened fashion and it anticipated public school changes by more than a generation: it also followed the Scottish tradition of Mill's day. Mill's curriculum also included Natural Science, especially in his 'outlines of a course for University College', but significantly, not because it was socially useful, or 'relevant' to contemporary needs, but because it was an established field of knowledge.

Mill, then, defies classification as a thinker on education: he was outside the tradition of progressive thought of his day and, to many, he will remain outside it today. The essential reason

for this is that his educational theories are based on his philosophy, and if his philosophy is in some respects influenced by the society of his day, and by the intellectual tradition of the nineteenth century, it is this philosophy and not the educational thought and practice of his day, which is the basis of his theory of education. In seeking a theory of education, Mill went back to first principles: he was surely right in supposing that those first principles must necessarily be philosophical ones. In his practice of education he may strike us as authoritarian in his outlook and methods, but the authority was really the authority of learning and not that of a man. For his teaching exemplified traditions of scholarship and learning which were, at the time, under attack from more than one quarter as, for example, irrelevant to the needs of the day or as contrary to the doctrine of 'education according to nature'. Utilitarianism is essentially a doctrine of social purpose—yet when it comes to education, Mill's achievement is to fuse the Utilitarian ideal with traditions of scholarship which are the product of many ages. This in the end may be its most important quality and the reason for its relevance not to one age or to one society, but to all.

BIBLIOGRAPHY

PRIMARY SOURCES

(a) *Manuscript*

British Museum Additional MSS. (Place Collection).
British Museum Additional MSS. (MacVey Napier).
British Museum Additional MSS. (Bentham Papers).
British Museum Reading Room (Place Collection, vol. 60).
Bentham MSS., University College London.
Brougham MSS., University College London.
Dumont MSS., University of Geneva.
James Mill's Commonplace Book, London Library.
Laurie and Whittle, New Map of London 1813 (British Museum).

(b) *Printed*

Bain, A., *James Mill: a biography*, London, 1882.
Bentham, J., *Chrestomathia*, London, 1817.
Bowring, J., *Memoirs and Correspondence of Bentham*, London, 1843 [Bowring edition of J. Bentham vol. 10].
British and Foreign Schools Society, *Manual of the System of Instruction in Model Schools*, London, 1831.
Edinburgh Review.
Grote, Mrs H., *Personal Life of George Grote*, 1873.
Elliott, H. S. R., *Letters of J. S. Mill*, 1910.
Knox, Vicesimus, *Works*, iv, 1824 (*Liberal Education* and *Remarks on Grammar Schools*).
Macaulay, Lord, *Miscellaneous Writings*, 1860.
Mill, James, *Commerce Defended*, 1807.
—, *Essay on Education* and *Schools for All, not Schools for Churchman only* in *James Mill on Education*, ed. W. H. Burston, C.U.P., 1969.
—, *Essay on Government*, ed. E. Barker, 1937.
—, *Essays on Government, Jurisprudence etc.*, 1828.
—, *Outline of a Course of Lectures* (University of London Library, Senate House).
—, *Elements of Economics*, 1823.
—, *Analysis of the Human Mind* (2nd edn), ed. J. S. Mill, 1878.
—, *Fragment on Mackintosh*, 1835.
Mill, J. S., *Autobiography*, ed. H. J. Laski, World's Classics, 1924.
—, *Autobiography*, ed. J. Stillinger, Urbana, Ill., 1961.
—, *John Mills, Boyhood Visit to France*, ed. A. J. Mill, Toronto, 1960.
Philanthropist, ed. W. Allen.

9

Roebuck, J. A., *Autobiography*, ed. R. E. Leader, 1897.
Solly, Henry, *These Eighty Years*.
Sraffa, P. (ed.), *Works and Correspondence of David Ricardo*, vi–ix, Cambridge, 1955.
Westminster Review, later the *London Review*.

SECONDARY SOURCES

Adamson, J. W., *English Education*, 1789–1902, C.U.P., 1964.
Ashton, T. S., *The Industrial Revolution*, O.U.P., 1954.
Aspinall, A., *Politics and the Press*, Home & Van Thal, 1949.
Bellot, H. H., *University College London*, University of London Press, 1929.
Bryant, A., *The Age of Elegance*, Collins, 1950.
Clapham, J. H., *Economic History of Modern Britain*, i, C.U.P., 1926.
Dicey, A. V., *Law and Public Opinion in England*, Macmillan, 1948.
George, M. Dorothy, *London Life and Labour in the 18th Century*, L.S.E., 1951.
Halévy, E., *History of the English People in 1815*, Benn, 1924 and 1961.
—, *Growth of Philosophical Radicalism*, Faber & Faber, 1928.
Hammond, J. L. and B., *The Town Labourer*, Longmans, 1925.
Hayek, F. A., *John Stuart Mill and Harriet Taylor*, 1951.
Hebb, D. O., *The Organization of Behaviour*, Chapman & Hall, 1955.
Hilgard, E. R., *Theories of Learning*, New York, 1965.
Humphrey, G., *Thinking*, Wiley, New York, 1963.
Levi, A. W., 'The Mental Crisis of J. S. Mill', *Psychoanalytical Review*, xxxii, 1945.
Morris, C. R., *Locke, Berkeley and Hume*, O.U.P., 1930.
Nesbitt, G. L., *Benthamite Reviewing*, Columbia University Press, New York, 1934.
Ogden, C. K., *Bentham's Theory of Fictions*, Routledge & Kegan Paul, 1951.
Packe, M. St J., *Life of John Stuart Mill*, Secker & Warburg, 1954.
Plamenatz, J., *The English Utilitarians*, Blackwell, 1949.
Reid, L. A., *Knowledge and Truth*, Macmillan, 1923.
Richards, I. A., *Interpretation in Teaching*, Routledge & Kegan Paul, 1949.
Russell, B., *Freedom and Organization, 1814–1914*, Allen & Unwin, 1934.
—, *History of Western Philosophy*, Allen & Unwin, 1946.
Steed, W., *The Press*, Penguin Books, 1938.
Stephen, L., *The English Utilitarians*, Duckworth, 1900.
Trevelyan, G. M., *English Social History*, Longmans, 1944.
Wallas, G., *Life of Francis Place*, Allen & Unwin, 1925.
White, R. J., *Waterloo to Peterloo*, Heinemann, 1957.
Woodward, E. L., *Age of Reform*, O.U.P., 1938.
Woozley, A. D., *Theory of Knowledge*, Hutchinson, 1949.
Young, G. M., *Early Victorian England*, O.U.P., 1934.

INDEX